ADVANCED-GUARD, OUT-POST,

AND

DETACHMENT SERVICE OF TROOPS,

WITH THE

ESSENTIAL PRINCIPLES OF STRATEGY,

AND

GRAND TACTICS

FOR THE USE OF

OFFICERS OF THE MILITIA AND VOLUNTEERS.

BY D. H. MAHAN, LL.D.,
PROFESSOR OF MILITARY AND CIVIL ENGINEERING, AND OF THE
ART OF WAR IN THE UNITED STATES MILITARY ACADEMY.

NEW EDITION, WITH TWELVE PLATES

NEW YORK:
JOHN WILEY, 56 WALKER STREET.
1863.

R. CRAIGHEAD,
Printer, Stereotyper, and Electrotyper,
Carton Building,
81, 83, and 85 Centre Street, N. Y.

PREFACE.

THE suggestion of this little compilation orig-
inated in a professional intercourse, some months
back, with a few intelligent officers of the Volunteer Corps of the city of New York.

The want of a work of this kind has long been
felt among our officers of Militia generally, as
English military literature is quite barren in systematic works on most branches of the military
art, especially so on the one known among the
military writers of the Continent as *La Petite
Guerre*, or the manner of conducting the operations of small independent bodies of troops; and
but few of these officers are able to devote that
time to military studies, which their pursuit in a
foreign language necessarily demands.

In making this compilation, the works in most
repute have been carefully consulted, and a selection made from them of what was deemed to be
most useful to the class of readers for which it
is intended. The object of the writer has been
to give a concise but clear view of the essential

points in each of the subjects introduced into the work; if he has succeeded in this, he trusts that the very obvious defects of the work will be over-looked.

An acknowledgment is here due from the writer to Major-General Sandford, commanding the First Division of the New York State Militia, and to H. K. Oliver, Esq., Adjutant-General of the State of Massachusetts, as well as to the officers gen-erally of the First Division N. Y. S. M., for their kind aid in bringing forward the work.

The previous editions of this work having met with very general circulation among the class of our offi-cers for whose use it was originally designed, and the approval of the most distinguished of our General Officers, it has been deemed well to enlarge the work by the addition of a concise statement of the *Princi-ples of Strategy and Grand Tactics*, with illustrations from several of the most celebrated campaigns of Napoleon.

This new matter has been chiefly drawn from the writings of Thiers and Dufour.

U. S. MILITARY ACADEMY,
    Dec. 1st, 1862.

CONTENTS.

INTRODUCTORY CHAPTER.

HISTORICAL SKETCH OF THE MOST REMARKABLE
EPOCHS IN THE MILITARY ART FROM THE
TIME OF THE GREEKS TO THE PRESENT.

----

1. No one can be said to have thoroughly mastered his art, who has neglected to make himself conversant with its early history; nor, indeed, can any tolerably clear elementary notions, even, be formed of an art, beyond those furnished by the mere technical language, without some historical knowledge of its rise and progress; for this alone can give to the mind those means of comparison, without which everything has to be painfully created anew, to reach perfection only after many cycles of misdirected mental toil.

2. To no one of the arts, that have exercised a prominent influence on the well-being of society, are these observations more applicable than to that of arms. To be satisfied of this, there needs only the most cursory glance at the grand military epochs of the ancient and modern world. Looking at the art as it was among the Greeks, under Epaminondas, Philip, and Alexander; and among the Romans, about the time of Julius Cæsar, of each of which epochs we have full authentic records; comparing it with the phases it assumed in the decline of the

Roman Empire and during the Feudal period; and following it, from the introduction of gunpowder down to the brief career of Gustavus Adolphus, its first great restorer in Europe,—it seems incredible that anything, short of the most entire ignorance of the past, could have led professional soldiers to abandon the spirit of the organization and tactics of the early Greeks and Romans, so admirably adapted to call into play the mental and physical energies of man, for the lumbering and unwieldy engines that clogged the operations of the Imperial armies of the Empire; or for the almost equally unwieldy iron-clad chivalry of the middle ages, whose *prestige* was forever obscured by the first well-organized infantry brought against it.

3. Coming to a more recent period, did we not remember by what slow and uncertain stages the march of improvement in other arts has proceeded, —how much has been seemingly owing to mere chance, rather than to well-directed investigation,— how rarely a master has arisen to imbody into simple formulas the often complicated processes and obscure doctrines of those who have preceded him, we should have still greater cause of astonishment, that, at a time of more general diffusion of science, art and literature, and particularly of the classical writers of antiquity, no master-mind should have evoked, from the campaigns of a Marius, or a Hannibal, the germ of the comparatively modern science of strategy; nor have gathered, from that almost horn-book of the school-boy, Cæsar's Commentaries, the spirit of those rapid combinations by which, with a handful of troops, the great Roman captain so uniformly frustrated the powerful and oft-repeated struggles of a warlike and restless people; but, that it should have been left to the great Captain of this

age to brush aside the mesh-work woven by routine and military pedagoguism ; while, by the development of gigantic plans, made and controlled with almost mathematical precision, he fixed immovably those principles which, when acted upon, cannot fail to command success, and which, when overlooked or neglected, lead to defeat, or else, leaving all to chance, make of victory only a successful butchery.

4. However desirable it might be to give to this branch of the military art the consideration to which it is justly entitled, it does not come within the scope of a work like this to do so. The most that can be attempted will be to make a brief recapitulation of the most marked epochs; with a view to draw the attention of the young military student to the importance of this too-frequently neglected branch, and to lead him into a field of research, where the spirit of inquiry will always be gratified, useful additions be made to his previous stock of acquirement, and hints be gleaned which he will find fully to justify the correctness of Napoleon's decision upon the influence which a study of the campaigns of Alexander, Hannibal and Cæsar, must have in the education of a thorough captain.

5. *Tactics of the Greeks.*—The Greeks, if not the earliest people who reduced the military art to fixed principles, are the first of whose military institutions we have any exact account ; and even of theirs, and of the system of their successors in conquest, the Romans, several points still remain obscure.

6. A Grecian army, at the period when the military art was in the greatest perfection among them, was composed of infantry and cavalry. The former was made up of three different orders of soldiers ;

termed, 1. The *Oplitai*, or heavily armed, who wore a
very complete defensive armor, and bore the *sarissa*,
or Macedonian pike, a formidable weapon either fo
the attack or defence, about 24 feet in length. 2.
The *Psiloi*, or light infantry, who were without defensive armor, and carried the javelin, bow, and
sling. 3. The *Peltastæ*, who were intermediate bə-
tween the other two, carrying a lighter defensive
armor, as well as a shorter pike than the oplitai.

7. The cavalry consisted of two kinds. 1. The
Cataphracti, or heavy cavalry, in which both rider
and horse were well covered with defensive armor;
the former armed with the lance, and a sabre slung
from a shoulder-belt. 2. A light cavalry of an ir-
regular character, who were without defensive
armor, consisting of archers and lancers, who also
carried a sword, javelin, and a small buckler.

8. The elementary tactical combinations, or *formations*, of the Greeks, were methodical but very simple. An army corps was composed, 1. Of a *Tetraphalangarchia*, also termed a grand phalanx, consisting of 16,354 oplitai. An *Epitagma*, of 8192
psiloi; and an epitagma of cavalry of 4096 men.
The heavy armed, or infantry of the line, bore to the
light infantry and cavalry the ratio of the numbers
2, 4, and 1.

9. The composition of the grand phalanx was as
follows: Tetraphalangarchia = 4 *Phalanxes* = 16
Chiliarchiæ = 64 *Syntagmata* = 256 *Tetrarchiæ* =
1024 *Lochoi* or files = 4096 *Enomitiæ* of 4 men each.
It is thus seen that, in the various formations, a
division of the whole could be made by the powers
of 2 or 4.

10. This body of infantry was thus officered.
Each tetrarchia, consisting of 4 files, or 64 men,

was commanded by a *Tetrarch*, who was file leader of the first file.

11. The syntagma of 16 files, which was the army unit, and corresponds to our battalion, was commanded by a *Syntagmatarch*, who was stationed in front of his command, having an adjutant on his left; a color-bearer immediately in his rear; on the right a herald-at-arms, to repeat the commands; and on the left a trumpeter, to sound the signals. In the rear of the syntagma was stationed an officer who was the second in command.

12. The phalanx was commanded by a general officer bearing the title of *Strategos*.

13. The formation of the peltastæ and psiloi was analogous to that of the oplitai, the number of files being 8, instead of 16 as in the last; and the subdivisions receiving different denominations also.

14. The epitagma of cavalry was divided into two equal parts, each composed alike, termed *Telea*. One was placed on each wing of the line of battle. The telos was subdivided into 5 divisions; the strength of each subdivision being the half of the one next in order above it. The lowest, termed *Ila*, of 64 horsemen, corresponding to the modern squadron, was drawn up on a front of 16 with 4 files, and was commanded by an officer with the title of *Ilarch*.

15. The grand phalanx, in order of battle, was divided into two wings, with an interval of 40 paces between them, and one of 20 between the phalanxes of each wing.

16. The oplitai, when formed for exercise or parade, were drawn up in open order; leaving an equal interval between the men of each rank and between the ranks. When ready to charge, each man occupied a square of 3 feet, and the six lead

ing ranks brought their pikes to a level; thus presenting an array in which the pikes of the sixth rank extended 3 feet in advance of the front one. In attacks on intrenchments, or fortified cities, the men of each rank closed shoulder to shoulder, a sufficient interval being left between the ranks to move with celerity; the leading rank kept their shields overlapped to cover their front; the others held them above their heads for shelter against the weapons of the enemy.

17. The peltast corresponded to our *élite* corps of infantry, selected for enterprises requiring both celerity and a certain firmness.

18. The psiloi performed all the duties usually devolved, in the present day, upon light infantry, both before and at the opening of an engagement.

19. The position of the cavalry, in line of battle, was on the wings. The duties of this arm were mainly to charge that of the enemy. The cataphracti, for this purpose, were drawn up on each wing, with a portion of the light cavalry on each of their flanks. The charge was made by the former, and the latter followed up any success gained by them.

20. The marches of the Greeks were usually made by a flank. Sometimes, when the character of the ground permitted, two phalanxes marched side by side, presenting a front of 32 men, and being in readiness to offer a front on both the flanks, if necessary.

21. Among the orders of battles among the ancients, that known as the *wedge*, or *boar's head*, is the most celebrated. In this disposition, the *point*, or *head*, is formed of a subdivision of the phalanx of greater or less strength, according to circumstances; this being supported by two, three, and

four subdivisions of the same force, one behind
another.

22. *Tactics of the Romans.* Up to the time of
Marius, by whom the germ of the decadence of the
military art among the Romans was sown, a Consular Army consisted of two *Legions;* and of two
Wings composed of social troops. The legion was
composed of infantry of the line, light infantry,
and cavalry. The infantry of the line was divided
into three classes. 1. The *Hastati.* 2. *Principes.*
3. *Triarii.* These classes wore a very complete
defensive armor; they were all armed with the
snort straight Spanish sword; the *Pilum,* a kind
of javelin, about 7 feet in length, used equally to
hurl at a distance and in hand-to-hand engagements,
was added to it for the two first; and the triarii
carried the pike.

23. The light infantry, termed *Velites,* used only
the casque, and a buckler of stout leather, and bore
the Spanish sword and a short javelin, termed the
Hasta, only half the length of the pilum, and used
as a missile.

24. The cavalry wore the helmet and cuirass,
and carried a buckler; their arms were a long sabre,
the Grecian lance, and a quiver with arrows.

25. The legion was officered by six *Tribunes,*
sixty *Centurions,* with an equal number of officers
who served as file-closers for the infantry; and
twenty *Decurions* of cavalry; besides these there
were the officers of the velites, who fought out of
the ranks.

26. Until about the period of the Civil Wars, the
legion was commanded by the tribunes in succession; the tour of duty for each being two months;
afterwards the rule was adopted of placing the
legion in command of an officer styled *Legatus*

14

Whilst the tribunes exercised the command, those, who were not on this duty, served on all occasions of detachment service generally.

27. Each class of the infantry of the line was subdivided into ten portions, each termed a *Manipu lus*. The velites were attached to these by equal portions. The cavalry were divided into ten troops, termed *Turma*. To each manipulus there were assigned two centurions, and two file-closers; and to each turma two decurions. The velites, although forming a part of the manipuli, had centurions assigned to them, to lead them in battle.

28. The normal order of battle of the Romans, prior to the time of Marius, was in three lines: the hastati in the first; the principes in the second; the triarii in the third; and the cavalry on the wings.

29. The manipulus, which was the unit of force, was drawn up in 12 files, with a depth of 10 ranks, in the lines of hastati and principes; in the line of triarii there were only 6 files. The right and left files of the manipulus were led by a centurion, and closed by an officer file-closer.

30. The manipuli of the three lines were disposed in quincunx order; the manipulus of one line opposite to the interval between the manipuli in the one in front, this being the same as the manipulus front. The intervals between the lines were the same as the depth of each line. An interval of about 3 feet was left between the ranks and the files of the manipulus.

31. The same order of battle was followed for the social troops on the wings. The two legions occupied the centre; but what interval was left between them, or between the centre and wings, or how far the cavalry was posted from the infantry, is not well ascertained.

32. The velites, before engaging, were posted usually between the intervals of the triarii, and, in part, between those of the turma.

33. In both the legionary and allied cavalry the turma were formed in 8 files and 4 ranks. An interval the same as its front, was left between each turma. Of the two officers commanding a turma, one was placed on the right, the other on the left of the front rank. Each wing of cavalry was commanded by an officer styled *Prefectus.* In some instances the cavalry was placed as a reserve, in rear of the triarii, and charged when necessary, through the intervals of the manipuli.

34. In their engagements, the velites performed precisely the same part as that of the light troops which form the advanced-guards and advanced-posts of the present day. Watching and occupying the enemy before the main body is brought into play; then retiring and taking position to harass him farther, as opportunity may serve.

35. The main body, from its organization, and formation, was admirably adapted to meet any emergency; presenting, if necessary, by advancing the manipuli of the principes into the intervals of the hastati, an unbroken impenetrable front; or, by throwing the manipuli of the different lines behind each other, leaving an unobstructed passage to the front, or rear.

36. From the preceding brief exposition of the phalanx and legionary formations, the respective properties of these two celebrated bodies, on the field of battle, may be readily gathered. The legion was evidently far better adapted to circumstances of locality than the phalanx, which could only move well and effectively on even ground. In the phalanx, the keeping together of the entire body,—

whether in moving onward to bear down the enemy
bv its pressure, or in waiting to resist his shock by
its inertia,—was everything. In the legion, individual activity and the ease with which the manipuli lent themselves to every requisite movement,
gave to the entire machine the volition and strength
of life. The attack with the pilum, cast on nearing
the enemy, was followed up immediately by the on-
slaught with the terrible short straight sword, equally
effective to hew, or thrust with. Each manipulus,
equal to any emergency, was prepared, by the celerity
with which its movements could be made, to improve
every partial advantage, and meet the enemy on all
sides. Against cavalry alone, was the impenetrable front of the phalanx, bristling with a forest of
sarissas, superior to the legion. The open order
adopted for the vigorous action of the individual,
who to the charge of the horse had only his pilum
to oppose, so inferior to the fire of the musket, that
dread of modern cavalry, proved fatal to the legion
on more than one sanguinary field; till experience
taught, that safety might be found in ranks more
serried, and by presenting a front of pike-heads,
borne by the first four ranks of the hastati.

37. Marius, urged either by policy or the necessities of the times, made a fundamental, and it is
thought fatal change, not only in the organization
of the legion, but in other parts of the military system of his country. By substituting for that glow
of patriotism with which an army drawn wholly
from the bosom of the people is ever found to be animated, the mercenary spirit and its consequences,
he aimed a vital blow against the only real safeguard of a nation's honor, a national army.

In a despotism, such as Prussia was under Frederick, the controlling power of an energetic will

may, for a season, not only ward off the attacks of powerful neighbors, but reap conquests, and struggle with fortitude against great reverses, with an army recruited from the scum of mankind; but so soon as a state with any pretensions to republican institutions, substitutes the mercenary wholly for the national spirit in its armies, its fate is sealed. Like Rome, during the brilliant career of Marius, Pompey, and Cæsar,—like Venice, under some of her able *condottieri*, as the Colonnas and Sforzas, it may, through the singular ability of particular leaders, still present to the world the dazzling *prestige* that military success, under all aspects, carries with it; but the result is as certain as the ashes that succeed to the flame; anarchy comes in with all its ills, from the rival pretensions of successful partisan leaders, and the spectacle is again seen which Rome exhibited at the period referred to; or else the imbecility and utter prostration which Venice presented, almost from the very moment when outwardly she had attained to her loftiest flight, down to the pitiable closing scene that wiped her name forever from the book of independent states.

38. In the truly great days of Rome, the days of the Scipios, the raising of her legions was done with all the best guards of a constitutional popular election. Six tribunes for each legion, having first been chosen, either by the consuls or by the popular voice, the conscripts to fill its ranks were designated in each tribe by the proper magistrate; these were divided by the tribunes into the following classes:—1. The youngest and least affluent were selected for the Velites; 2. The next in years and wealth for the Hastati; 3. The next in the same gradation for the Principes; and 4. The oldest and most wealthy for Triarii. The cavalry

or knights, formed a privileged class, into which only those were admitted who paid a certain tax. This classification being made, the tribunes named 10 *first* and 10 *second centurions* for the infantry; with 10 *first* and 10 *second decurions* for the cavalry; and then in concert with the officers thus selected, divided the classes into *manipuli* and *turma*, assigning to each its two proper officers; whilst these, in turn, selected the two officers in each maniple who acted as file-closers.

39. Besides the distinction of first and second centurion, these officers took rank according to class. The first centurion of the Triarii, termed *Primipilus*, was the highest in rank of his grade, and took command of the legion when the tribunes were absent.

40. In the time of the Scipios the legion was composed of 1200 velites. 1200 hastati, 1200 principes, 600 triarii, and 300 knights.

41. Polybius states that the Consular army contained 6000 legionaries of the line, 2400 velites. and 600 knights of Roman troops; and of social, or allied troops, 6700 infantry and 800 horse for the wings; with an additional extraordinary levy of 1700 infantry and 400 cavalry; making a grand total of 18,600 men.

42. Marius introduced the *Cohort* instead of the maniple as the unit of force; forming it of three maniples, and abolishing the ancient modes of classification. The cohort preserved both the number and designation of the officers attached to the maniples. It was commanded by the first centurion, until, under the emperors, it received a superior officer, termed the *Prefect of the Cohort*. The use was also introduced of making of the first cohort a

corps d'élite, to which was intrusted the eagle,
under the orders of its primiple.

43. The order of battle by cohorts depended upon
circumstances; usually five were placed in the first
and five in the second line. The number of ranks
of the cohort was also variable; depending on the
front necessary to be presented to the enemy.

44. With the settled despotism of the emperors
arose, as a necessary consequence, in still bolder
relief, the mercenary system. The substitution of
auxiliary cavalry for the Roman knights, and the
introduction of foreigners and of slaves, even among
the legionaries, soon left not a vestige of the ancient
military constitution of the army; and that train of
results was rapidly evolved in which defeat was
followed by all its ills but shame, and the once
proud legionary became an object of terror to his
master alone. Effeminacy led to the abandonment
of his defensive armor; and, too craven to meet the
foe face to face with his weapons of offence, the
legionary sought a disgraceful shelter behind those
engines of war which were found as powerless to
keep at bay his barbarian opponent, as was the lumbering artillery, chained wheel to wheel, of the
Oriental, to arrest the steady tread of the English
foot soldier.

45. *Feudal Period.* To follow down the military art through all the stages of its fall until the
rise of the feudal system, could not fail to be a
most instructive lesson, did the limits of this work
permit it. Grand as were the occasional deeds of
derring do of the chivalric age, they were seldom
more than exhibitions of individual prowess. Art
and consummate skill there undoubtedly were in
this period, but no approach to science. Countries
and provinces invaded and ravaged, cities ruined

and castles razed, accompanied b wholesale butchery of the frightencd peasant, mocked with the ap-
pointments and title of soldier, such, without other result, were the deeds of chivalry, and such they must
have continued, had not the Swiss pike, that broke
the Austrian yoke, opened the way to free Europe
from its wretched thraldom, and again to raise the
profession of arms to its proper level, in which mind
and its achievements have the first rank, and brute
force combined with mere mechanical skill a very
subordinate one.

46. *Rise of Art in Modern Times.* After the
decisive day of Morgaten, the Swiss name resounded throughout Europe; and in time it became
a point with the leading powers to gain these moun-
taineers to their side in their wars; and even to re-
tain a body of them permanently in their pay. The
same men who at home were patriot soldiers, were
known abroad, in foreign service, as the real mer-
cenaries; deserting, or upholding a cause, as the
one or the other party bid highest. The true rank
of infantry now began again to be appreciated; and,
with the more permanent military establishments
soon after set on foot, an organization on juster
principles gradually found its way in; and with it
some glimmering views of ancient art.

47. Although able leaders from time to time appeared, and order, with a rude discipline, was introduced among the hireling bands of which the permanent portions of armies in most European states
consisted, after the first essay of regularly paid
troops made by Charles VII. of France; still no
one arose who seemed to comprehend the spirit of
ancient art, until the period of the Revolt in the
Netherlands brought forward the Princes of Orange
and Nassau, William and his son Maurice, both of

whom, but particularly the latter, gave evidence of consummate military talent. The camp of Maurice became the school of Europe, from which came forth many of the most eminent generals of that day.

48. *Epoch of Gustavus Adolphus.* But the great captain of this age was Gustavus Adolphus; a man who combined the qualities of hero, warrior, statesman and philosopher; one who early saw, what in our day, and especially in our country, is still disputed, that war is both a science and an art, and that profound and varied learning—an intimate acquaintance with literature as well as science—is indispensable in the formation of the thorough soldier.

49. Since the invention of gunpowder, the military art had, in some respects, retrograded, owing to a misapprehension of the true value of this new agent. The apprehension expressed by the bravest of the old chivalry, that it would be the means of extinguishing noble daring, was soon seen to be not ill-founded, in the disappearance of individual prowess in the cavalry; whilst the cumbrous machines put into the hands of the infantry, and the unwieldy cannon, that but poorly replaced the old engines, rendered all celerity, that secret of success, impossible. At the fight of Kintzig, for example, which lasted from mid-day to evening, and which took place after the fork, that served the old musketeer as a rest, had been suppressed, and the cartridge been introduced by Gustavus Adolphus, it is narrated, that the infantry were drawn up in six ranks, and that the fire of musketry was so well sustained that the slowest men even discharged their pieces seven times.

50. Besides this improvement in small arms,

Gustavus Adolphus was the first to make the clas
sification of artillery into siege and field-pieces,
adopting for the latter the calibres corresponding
nearly to those used for the same purposes in the
present day. He formed a light regiment of artillery; and assigned to the cavalry some light guns.

51. Important changes were made by him in the
cavalry; its armor was modified, the cuirassiers
alone preserving a light cuirass, and being armed
with a long sword and two pistols.

52. By adopting a new disposition for battle,
which he termed the *order by brigade*, the idea of
which was clearly taken from the dispositions in
the Roman legions, he broke up the large unwieldly
bodies into which troops had hitherto been massed;
and thus gave not only greater mobility, but de-
creased the exposure to the ravages of missiles.
In his order of battle, each arm was placed according to its essential properties; so that ease of
manœuvring and mutual support necessarily followed; and peculiar advantages of position were
readily seized upon. To this end, his forces were
drawn up in two or three parallel lines; either behind each other, or in quincunx order; the cannon
and musketry combined; the cavalry either in the
rear of the infantry to support it, or else upon the
wings to act in mass. The cavalry was formed in
four ranks.

53. The dispositions made at a halt at night
were always the same as those to receive the enemy,
should he unexpectedly attack. The order of march
was upon several columns, at suitable distances
apart.

54. Such, summarily, were the main points in
the improvements made by this great captain, who,
on the field of battle, exhibited the same warrior

instinct, in perceiving and availing himself of the decisive moment. Betrayed, as every original mind that reposes upon its own powers alone must be into occasional errors,—such, for example, as interposing, on some occasions, his cavalry between bodies of infantry, he more than cancelled them, by being the earliest to perceive the true power of each arm, as shown, in massing his artillery, and by keeping it masked until the effective moment for its action arrived.

55. *Epoch of Louis XIV* The wars that preceded the period of the Spanish Succession, and those induced by it, developed the seeds sown by Gustavus Adolphus and the Princes of Nassau. The old chivalry having become a thing that was, there arose that young chivalry, equally distinguished by valor and courtesy, which, although sometimes assuming a fantastic hue, has transmitted some of its spirit even to this day, through terrific scenes of popular struggles, and the loosening of every evil passion engendered by such strifes, and converted the battle-field into an arena where glory is the prize contended for; and where, the contest over, the conquered finds in the victor a brother eager to assist him, and to sympathize in his mishap. At the head of this distinguished band we find the Montecuculis, the Turennes, the Condés, the Eugenes, the Marlboroughs, the Catinats, the Luxembourgs, the Vaubans, and a host of others. Still, with the exception of some improvements in the weapons in use, as the changes in the musket, by substituting for the old match-lock the one with the hammer and flint, the addition of the bayonet, and the introduction of the iron rammer, together with a better organization of the artillery, the progress made in the art during this period was in no

degree commensurate with the grand scale on which its military operations were conducted. The science of fortification, and its kindred branch, the mode of conducting sieges, form an honorable exception to this general stagnation of the art. Each of these were brought by Vauban to a pitch of perfection that has left but little for his successors to achieve, so long as the present arms and means are alone employed.

56. It was also in this period that the infantry pike was abandoned. This change was first made by Marshal Catinat, in the army which he commanded in Italy; and it was gradually adopted throughout the French service by the efforts of Vauban, who demonstrated the superiority of the musket and bayonet to the pike both as a defensive and an offensive weapon. At the same time the distinction between light and heavy infantry became more prominent, partly from the introduction of the hand-grenade, for the handling of which men of the greatest stature and strength were selected, who, from this missile, were termed *grenadiers*, and partly, from the practice of, at first, placing the improved musket only in the hands of the best marksmen.

57. With the more effective use of fire-arms, the necessity was felt of adopting a formation both of infantry and cavalry, that would present a less exposed mark to their balls; but the disinclination to innovation which seems natural to all professions, retarded this change, and it was only after the war of the Spanish Succession that the French gave the example of a formation of infantry in three ranks. The cavalry was still far from that point of efficiency which it subsequently reached. Its movements were slow and timid, and fire-arms, unwieldy im-

plements in the hands of horsemen, were still preferred by it to the sword.

58 The usual order of battle was in two or
three lines; the infantry in the centre, and cavalry
on the wings. The lines were from 300 to 600
paces apart; having intervals between their battalions and squadrons, in each equal to their front, so
as to execute with ease the passage of lines. The
importance of keeping some troops in reserve, to
support those engaged, and also to be used for special objects, as turning the flank of an enemy, began
also now to be acted on. Yet the trammels of routine were but slowly laid aside. Manœuvres and
marches made with a tediousness and circumspection difficult to be comprehended in the present day;
engagements commenced along the entire front at
once; the intermingling of cavalry with infantry;
the power of artillery but vaguely felt; little appreciation of the resources to be found in varied
ground; battles fought apparently with no other
view than to drive the enemy from the battle-field;
such were the prominent military features of this
celebrated epoch,—one of faults, which deserve to
be attentively studied for the lessons they afford
even to the present day.

59. The period intervening between the age of
Louis XIV., and the rise of the Prussian power under Frederick II., was one of comparative stagnation in the military art. The Duke of Orleans, the
afterwards celebrated Regent, on one or two occasions, gave promise of great military talents. The
mad career of Charles XII. of Sweden, and the
achievements of Marshal Saxe,—to whom we owe
the modern cadenced step, and the well-known
axiom, *that the secret of victory resides in the legs of
the soldiers*,—are the most instructive events of this

3

time; particularly as regards the use of fortified points as an element of tactics; shown in the destruction of Charles's force at Pultowa, and in the influence of the redoubts on the renowned day of Fontenoy, with which closed the military life of Marshal Saxe.

60. *Epoch of Frederick II.* With Frederick II. of Prussia arose a new order of things; a mixture of sound axioms and execrable exactions upon the natural powers of man, of which the latter, for years afterwards, in the hands of ignorance and military pedagoguism, became the bane of the art, and the opprobrium of humanity, through the cruel tasks and wretched futilities with which the private soldier was vexed; to convert a being whose true strength resides in his volition into a machine of mere bone and muscle.

61. What influence the early hardships to which Frederick was subjected by the half-mad tyrant to whom he owed his being, or the mercenary material, fashioned under the same regimen as himself, with which afterwards he was obliged to work, may have had, in creating this state of things, it is not easy to say; but it seems incredible that, without some such bias, a man who showed such eminent abilities, as a statesman and soldier,—who, in most things, thought wisely, and acted well,— should have fallen into an error so gross and lamentable; one that even the poor shallow philosophy, of which he made his plaything, ought to have detected and reformed.

62. Frederick's first attention was given to the drill, or the mere mechanism of the art, in which he attained a sad celebrity. Firing executed with a celerity that rendered aim impracticable, and with an *ensemble* which made a point of honor of having

the report from a battalion undistinguishable from that of one gun; manœuvres calculated with mathematical precision, applied with equal precision by human beings tutored as dancing-dogs; the cane of the drill-sergeant more dreaded than the bayonet of the enemy; the field of battle, that arena where genius and military instinct should be least trammelled, converted into a parade ground, for carrying on all the trivial mummery of a mere gala-day: such were some of the worst features of Frederick's system.

63. But whenever his mind was left free to carry out an original conception, the master of the art again shone forth. In his orders of march and encampment, his choice of positions to receive an attack, he seldom failed to exhibit the consummate general. In his appreciation of the powers of the oblique order of battle, by which he obtained such decisive results on the field of Leuthen; the perfect state to which he brought his cavalry, and the brilliant success with which he was repaid by it, for his exertions in restoring it to its essential purposes; his introduction of flying artillery, and his clear-sighted views as to the proper employment of this arm generally on the battle-field; Frederick has high claims upon the profession, as well as for his written instructions to his generals, which are a model both of military style and good sense.

64. Frederick adopted invariably the formation of three ranks for his infantry, and that of two for his cavalry. From the preponderating value given to the effects of musketry, his dispositions for battle were always with lines deployed, and so disposed as to favor an easy passage of lines. This, and the curious importance attached to preserving an exact alignment in all movements, deprived the troops of

the advantages of celerity, and the use of the bayonet, to which the present column of attack so admirably lends itself.

65. The great authority of Frederick overshad-
owe l, and kept down, the naturally rebellious
promptings of common sense against parts of his
system; and all Europe soon vied in attempts to
rival its worst features, without comprehending its
essence. In England, it was silently imposed upon
a hired soldiery without difficulty; and showed itself in a guise, in which, but for the painful features, the exhibition would have been eminently
ludicrous. Throughout Germany it made its way,
in spite of the impenetrable character of the institutions of the day. In France, a furious war of
words and writings was waged between the respective advocates for the true French *laissez-faire*,
and the Prussian tournequetism and strait-jacket-
ism; as well as upon the more important question
of the deep and shallow formations. If this contest did nothing more, it provoked discussions in
which the voice of the real soldier was occasionally
heard in the din of mere military pedagogues. It
produced the brilliant pages of Guibert, and the
whimsical scene, so graphically described by De
Ségur, of the *experimentum crucis*, to which he in-
voluntarily, and a comrade voluntarily were put, to
ascertain man's powers of endurance under the
punishment of the flat of a sabre. Then came
that event which swept all these puerilities and
most other futilities into one vortex,—the French
Revolution. The value of proper control, and the
evils arising from i's want, were here equally demonstrated; and a just medium at length hit upon,
which left to the individual his necessary powers
under all circumstances.

66. *Epoch of the French Revolution, and its Sequel.* With the emigration of her nobles, France saw herself deprived of nearly all those who were deemed capable of organizing and leading her armies. Her enemies were upon her, still brilliant with the *prestige* of Frederick's name and Frederick's tactics; and to these she had to oppose only ill-armed and disorganized masses, driven to the field, in some cases, more through apprehension of the insatiable guillotine, than through any other motive, dreading it more than the disciplined Prussian. But here the man, thrown on his own resources, lifted up and borne onward by an enthusiasm bordering on fanaticism, showed himself equal to the emergency. Like our own first efforts, so those of the French were the actions of individuals. Where the drill had done nothing, individual military instinct filled up the want. A cloud of skirmishers, soon become expert marksmen, harassed and confounded lines taught to fire only at the word of command; the compact column, resounding with the *Ca ira*, scattered to the winds feeble, frigid lines, torpid with over-management, and effected a revolution as pregnant to the military, as the political one to which it owed its birth was to the social system. Thus was laid the foundation of the tactics of this day; a system that partly sprung up in the forests of America; and upon which, a few years later, the ingenious Bulow would have had military Europe to base its system.

67. The frenzy of enthusiasm past, reason and discipline again claimed their rights; and the well-judging, able generals of France, brought both the system of skirmishers and the column of attack, to their proper functions; and the way was prepared for that Genius who swayed these two elementary

facts with a power that shook Europe to its centre, and caused her firmest thrones to reel.

68. Napoleon appeared upon the scene at a moment the most propitious for one of his gigantic powers. The elements were prepared, and although temporarily paralyzed by a state of anarchy, resulting from the political and financial condition of the country, they required only an organizing hand to call into activity their inherent strength. This hand, endowed with a firmness and grasp that nothing could shake, or unloose, was that of Napoleon. To him we owe those grand features of the art, by which an enemy is broken and utterly dispersed by one and the same blow. No futilities of preparation; no uncertain feeling about in search of the key-point; no hesitancy upon the decisive moment; the whole field of view taken in by one eagle glance; what could not be seen divined by an unerring military instinct; clouds of light troops thrown forward to bewilder his foe; a crushing fire of cannon in mass opened upon him; the rush of the impetuous column into the gap made by the artillery; the overwhelming charge of the resistless cuirassier; followed by the lancer and hussar to sweep up the broken dispersed bands; such were the tactical lessons practically taught in almost every great battle of this great military period. The task of the present one has been to systematize, and imbody in the form of doctrine, what was then largely traced out.

69. In an intimate knowledge of the peculiar application of each arm, and a just appreciation of their respective powers; in all that is lofty in conception, skilful in design, and large in execution, Napoleon confessedly stands unrivalled. But it has been urged that, for the attainment of his ends

on the battle-field, he has shown a culpable disregard of the soldier's blood, and has often pushed to excess his attacks by masses.

To do the greatest damage to our enemy with the least exposure to ourselves, is a military axiom lost sight of only by ignorance of the true ends of victory. How far this may have been disregarded by Napoleon, can be known, with certainty, only through Napoleon himself. He, who suffered no important fact, or its consequences, to elude his powers of analysis, could hardly have been unmindful of the fate of the grand column at Fontenay, nor have forgotten the imminent danger in which those squares were placed that, at the battle of the Pyramids, resisted like walls of iron the headlong charge of the reckless Mameluke, when he launched forth the formidable column of M'Donald on the field of Wagram.

CHAPTER I.

70. TACTICS may be defined to be *the art of draw-ing up, and moving troops systematically.* It admits of a classification into two divisions. 1. *Minor* or *elementary* tactics; under which head may be placed all that refers to the drill, and other preparatory instruction of troops, to give them expertness in the use of their weapons, and facility of movement. 2. *Grand* tactics; or the art of combining, disposing, and handling troops on the field of battle.

71. The manner of drawing up troops, or their disposition in their *primitive order of battle*, evidently must depend upon the kind of weapon with which they are armed, and their mode of fighting. A glance, upon the preceding pages, will show how the primitive order of battle has been modified by these circumstances, in different nations, and at different epochs. Without stopping to consider these, or to enter into an analysis of the once vexed question respecting the merits of the deep and shallow orders, we shall take it as practically solved, for the present, by the adoption in all civilized states, of the uniform system now in use; which is for infantry troops, either dispersed, or deployed in lines for firing; and in columns of march, or attack, for movements;—for cavalry, either deployed lines or dispersed order for attack, and columns for manœuvres, and exceptionally for attack. To this it may be added, that no soldier, who has made himself conversant with the resources of his art, will allow

himself to be trammelled by any exclusive system. What the case requires he will do, if confident of his troops; throwing a deployed line, with the bayonet advanced, upon his enemy, if he judges the moment propitious; or charging impetuously, with his horse in column, under like circumstances.

72. The systems of tactics in use in our service are those of the French; not that opinion is settled among our officers on this point; some preferring the English. In favor of the French, it may be said, that there is really more affinity between the military aptitude of the American and French soldier, than between that of the former and the English; and that the French systems are the results of a broader platform of experience, submitted to the careful analysis of a body of officers, who, for science and skill combined, stand unrivalled; whereas the English owes more to individual than to general talent; and therefore is more liable to the defects of individual pride of opinion, than where this can only be felt in discussion at the council board, at which its *morgue* is liable to be checked, and its fallacies exposed, by rival talent.

73. In all tactical combinations, experience has shown that for each arm there is a certain numerical force, which lends itself best to the essential conditions demanded in all troops;—which are strength, activity, and the faculty of moving in any direction. This force, termed the unit, varies in the different arms. In all cases, it should not be so great but that all the men of which it is composed may be overlooked by, and be known to, the officer in command of it; and also when drawn up in its order of battle, be within reach of his voice. These last conditions place a practical limit to the

tactical unit; owing to the extent to which the human voice can be distinctly heard; the space taken up by each combatant; and the form and dimensions of the figure covered on the ground by the unit in its order of battle.

74. The *battalion* is the unit of the arm of infantry; the *squadron* that of the arm of cavalry; and the *battery* of six guns that of the arm of artillery.

75. For each of these units, particular subdivisions have been adopted; and their command intrusted to officers of suitable grade, both to overlook and to lead them in the various combinations to which the unit may be subjected. For the details on all these points, as they do not come within the scope of this work, reference may be had to the systems of elementary tactics adopted in our service.

76. The order of battle of the unit is usually based upon the nature of the weapon used, and the space required for handling it freely.

77. The *habitual order of battle* of infantry is in two or three ranks. With us, that of two ranks is generally preferred, partly because our battalion is small, and therefore requires all the front that can be given without presenting a line liable to waver at every change of position; but mainly because every musket can be made to tell effectively: a point of great importance where the troops, like ours generally, are habituated to handling firearms almost from childhood.

78. Cavalry is now universally formed in two ranks, in order of battle. The efficiency of this arm resides in the power of its shock; and, as in a charge, the first rank alone is brought into actual contact with the enemy, the only reason for placing

a second is to close up gaps made in the front, by casualties whilst charging; and also in the melée that succeeds the charge, to have a sufficient number of sabres in hand to do good service.

79. The order of battle of artillery is necessarily a line of pieces in front; a second of caissons for the supply of immediate wants, and a third line of caissons in reserve to the rear, beyond the reach of casualties from the enemy's fire.

80. The subdivisions of the unit have their habitual position in the order of battle. This is necessary, in order that the mechanism of the unit may have that simplicity and uniformity in which there will be no difficulty in its being comprehended and retained by ordinary minds, to the end that every movement may be executed with promptitude. Still cases may occur in which the requisite rapidity to meet an attack, or to move in a given direction, cannot be attained without changing the habitual order. Such cases are provided for by what are termed *inversions*, in which the subdivisions temporarily change places and parts.

81. In all changes of position that demand a disturbance of the fundamental order of battle of the unit, it is broken into its subdivisions, which are placed in certain relative positions with respect to each other, according to the object in view. These combinations are termed *manœuvres*, and their chief object usually is to change the direction of the front of the unit, according to the particular exigency.

82. Manœuvres, like all the rest of the mechanism pertaining to the unit, should be stamped with simplicity and uniformity, for reasons already assigned. The tactics of the present day present, in this respect, a remarkable contrast to those of the period anterior to it; which is owing, in no small

measure, to the little scope left for individual fancy every proposal being submitted to the formal examination of an enlightened board. Stage spectacles alone now occasionally furnish some notions of those whimsies of olden times; so happily hit off in the well-known article of Salmagundi, where the street-pump figures as an almost impassable obstacle to the show soldier of that day.

83. The foregoing observations, upon the spirit of the actual state of tactics, can doubtless convey nothing more than a vague idea of the subject. They were introduced with this view only; so that the young student of the art might have some general notion, though a vague one, of what is proposed to be attained, before his mind gets more or less bewildered in what must seem, for some time at least, a maze of technicalities, and mere rote-work, —the systems of elementary tactics for conducting the drill.

84. *Army Organization.* Although not altogether within the design of this work, a few words here may be not out of place on army organization. Of all the civilized states of Christendom, we are perhaps the least military, though not behind the foremost as a warlike one. A sounder era, however, is dawning upon us. The desire for war, *as such,* is decreasing, whilst a feeling of the necessity for being always ready for it is becoming more general. All our battle-fields, up to the glorious feat at Buena-Vista, have proved to the world that the American soldier was wanting in no military quality, but combined the vivacity of the French with the tenacity of the English. But this, however, could make but little impression upon the soldier-statesmen of Europe. To be warlike, does not render a nation formidable to its neighbors

They may dread to attack it, but have no apprehensions from its offensive demonstrations. It was
reserved for the expedition to Vera-Cruz, and its
sequel, the victory of Cerro-Gordo, to bring into
strong relief the fact, that we were unostentatiously,
and almost silently, becoming a powerful military
state. The lesson will not be lost upon our neighbors, however slowly we, in the end, may profit by
it. A shout has gone forth from the Rio-Grande,
and the shores of the Gulf of Mexico, which, heard
on the Thames and the Seine, has resounded along
the far-off shores of the Baltic and Black Sea, and
will reach the farther Ind, bearing with it a signifi-
cance that no prudent statesman will hereafter
affect to misunderstand. What are the military resources of this great Republic is no longer a question ; a more thorough organization is alone wanting for their complete development.

85. Napoleon, at the period of the preparations
for his descent upon England, had a moment of
leisure which he could bestow upon his military organization. Then, for the first time, it is believed,
was introduced a systematic organization of grand
masses, termed *Army Corps;* each one comprising
within itself all the elements of a complete army,
and apt for any emergency.

Since then this has served as a type to France,
and other European states, in their organization.

86. An army is now composed of one, or more
army corps, made up of infantry and cavalry; an
artillery equipage, comprising several batteries ;
several artillery parks of reserve ; with a grand
one to which is attached a bridge-train.

87. Each army corps consists of one, or more
Divisions ; each division of several Brigades ; the
brigade comprising two Regiments.

4

Two batteries of foot-artillery, of six pieces each, are attached to each infantry division; and one of horse-artillery, of the same strength, to each division of heavy cavalry.

Besides, for each army corps of infantry, there is a reserve of several batteries; and a few served by foot artillery. In some cases, one of the batteries of reserve is served by the horse-artillery.

88. A company of engineer troops, termed *Sappers*, is generally attached to each infantry division; and to each infantry army corps a brigade of light cavalry; with a company of *Pontoniers*, which has charge of the bridge-train.

89. In France, each brigade is commanded by a *Maréchal de Camp*, a grade corresponding to our brigadier-general; each division by a *Lieutenant-General*, which corresponds to our major-general; and an army corps by a *Maréchal de France*.

90. The particular organization of the General Staff, and the different arms of service, would lead to details of no importance here. The proportion, however, of each arm of an army to the others, is a subject of great interest, as upon this depends, in a great degree, the more or less of excellence in the military institutions of a state.

91. The infantry, from its powers of endurance its capabilities for battle in all kinds of ground, and its independence of those casualties by which the other arms may be completely paralyzed, is placed as the *first arm;* and upon it is based the strength of all the others. It generally forms about *four-fifths* of the entire force.

92. In all states where the military art is justly appreciated, the cavalry arm is placed in the *second rank* to the infantry. To it an army is often indebted for turning the scales of victory, and giving

a decisive character to the issue. To it, the infantry, when exhausted by fatigue, or broken, often owes its safety, and through the respite gained by its charges, finds time to breathe and reform. Without it, much of advanced-post duty, patroles, and detachment service requiring great celerity, would be but badly performed.

But the arm of cavalry by itself can effect but little; and, in many circumstances, does not suffice even for its own safety. The smallest obstacles are sufficient to render it powerless; it can neither attack nor hold a post without the aid of infantry; and at night is alarmed, and justly so, at every phantom.

The proportion borne by the cavalry to the infantry should vary with the features of the seat of war; being greater in a champagne than in a broken, or mountainous country. The proportion of *one-fourth* of the infantry for the first, and *one-sixth* for the last, is generally admitted by received military authority as the best.

93. The artillery is placed *third in rank* among the arms. Its duties are to support and cover the other arms; keep the enemy from approaching too near; hold him in check when he advances; and prevent him from *débouching* at particular points. To perform these duties it is considered that an allowance of *one piece for each thousand men* of the other arms, and *one in reserve* forms the proper quota of this arm. It is to be remarked, however, that this proportion supposes the other arms in an excellent state of organization and discipline. In the contrary case, the quota of artillery must be increased; for it inspires poor troops with confidence, as they rely upon it, to keep off the enemy, and to cover their retreat. But here arises another disad-

vantage; as artillery is utterly incapable of defending itself, and therefore, when present in an over proportion, it must necessarily sustain great losses in guns and the other *matériel*.

94. The arm of engineering, although requiring more science and a higher grade of talent for its duties than any other, takes the *last place in tactical considerations*. To it is intrusted all that pertains to opposing passive obstacles to an enemy's advance, and removing those which he may have raised. To it is assigned that most difficult of all tasks to the soldier, patient endurance of manual toil, and a disregard of everything but the work in hand, whilst exposed to the enemy's fire. The proportion of engineer troops will depend in a great measure upon the character of the operations undertaken; being most in sieges, and least in those depending mainly on manœuvres. In the French service, the engineers are one-half the strength of the artillery; a large number, but rendered necessary by the peculiar military position of that country.

95. the troops which compose the three principal arms are generally subdivided into two classes, *heavy* and *light*; partly arising from the nature of their weapons, and partly from their destination on the field of battle.

96. This subdivision is less marked in the infantry than in that of the other arms; for although in most foreign armies, a portion of the infantry carries a sabre with the musket, still this additional weapon is of rather questionable utility; for the musket is the one which, under all circumstances of attack and defence, will be resorted to.

97. All infantry now receive the same instruction; but whether a portion of it ought not to be reserved especially for the duties consigned to light

troops, is still a disputed point. One thing is cer
tain, that perfection is more easily reached by con
fining the individual to one branch of his art, than
by requiring him to make himself conversant with
the whole. Still it might be often found inconvenient, at the least, if infantry were not able to
perform all the functions required of it.

98. The service of light infantry often demands
great individual address, intelligence, and well-developed physical powers; a combination of qualities
not easily found, and seldom, indeed, without careful habitual training. Whereas, in infantry of the
line, the qualities of the individual are of less importance, as results here depend almost solely upon
the action of the mass.

99. The habitual order of battle of light infantry
is the *dispersed order*; and whether acting offensively or defensively, it depends for its results upon
the effect of its fire, resorting to the close order,
and using the bayonet, only exceptionally. As
each individual, although immediately supported
by his own file-closer, and those on his right and
left, is still often thrown upon his own resources,
being obliged to take cover where he can most conveniently find it, he must be a good marksman,
cool, deliberate, and circumspect; since it may become necessary to keep an enemy occupied hours,
and even days together, pressing on him at one moment and yielding to him the next, or holding with
tenacity, and disputing inch by inch some particular point, as it may suit the views of the general in
command.

100. In infantry of the line, as success depends
upon the action of the mass, *ensemble*, coolness, and
determination should characterize all its movements,
whether it delivers its fire in line, forms in column

4*

to attack with the bayonet, or throws itself into
square, to await the charge of the enemy's cavalry.

101. The duties of light infantry are to open an
engagement, and, after it is fairly got under way,
to keep it going; turning it to advantage if successful, otherwise breaking it off. In its relations
to the infantry of the line, it should cover the
flanks of the latter; clear the way for its advance
by rooting the enemy out of all covers, and then
holding them if requisite. Upon it devolves all
advanced-post, detachment, and advanced and rear-
guard service.

102. To the infantry of the line is confided everything where firmness is the essential requisite;
as the attack or defence of key-points, the formation of all supports and reserves; whether on the
field, or in the attack and defence of posts.

103. There is a third class of infantry, termed
riflemen, which does not form a part proper of the
arm of infantry; partaking, when properly constituted, more of the character of partisan than of
regular troops; being chosen only from that portion of a population whose habits lead them *to* a
daily use of fire-arms, and give them an unerring
aim. As an auxiliary in the defence of particular
localities, where they are secure from the attack
of the bayonet, or of cavalry, and can deliver their
fire with that deliberation which their weapon demands, riflemen will often be found invaluable; as
nothing is more dreaded by troops generally than
this lurking, and often invisible foe, whose whereabout is only divined by the destruction he deals
around him.

104. In cavalry, the distinction between heavy
and light is more strongly marked, and the functions of each more clearly defined than in infantry

105. The *cuirassiers*, from their defensive armor and heavy sabre, which in both man and horse call for great physical powers, constitute the true heavy cavalry. The *dragoons* and *hussars* belong to the light, and the *lancers* indifferently perform the functions of either.

106. The most essential quality of all cavalry, which distinguishes it from all other arms, and gives it the faculty of taking an enemy frequently at disadvantage, is that of celerity. If to this the rider unites boldness, and even, when called for, recklessness, it makes of this arm a truly fearful one.

107. Cavalry, to attain its ends, should unite several essential conditions; horses and weapons in good condition; sufficient depth of ground both in front and rear to gather speed for the charge, or space for rallying; to be led boldly but skilfully into action; have its flanks covered against a surprise; and be followed by a support, or reserve, to cover the retreat, or secure from the effects of confusion the line charging, if brought up unexpectedly by the enemy.

108. There are qualities which are peculiar to each kind of cavalry, growing out of the duties required of this arm. To the heavy cavalry, the *cuirassier sans peur*, should belong the attribute of irresistibility. Apparently as careless and indifferent to the maddening strife around, as was *le Noir Fainéant*, in the "Gentle and Joyous Passage of Arms of Ashby-de-la-Zouche," whilst waiting the moment for action; the cuirassier, when, with sabre raised, he rushes on his foe, should, like the tornado, level all before him, and leave nothing of his task unfinished but the gathering of the wreck he leaves in his track.

109. The dragoon, when first instituted to combine the functions both of the foot soldier and cavalier, was found, like most mongrels, to have the qualities of neither in a very serviceable degree. He still retains his musquetoon, and on outpost duty, and skirmishing in broken ground, does a soldier's duty with this weapon. Apt for attacks, whether in close order or dispersed, he should lend himself to the charge kindly; and in cases where thrown on his own resources, display all the intelligence, activity, and circumspection of the best light infantry.

110. The dashing bold hussar, that epitome of military impudence and recklessness at the tavern, should present those qualities in a sublimated form on the field. Regardless of fatigue and danger, his imagination should never present to itself an obstacle as insurmountable. On the march, constantly at the enemy's heels; in position keeping him at all moments on the alert, harassing him either with fatigue, or apprehension for the security of his rear and communications; on the field careering with a falcon's speed and glance upon his quarry, however it may seek to elude his blow, such should be the hussar.

111. The lancer, like the poet, " is born not fashioned." In the hands of the Pole, the lance, whether used to charge in line or in the dispersion of pursuit, is a truly fearful weapon; but to those to whom long practice in its use has not made it a second nature, it is only embarrassing, and more to be avoided by a comrade than by a foeman. Still the apprehension of being run through has a powerful moral effect upon a man: and there is no sound more appalling to a flying enemy than " here come the lancers."

112. As the functions of heavy cavalry are to bear down all opposition, and present an impassable wall to the enemy's efforts, its duties are confined to the battle-field; there, placed in the reserve, it is held in hand until the decisive moment arrives, when it is launched forth to deal a blow from which the enemy hopelessly struggles to recover, either to achieve victory, or to fend off utter defeat.

113. To light cavalry are intrusted the important duties of securing from surprise the flanks of the heavy; to watch over the safety of horse artillery, and to perform the services required of them by infantry divisions, and those of detachment service in general.

114. The artillery, which had for a long period, and even still, preserves the character of eminent respectability, has of late years begun to infuse a dash of the dare-devil spirit of the cavalier into its ranks. If it has not yet taken to charging literally, it has, on some recent occasions in our service, shown a well-considered recklessness of obstacles and dangers, fully borne out by justly deserved success.

115. The distinction between light and heavy in this arm arises, not only from the difference of calibre in the pieces, but also in a difference of their tactical application.

116. The heavy field calibre is the 12-pounder, which is reserved for batteries in position, and is seldom shifted during the action.

117. The light field calibre is the 6-pounder, and the 24-pounder howitzer, which are served either by foot or horse-artillery, and follow the movements of the other arms.

118. Improvements both in the *matériel* and the tactics of artillery have been very marked within

late years. Formerly, considered only in the light of an auxiliary on the battle-field, artillery now aspires, and with indisputable claims, to the rank of a principal arm. Its decisive effects, at the late battles on the Rio-Grande,* are supported by testimony too emphatic to be overlooked.

119. From the studies required of him, the artillerist is well trained to maintain the characteristics of his arm; courage of the highest order, in which the physical is always under the control of the moral element, producing, as a necessary result, unbounded devotion to the task assigned; a presence of mind that nothing can disturb; and that coolness which no danger, however appalling, can impair.

120. The tactical applications of artillery on the field depend on the calibre. To the heavy are assigned the duties of occupying positions for strengthening the weak points of the field of battle; for securing the retreat of the army; for defending all objects whose possession might be of importance to the enemy, as villages, defiles, &c.; and for overturning all passive obstacles that cover the enemy, or arrest the progress of the other arms.

121. The light pieces, served by foot-artillery, follow the movements of the infantry; covering the

* In alluding to the late brilliant achievements of our artillery, it is but just to call attention to the fact, that the country is indebted for it to the Hon. Joel R. Poinsett, late Secretary of War under the administration of President Van Buren. Without the forethought and military sagacity of this accomplished gentleman, and his untiring efforts, while in office, to promote the public good and insure its safety if suddenly brought into a state of war; the country, in all probability, would have been found, on the breaking out of the Mexican difficulties, in the same dilemma with regard to this most important arm, as it was in some other hardly less essential points. It is to be hoped that the maxim so often idly repeated, and the value of which was here forcibly illustrated, *In Peace prepare for War*, may not again be used in vain.

flanks of its position, preparing the way for its onset, and arresting that of the enemy. It is of this
that the principal part of the artillery in reserve is
composed.

122. The horse-artillery is held in hand for decisive moments. When launched forth, its arrival
and execution should be unexpected and instanta-
neous. Ready to repair all disasters and partial
reverses, it, at one moment, temporarily replaces a
battery of foot, and at the next is on another point
of the field, to force back an enemy's column. In
preparing the attacks of cavalry, this arm is often
indispensable and always invaluable; brought with
rapidity in front of a line, or opposite to squares of
infantry, within the range of canister, its well-
directed fire, in a few discharges, opens a gap, or so
shakes the entire mass, that the cavalier finds but a
feeble obstacle, where, without this aid, he would in
vain have exhausted all his powers.

CHAPTER II.

INFANTRY.

123. *Position and Formation.* On the field of battle, whether the object be to attack, or defend, the infantry is divided into three bodies; an advanced-guard, the main-body, and a reserve. Their relative proportion will depend upon the total force, and the character of the position occupied. The advanced-guard must be of sufficient strength to hold the enemy in check, but, at the same time, the main body, upon which the brunt of the action should fall, must not be left of insufficient force, by unnecessarily increasing the advanced-guard; and the reserve should be strong enough to repair any disaster that may befall the main body; or to profit by its success in accomplishing the complete over-throw of the enemy.

124. These three bodies are separated from each other by intervals which will depend upon the nature of the ground. The advanced-guard occupying the front; the main-body at a distance from 150 to 300 paces in its rear; and the reserve at a like interval to the rear of the main body. Where the ground, for example, is undulating, and therefore favorable to masking the troops from the enemy's fire, these intervals may, if requisite, be reduced to 80 or 100 paces.

125. The troops composing these three bodies will be formed either in columns of battalions, or

be deployed, according to the circumstances under which they may be placed. For an attack, for evolution, or for defence against cavalry, the formations of columns of battalions is best. To repel the enemy's attack by a fire, and in some cases, to present a less favorable mark to his artillery, the battalions are deployed. The battalions, whether deployed or in column, preserve the proper intervals for evolutions; these intervals may be increased in obstructed ground without weakening the defence.

126. The battalions composing the main-body may be drawn up in one or two lines. The latter usually obtains only when a large force is present. In this case the reserve no longer holds the position of a third line, as in the other; but forms an independent body, to be used according to the emergency; the second line supporting the battalions of the first, and, for this purpose, occupying positions to the rear, opposite to their intervals.

127. *Defence.* When the position is taken up to receive the enemy's attack, and then either to remain on the defensive, or to assume the offensive, as circumstances may justify, the advanced-guard will be posted on the ground most favorable to hold the enemy in check, and so force him, by disputing it with tenacity, to develope his means and plans. This is best done by a judicious combat of skirmishers, who, for this purpose, are thrown forward 300 or 400 paces, to feel the enemy, and are only reinforced when closely pressed.

128. Whether the advanced-guard shall maintain its ground obstinately until reinforced by the main-body, or whether it shall fall back, either on the flanks or to the rear of the main-body, must be determined by the strength of its position. If this be so strong that the enemy's loss in carrying it must

be great, then it should be pertinaciously maintained; in the contrary case it must, after a suitable show of resistance, be abandoned.

129. As a general rule, troops should be placed as much out of view as practicable before they go into action, by taking advantage of covers offered by the ground. The main-body should be kept masked in this way until it is called to engage the enemy. If it advance to support the advanced-guard, it will usually attack with the bayonet; if the advanced-guard is called in, the main-body will usually receive the enemy by its fire; the battalions being deployed for this purpose. If the enemy is staggered by this fire, or, in advancing, shows, by the wavering or confusion of his line, a want of confidence, the fire may be followed up either by a charge of the troops in line; or they may be formed in columns of attack before charging, if the enemy perseveres in his onward movement. A charge by a column, when the enemy is within 50 paces, will prove effective, if resolutely made.

130. The reserve is composed of the most reliable troops. It should be distinguished for cool courage; acting under all circumstances, either defensive or offensive, with circumspection and determined resolution.

As the object of the reserve is to infuse greater energy into the action of the main-body, and, if necessary, to strike a last and decisive blow, it should be kept masked from the enemy's fire and view until called into action. The proper moment for engaging the reserve is either when the enemy has been shaken in his attack by the resistance offered by the main-body, or when the latter is unable farther to resist the enemy's efforts. If engaged too soon, the resistance offered to the reserve may prevent its making a decisive blow; if not engaged in time, the main-body may be too far exhausted and disorganized to rally.

In cases where the reserve forms a second line, to support the main-body, it should approach the first line when it becomes engaged, to be ready to replace it when circumstances may render it necessary. The advanced-guard, in such cases, should retire to the rear, to act as a reserve.

131. *Attack.* In the attack of infantry, the same fundamental dispositions are made as for the defensive. The advanced-guard will not throw forward its skirmishers until they are near enough to engage the enemy. The line of skirmishers should be strongly supported, and will press the enemy with vigor and without relaxation. If the force engaged be small, the main-body will regulate its movements by those of the line of skirmishers; if considerable, the reverse will obtain.

132. The main-body and reserve follow in column the advanced-guard, preserving the requisite intervals. The columns should take every advantage of the ground to mask their movements; getting rapidly over any where they are much exposed to fire. So soon as the advanced-guard is checked, it will fall back either on the flanks of the columns, or to the rear; and the main-body will be immediately brought into action, either by deploying and opening its fire, or by a vigorous charge with the bayonet. If the main-body falters in its attack, or gives any signs of want of resolution, the reserve should advance at once through the intervals, and make a vigorous charge with the bayonet.

133. If the attack by the main-body is made with the bayonet, the interval between it and the col-

umns of the reserve may be lessened to 80 or 100
paces. The flanks of the columns of attack, and
the intervals between them, should be occupied by
skirmishers. This is an important precaution; as,
by forcing the enemy to deliver his fire before the
columns have reached within a destructive range,
the main obstacle to their onward movement will
be removed.

134. *Pursuit.* If the assailed retires, the pursuit must be conducted with system and in good
order. The line nearest the enemy will throw forward a few troops in pursuit; which, in most cases,
will be preceded by skirmishers. The line in close
order, will follow these troops until it attains a good
position to receive the enemy, should he make an
offensive movement, when it will be halted and
formed in readiness for action. A pursuit by infantry alone cannot be pushed far, even should the
enemy retire without any order, or show of resistance, as the retreating force will soon distance their
pursuers.

135. *Retreat.* When, either in the defensive, or
offensive, it becomes necessary to retire, the first
point to be attended to is to withdraw the troops
engaged; either to a good position to their rear,
where they can halt and face the enemy, or else
behind the line in their rear, which should hold the
assailants in check, and allow the retreating troops
to fall back in good order. Having fairly got dis-
engaged, dispositions must be promptly made tc
withdraw from the field. This may be done by
the entire force moving off together, if the enemy
shows no disposition to follow up his success with
energy; or, in the contrary case, by retiring by
successive portions; the line which withdraws falling some 150 paces to the rear of the one by which

It is covered, whilst falling back, and then forming, to cover in turn the retreat of the latter.

The dispositions made in the retreat will depend entirely upon the character of the enemy's pursuit, and the features of the ground. It will usually be made in columns, covered by skirmishers, if the pursuit is made by infantry alone; if by cavalry, the retreat must be made with great circumspection; the troops retiring slowly and in good order, adopting the formation against cavalry; never hastening the march, unless very near a good position for defence, which should be attained as rapidly as possible, unless closely pressed by the cavalry.

136. If it be necessary to continue the retreat for some marches, under the eye of the enemy, a rear-guard must be formed; selecting, from a fourth to a third of the entire force, for this service. The main duty of the rear-guard is to hinder the enemy from pressing too closely on the main-body; and it should therefore, under no circumstances, allow itself to be forced back upon the main-body. The dispositions adopted by the rear-guard will depend upon the features of the ground; its rear will usually be covered by a line of skirmishers. The rear-guard will keep within good supporting distance of the main-body; and, when pressed by the enemy, the latter, whenever a favorable position offers, will halt and form; to cover the former, and force the enemy to greater circumspection.

137. *Measures for protracting an Engagement.* In the attack, as in the defence, it may frequently become an object to protract an engagement, without coming to any decisive result; either for the purpose of holding a position for a certain time, to favor other objects, as the arrival of reinforcements; or to occupy an adversary upon one point whilst a

5*

54

decisive blow is preparing on another. This game can be played only upon ground favorable to alternations from the defensive to the offensive; and should only be intrusted to troops thoroughly conversant with the duties of skirmishers. The main-body is kept some two thousand paces to the rear of the skirmishers in such affairs; taking advantage of the ground, and making suitable dispositions of the troops to avoid the effects of the enemy's artillery. Small columns are thrown forward between itself and the troops engaged, which take post in covered ground, to be at hand to support the skirmishers. The troops engaged should be promptly reinforced, when the enemy presses onward; and attempts should be made, by charging him in flank, to force him to retire. The troops in action should be frequently relieved, and the opportunity should be seized, when the fresh troops come up, to make an onward movement on the enemy, and force him from any points he may have gained.

138. *Defence against Cavalry.* When infantry is threatened by cavalry, the proper formation to repel its charge is that of squares. If but one square is formed, it must rely on its own resources to beat off the enemy; but when there are several they may give mutual support, by bringing a flank fire from one upon a force advancing on either of the two contiguous to it. The safety of infantry against cavalry will depend upon the preservation of perfect coolness, good order, and connection in the ranks; the avoidance of any precipitate movements which might bring about a surprise; and the husbanding of its ammunition, and reservation of its fire until the enemy is within a deadly range. Well disciplined infantry, whilst in position, and when not exposed to a fire of artillery, may securely trust to its

own resources to repulse the best cavalry, so long as it adopts the proper precautions. If annoyed, as sometimes may happen, by the fire of a few horsemen, advanced to draw the fire of the squares, it will be better to throw out some skirmishers, ten or twelve paces from the squares, to keep off such attacks, than to open a fire from the squares.

139. *Defence, &c. against Artillery.* Infantry may take advantage, either of covers presented by the features of the ground, or of occasionally shifting its position, to avoid the fire of artillery. Very slight undulations, or obstructions, like the low banks along the borders of ditches, will serve to cover troops, by causing the shot to rise above them. If no covers are at hand, the chances of casualties, when within point-blank range, may be diminished by moving forward, or backward, some 50 paces; if the fire be a ricochet, the position should be shifted some 50 paces to the right or left. The enemy's batteries may be annoyed, and sometimes be forced to change their position, by sending out good marks-men, who advance singly to within some 250 paces of them; where, lying down, they can pick off the officers, men and horses.

140. *Attack of Artillery.* Whenever it is found necessary to carry a battery by the bayonet, the troops for this duty are divided into two detachments; one of which is charged with capturing the guns, and the other with attacking the supports of the battery.

The dispositions made by the detachment which moves against the guns will be the usual one of skirmishers; the line surrounding the battery, and opening their fire upon it when within about 250 paces, taking advantage for this purpose of any covers, to screen the men. The supports of the

.ine of skirmishers should be kept well to the rear
to be ready against a flank movement on the line.
If this manœuvre succeeds in drawing the fire of
the guns, and any confusion is observed among the
men, then a rush must be immediately made upon
them with the bayonet.

The detachment against the supports of the battery will make its dispositions according to the kind
of troops which compose the supports. If of infantry, the detachment to seize the guns, divided into
two portions, will advance either in line, or column,
as may be best, on the flanks of the line of skirmishers; gradually getting in advance of it, and
closing on the flanks of the battery, so as to attack
the supports in flank; or else they may keep to the
rear of the line of skirmishers, in order to tempt the
supports to move forward, and thus mask the fire
of their guns. If the supports are of cavalry, the
detachment, divided into two columns, will follow
the line of skirmishers. in rear of the flanks; to cover
it against a charge of the cavalry.

CAVALRY.

141. *Position.* This arm is usually placed in
the rear of the infantry, on ground favorable to its
manœuvres, and where it will be masked from fire
until the moment arrives to bring it into action;
here, if acting on the defensive, the cavalry watches
its opportunity to support the other troops, driving
back the enemy, by prompt and vigorous charges,
when these are hard pressed; or, if on the offensive,
biding its time, to rush upon the assailant, and complete his destruction; when his ranks commence to
waver or show signs of disorganization from the
assaults of the other arms

142. *Formation.* The habitual formation of cavalry for the attack is in a line of two ranks, with a reserve, or support to its rear. The supports are indispensably requisite to guard against those chances of danger to which cavalry is particularly exposed, if attacked in turn, when in a state of partial disorganization, after a successful charge; or when threatened by an offensive movement against its flanks. The supports offer a safeguard against either of these dangers; for, if the front line is brought up by the enemy, after a successful charge, it can retire and rally in the rear of the supports; and if the enemy makes a movement against the flanks, the supports, placed behind them and in column, can form and anticipate the enemy's charge. For the foregoing reasons, cavalry should not give way to a headlong pursuit after a successful charge, unless its supports are at hand; and, in cases where a charge is made without supports, a portion only should engage in pursuit, the rest being rallied to form a support.

143. Cavalry is seldom called on to use fire-arms. When on out-post service, or acting on the defensive on ground unfavorable to charging, a portion of the force may be dispersed as flankers, to hold the enemy in check by their fire. In this case their movements are regulated in the same way as other skirmishers.

144. *Defence.* The defensive qualities of cavalry lie in the offensive. A body of cavalry which waits to receive a charge of cavalry, or is exposed to a fire of infantry, or artillery, must either retire, or be destroyed. This essential quality of cavalry renders its services invaluable in retreats where the enemy pursues with vigor. In such cases it should be held in constant readiness to take advantage of

every spot favorable to its action; and, by short and
energetic charges, force the enemy to move with
circumspection.

145. *Attack against Infantry.* So long as infantry maintains its position firmly, particularly if
the ground is at all unfavorable to the movements
of cavalry, the chances are against a successful attack by the latter. Cavalry should therefore either
wait patiently until a way is prepared for its action, by a fire of artillery on the enemy's infantry;
or until the infantry has become crippled and exhausted by being kept in action for some time; or
else, watching its opportunity, make a charge whilst
the infantry is in motion, so as to surprise it before
it can form to receive the attack.

Cavalry should direct its charge on that point of
the enemy's infantry where it will itself be exposed
to the least column of fire. If the infantry is in line,
the charge should be made on one of its flanks; if
in square, on one of the angles of the square; and
when several squares are formed, so as to afford
mutual support by their fire, selecting the squares
on the flanks as most vulnerable, from their position.

146. The formation usually recommended for
charging against squares, is that of three squadrons
in line at double distance; the leading squadron
being followed by the others, either directly in its
rear; or else the squadrons may be formed in echelon, successively overlapping each other by about
the front of a platoon. The angle of the square is
charged by each squadron in succession, if the
charge of the one preceding it fails; the repulsed
squadrons each wheeling to the right, or left on retiring; to leave the way clear for its successor. A
fourth squadron in column follows those in line; to

surround the square and make prisoners if it should
be broken by the charge.

147. To draw the fire of the infantry before
charging, a few skilful flankers may be thrown
forward, to open a fire on the square. Stratagem
may also be tried, by moving along the front of the
infantry, at some 400 paces, and then charging, if
it is tempted to throw away its fire at this distance.
In an attack where several squares are in line, if
one fires to second another it should be instantly
charged.

148. *Attack against Artillery.* In attacks against
artillery, the detachment of cavalry should be divided into three bodies; one-fourth of the detachment being charged with carrying the guns; one-
half to attack the supports of the battery; and the
remaining fourth acting as a reserve, to cover the
parties in advance, from an offensive movement
against their flanks, or rear.

The party to secure the guns make their attack
in dispersed order, and endeavor to gain the flanks
of the battery. When the battery has a fair sweep
over the ground along which they must advance,
they should, by manœuvring and false attacks, try
to confuse the artillerists, and draw their fire before
making their charge.

The attack against the support of the battery
will be directed in the usual manner; the party
manœuvring to gain their flanks.

ARTILLERY.

149. *Position.* The manner of placing artillery and its employment must be regulated by its
relative importance under given circumstances,
with respect to the action of the other arms.

In the defensive, the principal part is usually assigned to the artillery; and the positions taken up by the other arms will, therefore, be subordinate to those of this arm. In offensive movements the reverse generally obtains.

150. *Defence.* In defensive positions the security of the batteries is of the last importance. Unless the batteries are on points which are inaccessible to the enemy's cavalry and infantry, they must be placed under the protection of the other troops, and be outflanked by them.

As in the defensive, we should be prepared to receive the enemy on every point; the batteries must be distributed along the entire front of the position occupied, and on those points from which they can obtain a good sweep over the avenues of approach to it; the guns being masked, when the ground favors, from the enemy's view, until the proper moment arrives for opening their fire.

151. The distance between the batteries should not be much over 600 paces; so that by their fire they may cover well the ground intervening between them, and afford mutual support; the light guns being placed on the more salient points of the front, from their shorter range and greater facility of manœuvring; the heavier guns on the more retired points. Guns of various calibre should not be placed in the same battery. A sufficient interval should also be left between batteries of different calibre; to prevent the enemy from judging, by the variations in the effect of the shot, of the weight of metal of the batteries.

Those positions for batteries should be avoided from which the shot must pass over other troops, to attain the enemy. And those should be sought for from which a fire can be maintained until the enemy has approached even within good musket-range of them.

Where the wings of a position are weak, batteries of the heaviest calibre should be placed to secure them.

152. A sufficient number of pieces—selecting for the object in view horse-artillery in preference to any other—should be held in reserve for a moment of need; to be thrown upon any point where the enemy's progress threatens danger; or to be used in covering the retreat.

153. The collection of a large number of pieces in a single battery, is a dangerous arrangement; particularly at the outset of an engagement. The exposure of so many guns together might present a strong inducement to the enemy to make an effort to carry the battery; a feat the more likely to succeed, as it is difficult either to withdraw the guns, or change their position promptly, after their fire is opened; and one which, if successful, might entail a fatal disaster on the assailed, from the loss of so many pieces at once.

154. In all defensive dispositions the ammunition should be most carefully husbanded. A fire should never be opened until the enemy is within good range; and, when once opened, be continued with perseverance and coolness up to the last moment in which it can be made effective.

155. *Attack.* In the outset of offensive movements, good positions should be selected for the heaviest pieces, from which they can maintain a strong fire on the enemy until the lighter pieces and the columns of attack are brought into action. These positions should be taken on the flanks of the ground occupied by the assailant, or on the centre, if more favorable to the end to be attained. In all

cases, wide intervals should be left between the heavy batteries and the other troops; in order that the latter may not suffer from the return fire which the assailed will probably open on the batteries. For the same reason, care should be taken not to place other troops behind a point occupied by a battery, where they would be exposed to the return fire of the assailed; when this cannot be avoided, the troops should be so placed as to be covered by any undulation of the ground; or else be deployed in line to lessen the effects of the shot.

156. The artillery which moves with the columns of attack, should be divided into several strong batteries; as the object in this case is to produce a decisive impression upon a few points of the enemy's line; by bringing an overwhelming fire to bear upon these points. These batteries should keep near enough to the other troops to be in safety from any attempts of the assailed to capture them. Their usual positions will be on the flanks and near the heads of the columns of attack; the intervals between the batteries being sufficient for the free manœuvres of the other troops, in large bodies. The manœuvres of these batteries should be made with promptitude; so that no time may be lost for the action of their fire. They should get rapidly over unfavorable ground to good positions for firing, and maintain these as long as possible; detaching, in such cases, a few pieces to accompany the columns of attack. In all the movements of the batteries, great care should be taken not to place them so that they shall in the least impede the operations of the other troops.

CHAPTER III.

157. Among the most important modern additions to the military art, is that of *topography*, or the study of the natural features of positions, with a view to turn them to account in the first dispositions for battle, and its various succeeding phases.

158. It is only by this study that the *coup d'œil militaire*, or the art of disposing troops in harmony with the ground on which they are to act, can be brought to any high degree of perfection; whatever may be the natural gifts of the individual.

159. This study is not altogether of modern origin. Among the ancients, some of the Greek generals have given evidence of a feeling of its importance; as in the examples of Épaminondas, Xenophon, Alexander, and particularly of Philopœmen. The Romans, although having adopted an order of battle which lent itself better to varied features of ground than that of the Greeks, still showed but little knowledge of this branch, until after the wars with Pyrrhus, when the art of *Castrametation* underwent some change with them.

160. The tactics which grew out of the French Revolution gave to topography great prominence; and no general perhaps has ever displayed more consummate attainments in this respect than Napoleon; whose descriptive memoirs, particularly of the Alps, are considered as models for all graphic writings; presenting with clearness and comprehensiveness, a picture that the mind's eye cannot fail to seize.

161. The term *Position* is applied to any grouno taken up by a body of troops either to make, or to receive an attack.

162. To select a position understandingly, an officer must possess a thorough practical knowledge of the tactical combinations of the different arms; their respective qualifications for the offensive and defensive; and of the adaptation of ground to their particular manœuvres.

163. In choosing a position, the ground must be examined not only with respect to its peculiar suitableness to the object in view, but also with reference to the influence of that in its vicinity upon this object.

164. The first point to be looked to is the extent of the position. This should be such that, deduction made of the advanced-posts, and of the reserve, its front and flanks shall present an unbroken line of troops, from which a close and well-sustained fire can be brought upon all points by which these can be approached.

In estimating the front of a position, an allowance of about 180 yards may be made for each battalion, from 600 to 700 strong; about 60 yards for each squadron of horse of 48 files, the necessary intervals between these units being included in this estimate; and from 12 to 20 yards for the interval between the pieces of a battery.

In estimating the depth, an allowance of 600 to 800, yards at least, should be made from the front to the rear; in order that the two lines and the reserve may be posted in suitable relative positions for good support.

165. The position should offer no features by which the prompt movement of troops from one point to another, for mutual support, might be ob-

structed. Its *débouches* to the front for offensive
movements, as well as those to its rear in case of
retreat, should be ample. It should be beyond the
effective cannon range of commanding heights both
on its front and flanks.

166. The flanks, being the weakest point• of a
body of troops, must be secured from being turned,
or attacked; by resting them upon some strong
natural feature of the position, as a river, precipice,
&c., which the enemy can neither turn, nor seize
upon; or else on some point that will afford sufficient means of prolonging the resistance to enable
reinforcements to reach it in time, as an intrenched
village,* a field work, &c. When the flanks cannot be secured in either of these ways, they must
be strengthened by an accumulation of troops upon
them; to offer a vigorous resistance to the enemy
should he attempt an attack.

167. *Positions for the Defensive.* When a position is taken up to maintain a strictly defensive
attitude, the natural features of its front should be
of a character to prevent an enemy from approaching in good order; and to enable the assailed to
dispute, with advantage, every foot of ground.
The enemy, moreover, should not be able to turn
the position, when it is unavoidably exposed to this
manœuvre, without great risk to his own safety, by
an offensive movement of the assailed on his flanks,
or rear.

168. The manner of disposing and handling
troops in a defensive position will mainly depend
upon its natural features. The only rule that can
be laid down is, to post the different arms upon
ground best adapted to their respective tactics ·

* See Chapters VII, IX. X, and XI, Mahan's Field Fortifica
tion, on Intrenchments, &c., of Positions, &c.

and in such relative positions as to afford mutual
support, and not impede each other's movements.

169. The obstructions on the front and flanks of
the position will be occupied by the advanced-guard,
formed of light troops of each arm, if the ground is
favorable to their combined action; for the purpose
of observing the enemy, and holding him in check
if he makes an onward movement.

170. The main-body of the infantry will occupy
every point, between the obstacles on which the
flanks rest, in such a manner that no intervals
shall be presented through which the enemy can
penetrate without being exposed to a close and
powerful line of fire.

171. The artillery will be placed on those points
where it can have a commanding view of the ground
in advance of the position, and sweep by its fire the
approaches of the enemy, both in front and flank.

172. The cavalry, posted in rear of the infantry,
should occupy ground upon which it can make
effective charges, to support the infantry when
pressed by the enemy.

173. In posting troops on obstructed ground, care
should be taken not to place them on points where
they can only be idle spectators of the combat;
either from the impossibility of their being approached by the enemy, or from their not being
able to join the enemy at the proper moment. In
like manner, those points should be avoided where,
from obstacles in their rear, the safety of the troops
might be compromised in case of retreat. Whenever it becomes necessary to dispute the possession
of the latter class of points with the enemy, the
avenues to the rear must be occupied by detachments of suitable strength, to secure the retreat of
the troops in advance.

174. In order that the necessary manœuvres may be promptly executed, without confusion; and to avoid offering a mark that might attract the enemy's fire, and occasion useless exposure; no more troops should be placed on any point than its defence may indispensably require; and whenever it becomes requisite to strengthen a weak point, by an accumulation of troops upon it, every advantage should be taken of the undulations, or other accidents of the ground, to mask them from the enemy's fire until the moment arrives for bringing them into action.

175. The value of obstacles, as supports for the flanks, or as obstructions in the front, or rear of a position, is altogether relative; and depends on the number of troops. A very slight obstacle on a flank, which will serve to hold the enemy in check but a few minutes, may answer all the purposes of a small body of troops; by enabling them to make such changes in their dispositions as the nature of the case may call for; whereas a larger body, under like circumstances, might be overwhelmed on their flank before they could make suitable manœuvres to prevent it. A broken, obstructed country to the rear, presenting few and narrow avenues of retreat, might be fatal to a large body of troops forced to retire in the face of an enemy; whereas, to a small body, the same features of ground might present many points where strong positions could be momentarily taken up to hold the enemy in check, and force him to pursue slowly and circumspectly.

176. When it is found that the enemy is moving upon the position, the advanced-guard makes suitable dispositions to hold him in check; by occupying with its skirmishers all the obstacles in its front

and flanks; when forced to retire upon the main position, these troops concentrate more and more as they approach it, taking care not to mask the fire, or impede the action of the main-body.

177. The artillery will only open its fire when the enemy is within a destructive range; it will then concentrate its efforts against the columns of attack; not replying to the fire of the enemy's batteries, unless it becomes urgent to do so, from their effects upon the other troops. The artillery will maintain its positions with pertinacity, as long as possible; watching its opportunities, during the different phases of the action, to support and succor the other arms; as, for example, when it becomes necessary to replace the front line of infantry by the reserve; to advance the cavalry; when the other arms are obstinately disputing a decisive point; or when the enemy abandons the attack. The great mobility of field-artillery, owing to the more recent improvements, places it in the power of this arm to act with great boldness in support of the others. The ground over which the guns may be required to move, for this purpose, should be well examined, before the attack commences, by the officer commanding the artillery; that no delays may occur in bringing them into action upon the proper point at the proper moment.

178. The main-body of the infantry should not open its fire until it can be thrown in with deadly effect. If the enemy, unchecked by the fire, still pushes forward, he must be met by a charge, either in line, or column, from the point menaced; a portion of the reserve immediately closing the interval left by the troops making the charge.

179. The reserve should not be brought into action unless its co-operation is indispensable for ob-

taining some decisive result; as forcing the enemy back from some important point from which the main-body has been compelled to retire; or covering the retreat of the main-body, until it can rally and form again in the rear.

180. The cavalry must be in readiness, from its position, to act promptly, either against any attempt upon the flanks of the infantry; or to profit by any faults, or disorder of the enemy. If the enemy throws forward small detachments without supporting them properly, or advances his main-line without securing his flanks, or shows symptoms of confusion in his infantry, the opportunity should not be lost by the cavalry. In all movements of the infantry, either in advancing or retiring, the cavalry should be at hand to cover it from a sudden attack.

181. If the enemy is beaten off, pursuit is made, either by the cavalry or by detachments of infantry, according to the features of the ground; whilst the main-body is promptly rallied, and placed in position, to receive the enemy should the attack be renewed.

182. The dispositions for a retreat will depend upon the circumstances under which it may be made. When the troops retire by successive lines, the greater portion of the artillery should always be in the line nearest the enemy, and between the battalions; the remainder being in the second line, ready to repulse any flank attack. The cavalry is posted in rear of the second line, either upon one, or both wings, to be in readiness for a charge at any moment.

183. When the entire force moves off together, the rear is secured by a rear-guard of the best troops, composed of one, or several arms, as the circumstances of the ground may require. The

rear-guard will profit by the features of the ground to check the enemy; but will be careful not to lose time, by prolonging unnecessarily the resistance on any point; as this might bring the main force of the enemy upon it.

184. Great circumspection should be shown in retreating through obstructed ground; in watching the enemy's movements on the flanks; and in timely securing defiles leading to the rear; to prevent the enemy from cutting off the retreat.

185. *Attack.* An enemy may be made to abandon a defensive position, either by driving him from it; or by manœuvring to turn it, and so force him to fall back to secure his line of communications. In attempting the latter plan, it should not be forgotten that the assailant is, to a greater or less degree, exposed to the same danger as his adversary, who, if active and enterprising, may turn the tables on him.

The celebrated battle of Rivoli, in which a portion of the Austrian force turned the flank of the French position, and was there obliged to lay down their arms,—Napoleon, using on that occasion, when these troops were discovered in his rear, one of those magical expressions, " *Those are ours,*" by which he so well understood how to electrify the soldier,—is a remarkable example on this head. The battle of Buena-Vista, where the Mexicans, after turning the flank and gaining the rear of our troops, barely escaped a similar fate, is another; whilst that of Cerro-Gordo is as remarkable for the masterly and admirable manner in which the enemy's position was turned and carried, although resting upon ground which was fairly deemed impracticable by him.

186. In planning the attack of a position, atten-

tion must, in the first place, be directed to those points in which its main-strength resides, and for this reason termed the *key-points*, the loss of which will force the assailed to retire. As the assailed will probably put forth all his efforts to maintain these points, their attack will demand corresponding exertions on the part of the assailant; and should be made only with troops of the best character.

187. In the second place, those points must be carefully examined, which, by their fire, flank the position; as an advance upon its front cannot be made without great loss and hazard of success until the assailed is dislodged from them.

188. Finally, points which are weak, either from the features of the ground, or from a faulty disposition of the troops; as approaches which are badly swept by the fire of the assailed; an exposed flank with too few troops; or a point where they are not properly placed for mutual support.

189. The main effort of the assailant is seldom directed against more than one point of the position; that one being usually selected which, if carried, will lead to the most decisive results; as, for example, one of the flanks, when not resting upon any strong obstacles. But the main attack is always combined with demonstrations upon some other point; both with a view of deceiving the assailed as to the real point of attack, and to prevent him from withdrawing troops from other points to strengthen the one menaced.

190. These demonstrations, or false attacks are, in some cases, made by the advanced-guard of the assailant, after driving in that of the assailed; in others, by a special detachment. In the latter case, the detachment should seldom exceed a fourth of the entire force; and should be composed of troops

of each arm; both for its own safety against any
offensive movement, and to present to the assailed
a likelihood of danger.

191. The advanced-guard, composed of light
troops of each arm, commences the attack, by driving in the advanced posts of the assailed; keeping
within supporting distance of the main-body, and
occupying such points as may be necessary to
cover its manœuvres, or to secure its retreat in
case of failure. If a reconnoissance of the position has not been previously made, it will be effected under cover of the movements of the advanced-guard.

192. The artillery takes position where it can
silence the batteries of the assailed, and prepare
the way for the advance of the other troops. The
infantry is usually formed in two columns for the
real attack; the leading column being sometimes
preceded by an advance. A part of the artillery
advances either in one body, or in echelon, on the
flank of the column of attack; the leading section
preceding, by about a hundred paces, the head of
the column of attack. If the column of attack de-
ploys to open its fire, the artillery moves to one of
its flanks and seconds it by a fire of case shot. If
the column charges with the bayonet, the advanced
portion of artillery retires to the position of that in
the rear; to be ready to cover the infantry by its
fire, if the attack fails. The cavalry follows in the
rear of the infantry; to secure its flanks from any
offensive movement, and to hold the assailed in
check, should he attempt a pursuit after beating
off the infantry.

193. If the attack is successful, the artillery and
the greater portion of the infantry are immediately
formed in good order, to be in readiness for any

emergency; the pursuit being left to the cavalry and some detachments of infantry. In 'case of failure the troops engaged fall back under cover of those in their rear; the artillery, by a well-directed fire, and the cavalry by opportune charges, holding the enemy in check, until order is re-established in the retiring troops, as a preliminary to a retreat, or to a renewal of the attack.

194. *Positions in obstructed Ground.* This term may be applied to localities where the ground, although level, is cut up by ditches, hedges, broken roads, &c., which obstruct the free movement of troops.

195. Positions of this character are more favorable to the defensive than the offensive. As, from the nature of the case, connected movements are, for the most part, impracticable, the commander will find it difficult to direct the engagement, and must rely upon the judgment and skill of his subordinates for its successful issue.

196. The general disposition of the troops will be in dispersed order. There will be but few opportunities for the action of cavalry; and the artillery can seldom find positions to act in mass. The light cavalry and light pieces may be placed in front, wherever they can act with advantage, and support the infantry. The supports and reserves should be kept well to the rear of the troops engaged; to be ready to meet the enemy should he attempt to turn the flanks, a manœuvre to which obstructed ground is frequently favorable. The heavy cavalry and heavy artillery take post to the rear, at any point which may offer a good position to cover the retreat.

197. The attack, like the defence, will be mainly conducted by the infantry, and some light pieces;

7

the infantry, acting as skirmishers, and the artillery
being employed to force any opening, that may
offer, for the advance of the infantry. Whenever
the artillery gets a good position it should endeavor
to keep it as long as practicable. The cavalry
can effect but little; as the enemy's, even if inferior in strength, may watch its opportunities, from
behind obstacles, to make short and successful
charges. The artillery not in action will occupy
the roads, at points to the rear most suitable for
covering the retreat, if the attack fails.

198. In positions of a mixed character, presenting alternations of open and obstructed ground, the
troops on the defensive must guard, with great care,
every accessible point at which the assailant can
débouche from the obstructed upon the open portions. A strong fire of heavy artillery should be
brought to bear upon these points; and cavalry
should be posted in places where they can be
masked from the enemy's fire, and be at hand to
charge the assailant, as he attempts to débouche.
These efforts should be seconded by the bayonets
of the infantry, if a favorable opportunity occurs.

199. The obstructed ground to the rear must be
strongly occupied, to secure the retreat; by posting light troops under the cover afforded by the
skirts of woods, by ditches bordered with trees and
hedges, &c.; and advantage must be taken of every
small defile, to dispute the ground inch by inch.

200. In the phases of engagements in positions
of this character, the defence must frequently be
accommodated to the troops at hand; as in the confusion of the most orderly retreat, in such cases, it
is impracticable to preserve that connection between
the movements of the different arms which would
be best for mutual support. If the assailant, by

disconnected movements, or a disorderly pursuit,
.ays himself open to an attack, it should be made
and pressed with vigor, or not at all.

201. In the attack of mixed positions, the supports and reserves should be kept well to the rear,
whilst the troops are engaged in the obstructed portions; to guard against offensive movements on the
flanks by the assailed. Those engaged should close
in as the ground opens, to prepare to *débouche* upon
it in force; in which operation the infantry must be
covered by the cavalry and artillery. In advancing
upon the obstructed ground, the way must be prepared for an attack with the bayonet, by a heavy
fire of the artillery, directed particularly upon the
most accessible points.

Operations of this character demand extreme prudence and forethought. Every forward movement
must be made with great caution; every point
gained must be well secured; and its possession
disputed with tenacity if the assailed attempts to
repossess himself of it. In no other way can the
troops engaged be kept well in hand, and be pre-
vented from the confusion and dangers of a hasty
pursuit.

202. *Positions in Forests.* In occupying a forest defensively, the skirts and the openings to it,
as roads, &c., must be strongly guarded by a line
of skirmishers with its supports and reserves, and
by artillery so placed as to sweep in flank those
points which are most accessible, as the salient
portions, and the roads. The line of skirmishers,
besides availing themselves of the natural covers
of the position, as trees, ravines, &c., will form
abatis in front of the more accessible points; and
the cannon, in like manner, should be covered by
epaulments, when suitable means are at hand.

203. The main-body will take up a central position, on ground favorable to the defence; covering its flanks by marshes, or other like obstacles, strengthening, if requisite, its front by abatis; and guarding all the approaches by a suitable disposition of its heavy artillery. The points of junction of roads leading to the front should be strongly occupied, and strengthened, when practicable, by field-works.

204. The space between the skirts of the wood and the central position should be obstinately disputed; advantage being taken of any clearings that may occur, to post light pieces and cavalry in ambush near them, to drive back the assailant, as he *débouches* on the open ground.

205. As cavalry can only act, under such circumstances, in small detachments, the main body of it will take position to the rear, to cover the retreat of the other troops from the forest, and check the assailant in *débouching* from it.

206. The attack will be directed on the salient portions, and upon the entrances of the forest; first by a heavy fire of artillery, to drive back the infantry, and force the guns of the assailed to retire. This will be followed up by a rapid attack in line, with the bayonet, on those points, whilst demonstrations are made against the others occupied by the assailed.

If the attack with the bayonet succeeds, the troops must secure the points seized before pushing forward in pursuit; placing some cannon and troops at the most suitable points, to cover the retreat, should the assailed make a strong offensive movement.

207. The pursuit should be made firmly but cautiously; the skirmishers leading and rooting out the

assailed from every strong cover; some field-pieces, and a column of infantry, each secured by skirmishers on their flanks, following upon the main road, with a detachment of cavalry well to the rear but within supporting distance, to act according to the emergency.

208. If the assailed makes a firm stand at his central position, an attack upon his front will not only be bloody but of doubtful success; an attempt should therefore be made to turn his flanks, whilst he is occupied in front by demonstrations and false attacks.

If the assailed retires, the pursuit will be made by some light pieces followed by the infantry and cavalry; the different arms being employed according to the varying circumstances of the ground.

209. *Positions in Mountains.* The best and only safe system of defence in mountainous positions is to occupy, with the main-body, a central point, at which the principal passes meet; and be always in a state of readiness to act offensively against the enemy, on whatever point he may advance; throwing forward strong detachments in the principal passes to observe the enemy, and offer a vigorous resistance, in order to force him to develop his plan of attack. So soon as it is ascertained on what point the principal force of the enemy is concentrated, the main-body will advance, from the central position, to a point where it will be secure from a flank attack, to act offensively. The detachments on the other passes will act on the flanks of the enemy, by cross-roads, if they can do so, or will try to fall on his rear.

210. When circumstances constrain to a passive defence, a position must be taken up either across

73

or along the valley, which will best secure the flanks, and cover the line of communication.

211. The attack in mountainous positions is conducted on the same principles as the defence. The assailed must be threatened on every point; by throwing columns into the several passes, whilst the main-body advances along one of the principal lines. If the assailed maintains a strict defensive, the several columns unite and make the attack; if he assumes the offensive, the principal columns must be reinforced, and an attempt be made to throw detachments on his flanks and rear, to force him to fall back. The flanks of the troops in column, advancing in the valleys, must be covered by detachments of skirmishers on the heights.

212. The attack will be made mainly by the infantry, as skirmishers. A strong line of fire must be maintained with great pertinacity; the supports must be kept well to the rear; the reserve and main-body holding the points of junction of the roads leading to the front, and not advancing until the engagement is well under way.

Great prudence must be shown in advancing; as the troops engaged are liable at any moment to an attack on their flank. If the assailed attempts this manœuvre, the line of skirmishers must hold on pertinaciously to the ground gained, whilst the supports display and keep the enemy in check, until the reserves can be brought up to repel the attack with the bayonet. As the line of skirmishers force back the assailed, the main-body follows in column along the valley; its flanks being secured by skirmishers on the heights. If opposed by the assailed, the main-body must attack with vigor, to carry its point promptly; as those engaged in front have no chance of being relieved.

213. There is here seldom any field of action for cavalry; the main portion of this force will therefore be kept to the rear; occupying the points of junction of the passes. Small detachments of dragoons may occasionally do good service in front; making charges, or fighting on foot, as the opportunity offers.

214. The artillery can seldom find positions off the roads. A few light pieces, which can be placed in position on the heights and be well served, may frequently produce very decisive results. When it is necessary to open a way, for the mainbody to advance, at points of peculiar strength, it should be done by the heaviest pieces. The horse-artillery will usually be attached to the troops charged with making a demonstration on the flanks of the enemy's position, through the secondary passes.

215. As the assailed will probably obstruct the passes by abatis, or other obstacles, a detachment of engineer troops should accompany each column, being kept always at hand to clear away the obstructions.

216. *Positions near Rivers.* Positions may be selected near rivers either for the defensive, to prevent an enemy from passing; or for the offensive, to force a passage.

217. A position for guarding a river should be selected at some central point, from which the troops can be rapidly marched to oppose the enemy wherever he may attempt to cross. Small posts are established along the course of the river, at the most suitable points for observing the enemy; and communicating to the rear intelligence of his movements.

So soon as it is known that a decided attempt is

to be made at any point, the cavalry, with some batteries of horse-artillery, will move to oppose it. If, on reaching the point, it is found that the enemy has succeeded in throwing over a portion of his forces, they must be vigorously attacked, by successive charges of cavalry, and by a persevering fire of the artillery. If the ground is obstructed, so that the cavalry cannot charge, the dragoons should dismount and act as skirmishers. Positions should be selected by the artillery, where it can take that of the enemy, on the opposite bank, in flank; the object being to silence it, or to draw off its fire, to enable the cavalry to act. Everything here depends on lengthening the affair; and preventing the enemy from reinforcing the troops that have passed, until the main-body can arrive from the central position, to support the cavalry and artillery engaged.

218. The passage of a river in the face of an enemy is an operation of extreme difficulty; and every means should therefore be employed to deceive the enemy, and draw off his attention from the point selected for the passage. The bridge-train and other requisites being in a state of readiness, the night-time is selected as most favorable to a successful issue.

The point, selected to pass a river in the face of an enemy, should combine several properties, as a position; to give the assailant a decided advantage over the assailed. The river at this point should be narrow, so that the bridge may be rapidly constructed; the banks should form a bend towards the assailant, to enable him to plant his batteries in a position to concentrate their fire on that part of the ground, on the opposite bank, where the troops must form; care being taken that these batteries are not exposed to an enfilading fire from those of the assailed, within the proper range for this fire; the ground near the landing place, on the opposite shore, should present covers, in order that the troops, passed over in boats, before the bridge is ready, may not be exposed to the artillery and cavalry of the assailed, and may be enabled to maintain their position until reinforced by the main-body. If there are islands, near the point of landing, from which a fire of artillery and infantry can be brought to bear on the assailed, they should be occupied by infantry, and some field-pieces; particularly if they are wooded, or offer other covers.

219. In moving upon the point, silence and perfect order should be preserved throughout. Batteries of the heaviest guns are placed at the most suitable points, to bring a converging fire to bear upon the approaches to the landing on the opposite shore. Light troops are thrown over in boats, to occupy the ground in advance of the landing; which troops, if discovered by the advanced posts of the enemy, should be rapidly reinforced. So soon as the bridge is ready, an advanced-guard, composed of troops of all arms, will pass and take position, to cover the formation of the main-body. The advanced-guard will mainly keep on the defensive, acting with great prudence, not to offer any advantage to the enemy; its task being to gain time for the rest of the forces to pass.

220. The order in which the main-body should pass must be regulated by the character of the ground, and the resistance offered by the enemy. Usually a portion of the heavy guns follow the advanced-guard, and take position to check the enemy; and these are followed by the main-body of the infantry; the main-body of the cavalry with its batteries of horse-artillery passing last. In other

cases, it may be best to throw over the cavalry and horse-artillery before the other troops.

221. The task, imposed upon the batteries, of covering the passage, is of the greatest moment. Careful attention should be given to the management of their fire; directing it, in all cases, upon that portion of the enemy's force whose presence is most threatening.

222. A retreat across a river, when pressed by the enemy, is of all operations the most difficult; and requires every auxiliary means to save the retreating force from destruction. The point selected for the passage should have the same requisites as one for the offensive; and its natural strength should be increased by field works; in order that the enemy may be kept from pressing too hotly upon the rear of the troops that pass the last.

In a retreat of this character, all the usual stratagems for deceiving an enemy must be resorted to before commencing the movement; so that time sufficient may be gained for making the necessary dispositions to secure the point of passage, as well as to gain a march, or two, in advance. The heavy artillery should be dispatched at an early moment to the rear, to take a position on the opposite shore, for covering the passage. The rest of the force, covered by a strong rear-guard, formed of the best troops, will effect their passage generally in an inverse order to that followed in one for the offensive.

One of the worst dangers to be guarded against is the confusion caused by hurry. To avoid this, the arrangements for the march of the different bodies should be made with the greatest care; so that each may reach, at the proper moment, the point of passage.

CHAPTER IV.

223. To keep an enemy in ignorance of the state of our forces and the character of our position is one of the most indispensable duties in war. It is in this way that we oblige him to take every possible precaution in advancing; forcing him to feel his way, step by step, and to avoid risking his own safety in hazarding those bold and rapid movements which, when made against a feeble, or an unprepared enemy, lead to the most brilliant results.

224. This object is effected, by placing between the position occupied by the main force, and the presumed direction of the enemy, a body detached from the main force, but acting always with reference to it, termed an *Advanced-Guard*.

This term is used for any body of troops so separated from the main-body; whatever its strength and composition; and whether the troops be in position, or on a march.

225. For a large force, the advanced-guard is necessarily composed of troops of all arms; its strength being proportioned to that of the main force;—the more or less resistance of an independent character it may be required to make ;— and the greater or less extent it may be found necessary to embrace, by its advanced-posts, on the front and flanks, to watch and anticipate every movement of the enemy.

The proportion of the advanced-guard to the

main-body may vary from a third to a fifth of the total force. In armies of some strength, or large *corps-d'armée*, particularly where the nature of the country requires a wide development of advanced-posts, the larger proportion is demanded; as at least one-third, or even one-half of its strength will be required for the advanced-post service. In a small force of two or three thousand men, one-fifth will usually be all that can be well spared for the same purposes.

226. Our purpose, in all cases, should be to keep the enemy in a state of uncertainty as to our actual force, and movements; and this can be effected only by keeping constantly between him and our main-body a force of sufficient strength to offer an obstinate resistance, if necessary, to every attempt he may openly make to gain information; and even to act offensively against him, when occasion offers, so as to keep him in doubt as to the actual character and number of the troops before him; the old military axiom, being always kept in mind, that " *a sword opportunely drawn frequently keeps another back in its scabbard.*"

227. In all defensive positions, the advanced-guard and its advanced-posts should retire slowly but circumspectly; so that the main-body may have time to take all its defensive measures. In the offensive, the attack of the advanced-guard should be decided and vigorous; pressing upon the enemy at every point; and leaving nothing undone to demoralize him, by the confusion which so often follows from an impetuous onset.

228. Whilst in position, the advanced-guard should take advantage of the natural, or other obstacles on its front and flanks which are within supporting distance; to strengthen itself, and gain

supports for its advanced-posts. In this way, its means of resistance, whether acting offensively, or otherwise, may be greatly augmented. Ground of this character, taken up by the troops, should not be abandoned without very cogent reasons for it; since, should circumstances bring about a forward movement, it might cost more to regain what was given up than to have maintained it obstinately at first.

229. The ground to be taken up by an advanced-guard, and embraced within its advanced-posts, should be carefully chosen. To take position where the movements of the enemy can be well watched, whilst our own troops are kept concealed, and not liable to a sudden attack, either in front or flank, are the *desiderata* in such cases. If, in following this guide, it should lead to a development of advanced-posts which would be too weak at any point for a tolerable resistance, there remains but the alternative to retire slowly before the enemy,—taking care that he do not slip behind the out-posts and their supports,—upon some central point to the rear, where the advanced-posts, united to the troops in reserve, may make a good stand; and from which, if the chances are favorable, they may advance upon the enemy, and make him pay dearly for his temerity.

230. In all affairs of advanced-guards great circumspection is to be shown, both by the officer in command of the advanced-guard, in throwing forward fresh troops to strengthen a point assailed, as well as on the part of the general-in-chief, in sustaining the advanced-guard by weakening his main-body. These are points that can only be decided on the spot. The safer rule, in all cases, is not to weaken the main-defence, or main attack,

8

by detaching from it, to support a feeble point If the force engaged, under such circumstances does not suffice for its own defence, it is best for it to fall back in time; and, taking position with the main-body, endeavor, by their combined efforts, to turn the scales of victory in their favor.

231. The duties of advanced-guards being so much more frequently to feel and occupy an enemy, preparatory to some decisive blow by the main-body, than to engage him with a view to follow up any advantage gained, it follows, as a matter of course, that they should be composed of the most efficient and active light troops at the general's disposal. Such troops, in the hands of a bold, energetic, but prudent leader, will be the right arm of an army. Prompt on all occasions; never taken at fault, they keep the enemy constantly occupied; harass him with fatiguing precautions, to secure his flanks and rear; whilst their own force is kept relieved from these annoyances, and always fresh for any great emergency.

232. *Advanced-Posts.* The duties of the advanced-posts are the same whether the troops are stationary, or in movement; they are, 1. To keep a good look-out for the enemy, and when in his immediate presence, to take all means to be accurately informed of his strength, position, and movements; 2. Should the enemy advance, to hold him in check long enough to give the main-body ample time to be prepared for his attack.

233. By a faithful discharge of these duties, the whole army can, at all times, and under all circumstances, be kept in a state of readiness for action without subjecting the soldier to any fatigue beyond the ordinary physical endurance of a well-developed manhood; as but a small portion, comparatively, of

the force present is required to watch over the safety of the rest, and can t' refore be frequently relieved, so that every one may have time sufficient for the repose demanded after extraordinary exertions.

234. The object being to secure the front and flanks of the position, occupied by the main-body, from any attempt either to reconnoitre, or attack it, the detachments which form the advance-posts must be so distributed as to embrace all the avenues by which the enemy can approach the position. The system adopted, in most services, to effect this object, consists of two, or three concentric lines of posts, disposed in a *fan-shaped* order. The exterior line, which forms the *Out-Posts*, embraces a wide circumference; and by means of a chain of *Sentinels*, posted in advance, prevents any one from penetrating to the rear between the posts, without being seen.

235. The second line, which is one of *Grand-Guards*, embraces a narrower circumference than the line of out-posts; occupying the more important avenues from the out-posts to the interior; so as to be in a position to support the out-posts in case of necessity; and to receive them if driven in.

236. The interior line consists of several strong detachments, termed *Pickets*, posted upon the main-avenues to the position. They serve as supports to the two exterior lines, upon which they rally if forced to retire before the enemy.

237. Besides these dispositions for security, *Patroles* are kept up between the line of posts, to keep the one informed of the state of the other; and also between the out-posts and chain of sentinels, to see that the duties of the latter are well performed; and to search any ground not brought well under the eyes of the sentinels. The whole, in this way

See Plate L for Articles 234, 317.

rms a connected system, for observin; the enemy and for mutual support in case of attack.

238. The duties of the out-posts, and of the grand-guards which form their supports, are strictly those of observation. If attacked, they offer no resistance further than to enable them to feel the enemy perfectly, and never lose sight of him. The task of holding the enemy in check by a vigorous resistance, so as to procure sufficient time for the main-body to make its dispositions for battle, is consigned to the pickets.

239. The ground taken up by the advanced-posts will depend on the capabilities which its natural features offer for defence; on the number and character of the approaches it presents to an enemy for attacking the front, or flanks of the position occupied by the main-body; and upon the facilities it may afford for communication between the posts.

240. *Out-Posts.* The position of the out-posts, with respect to the main-body, will be regulated by the more or less broken character of the country. As a general rule, the mean distance may be taken at about two miles. The line occupied by these posts should take in all the approaches to the front and flanks of the main position. When a position is to be held for some time, or is taken up after a battle, the out-posts may be thrown farther in advance; to procure greater repose and security for the main-body.

241. The ground on which the line of out-posts is established should be carefully examined; with a view both to observation and defence. As far as practicable, those points should be selected for posts which present some natural advantages for the defence; will screen the troops from the enemy's

view; and enable them to watch all his movements. Whenever the features of the ground do not offer natural obstacles to cover the posts, artificial means of a slight character should be resorted to. The flanks of the line should rest upon strong natural obstacles; when such cannot be found, without giving the line too great an extent, these points must be secured by strong pickets of cavalry or infantry, thrown back to form crotchets; from which patroles must be constantly kept up on the flanks, in the presumed direction of the enemy.

242. The strength of each out-post, and the distance from one to the other, will be regulated by the features of the ground, and the number of sentinels, or vedettes that each post must throw out. The posts should, as far as practicable, be within sight of the grand-guards to which they belong; and the sentinels of their respective posts. When the ground does not permit this arrangement, sentinels should be placed at intermediate points, to communicate promptly whatever may happen at the line of posts, or of sentinels, to the rear. Posts of infantry should not, as a general rule, be placed farther apart than 600 paces; nor their sentinels more than 300 paces in advance of the posts. Those of cavalry may be some 1500 paces apart; and their vedettes from 600 to 800 paces in advance. The strength of each post should be calculated at the rate of four men for each sentinel, or vedette.

243. *Sentinels.* The sentinels and vedettes form a chain in advance, and are posted on points from which they can best watch the enemy, without being seen by, or exposed to him, in any way. As one of their main duties is to prevent any one from passing their chain, they should be so placed, with respect

8*

to each other, that they can see all the ground between their respective posts, and be able to stop any one who may attempt to pass between them. At night and in misty weather, the sentinels should be doubled and be drawn in nearer to the out-posts.

Whenever it may be deemed necessary to post sentinels on points beyond the line of out-posts, they should be furnished by posts detached in advance of the line.

244. *Grand-Guards.* As the grand-guards furnish the out-posts, and serve as their supports, not more than one-third of their force should be taken for the out-posts. The grand-guards are posted on the principal avenues leading to the detachments on which they are to fall back, if driven in; and, when of infantry, about 200 paces, and of cavalry, 600 to 800 paces, in the rear of the out-posts. The points which they occupy should be selected, both to secure them from the enemy's view, and to give a ready communication between them and their respective out-posts. No difficult, or broken ground, should lie between the grand-guards and their out-posts; if any such occur, particularly if it be of a nature to offer facilities to an enemy to penetrate to the rear, the whole should be posted on the farther, or hither side of it; and in preference in the latter position, if by it the chain of posts can be preserved unbroken.

245. *Pickets.* The main-detachments or pickets, which form the supports to the grand-guards and out-posts, occupy the principal avenues to the position of the main-body. As their duty is to hold the enemy in check; the points which they take up should be susceptible of a good defence; such, for example, as villages, defiles, &c.; whenever these advantages are not found at hand, resort should be had to any temporary obstacles, as abatis, &c.

which can be readily procured, to place the troops under shelter. The points thus occupied should, as a general rule, be about midway between the line of out-posts and the position of the main-body.

246. Small posts should be thrown forward by the pickets, between their position and the line of grand-guards; both for the greater security of the detachments, and as supports to the grand-guards In like manner, when the line of pickets is of considerable extent, intermediate posts must be established, to keep open a communication between them.

247. No pains should be spared to obstruct the approaches of the enemy to the points occupied by the pickets; particularly those which lead to the flanks; leaving open such only as will oblige the enemy to attack under the most unfavorable circumstances; and if, between the advanced-posts and the main-body, a defile, or other unfavorable pass should occur, which the enemy, by turning the line of the advanced-posts, might seize upon, and thus cut off their retreat, it should be occupied by a strong detachment; both to prevent such a manœuvre, and to favor the retreat on the main-body.

248. *Strength of Advanced-Posts.* The entire strength of the advanced-posts, as well as the relative strength of the pickets, grand-guards, and out-posts, will depend upon the character of the ground covered by them; as being more or less open; and presenting more or less facilities for circumscribing the approaches of the enemy to the main-position. It rarely occurs that sufficient troops can be detached to cover all the accessible ground, and perform the duties in a thorough manner.

249. The strength of each picket, and the kind of troops of which it is composed, will depend on the degree of resistance to be offered to the enemy's

See Plate II. for Article 247.

attack; and the character of the position occupied. In most cases, where a vigorous defence is called for, they will consist of troops of all arms; and an aggregate of several hundred men. The grand-guards, out-posts, and patroles, should not exceed one-third the strength of the pickets to which they belong. They will be composed of cavalry, or infantry, according to the more or less broken features of the ground.

250. It rarely occurs that artillery is placed at the out-posts. Whenever it happens that a piece, or two, may be deemed necessary, to sweep some passage, or defile, in advance of the line of out-posts, the guns must be protected by a strong post, to insure their safety in a retreat.

251. If, from the character of the ground, the out-posts are mainly of infantry, some cavalry should always be attached to them, to patrol in advance of the position, and to convey intelligence to the rear of what may be passing in the neighborhood of the out-posts.

252. When the advanced-posts cover an advanced-guard, the commanding officer of the whole should take a position, with his artillery and the main-body of his command, at some central point, in the rear of the pickets; in order to be ready to support them if hard pressed by the enemy. The choice of this position is an object of the greatest importance; as the safety of the advanced-posts as well as that of the main-body may depend upon the degree of judgment shown in this selection.

253. So soon as the advanced-posts have taken up their stations, instructions should be given to the officers of the different posts, with respect to the points upon which they are 'o fall back, in case of being forced in; the lines of communication they

must retire by; and the position they must take up, in joining the supports to which they respectively belong.

254. *Duties of Officer commanding an Out-Post.* An officer in command of any of the out-posts must be capable of untiring vigilance and activity; to perform the various duties which devolve upon him.

He should be provided with a good map of the country, a telescope, and writing materials.

255. He will thoroughly reconnoitre the ground upon which he is to dispose his command; and also as far in advance as circumstances will admit; questioning closely any inhabitant he may find. After taking up his position, he should go forward, with the half of his command, and post each sentinel himself. If, however, he relieves 'another in the command, and deems it advisable to make any changes in the dispositions of his predecessors, he should promptly report the facts to the commanding-officer in his rear.

256. When the officer finds that the enemy is not in his immediate neighborhood, he should endeavor to feel his way cautiously towards him by patrols; and when in immediate presence, he should omit no means to watch the enemy's movements; and from the occurrences of the moment, such as noises, the motion of clouds of dust, camp fires, conflagrations, &c., endeavor to divine what is passing in his camp, and his probable intentions.

257. Accurate written reports should be promptly sent to the officer in command, in the rear, on all these points. The reports should be *legibly* written, and should clearly, but *concisely*, state what has fallen under the officer's eye; what he has learned from others; and the character of the sources from which his information is drawn.

258. He will particularly see that no communication with the enemy be allowed; and that no flag be permitted to pass the line of posts, without orders from the rear.

259. The post under the officer's command, whether horse or foot, should not all be allowed to sleep, or eat at once. The horses, when watered, should be taken singly, or by pairs, and always mounted. At night, one-half of the command should be under arms, prepared for an attack; the other seated, their arms and the bridles of their horses in hand. The men should never be permitted to occupy a house; and if the weather is such that a fire out of doors is indispensable, it should be as much concealed as practicable; one-half only being allowed to sit near it; the other posted, at a convenient spot at hand, to fall on the enemy should he attempt a stroke.

260. When the position taken up is to be held for some time, it will be well to change the locality of the posts occasionally; this should be done, particularly at night, in a hilly district; changing the post from the brow of the hill, where the men can best keep a look-out by day, to the low ground at night, as more favorable to detect any movement above.

261. The out-posts are usually relieved at daybreak, as, being the most favorable moment for the enemy to attempt a surprise; the new-guard will serve to reinforce the old. For the same reason, the old guard should not be suffered to retire before the patrols come in, and report all safe.

262. As a general rule, no post should ever retire before an inferior force; and, if attacked by one superior to it, resistance should be cautiously made with a view solely to give time to the grand-guard

to be in readiness to receive the enemy. When it is seen that the movement of the enemy is serious, the officer should draw in his sentinels as skirmishers, and retire upon the grand-guard ; the latter will usually be divided into two divisions, one of which will be sent to take up a position to the rear, to cover the retreat; the other will act as as upport to the line of skirmishers, so as to feel the enemy. In all cases of retiring, whether of sentinels upon their posts, or of posts upon their supports, care should be taken to assume a direction towards the flank of the force in rear; so as to unmask its front and not impede any forward movement it may make, if necessary.

263. The degree of resistance to be offered by the pickets will depend on the object to be obtained, and the importance of the point occupied. They should not retire until they have received the whole of their grand-guards, out-posts and patrols.

264. At night the precautions should be necessarily redoubled ; and every movement be made with extreme caution. Whenever any noise is heard in the direction of a sentinel's post, the officer should proceed, with a part of his command, in its direction ; to ascertain the cause of it. If he finds that it arises from an onward movement of the enemy, he should only fall back upon his grand-guard when he sees that resistance would be unavailing; retiring slowly and cautiously, and taking every advantage, which the ground offers, to check the enemy's advance. Should the enemy fall suddenly upon his command, he must endeavor to cut his way through, and reach his position in the rear by the best circuit he can find.

265. *Advanced-Guards.* Measures of precaution, for a force in position, are far more easily arranged than for one in motion. At a halt of some

days, but slight changes in the first dispositions, arising from a more thorough knowledge of the ground taken up, will be requisite; on a march, the scene is continually shifting; and the enemy may fall on just at that point, or under those circumstances in which we are least prepared to meet him. Hence a necessity for doubling the ordinary precautions on a march, and keeping the troops more in hand, so as to be, at all moments, prepared for any emergency.

266. The spirit of the dispositions is the same in both cases; changes in the details, so as to adapt our force to the changing features of the ground passed over, present the real difficulty. On a march, we may have to guard against an attack on the head of the column; on either flank, or both; and in the rear. Hence a necessary disposition of movable advanced-posts, in each of these directions, keeping pace with the progress of the main-body, and far enough from it to give it timely warning of a threatened attack.

267. The dispositions in front is termed the *Advanced-Guard;* those on the flanks, the *Flankers;* and those in rear, the *Rear-Guard.*

268. As the head of a column in march towards the enemy is the weak point, it is here that the principal strength must be accumulated, so that, if threatened with an attack, sufficient resistance can be offered, to enable the rear divisions to come up and take timely position for battle. The advanced-guard should therefore be composed of troops of all arms, and be always in a suitable state of readiness to receive the enemy, according to the nature of the ground upon which it may be formed. To watch the enemy; resist him with obstinacy, should he suddenly attack, until time is gained for the

main-body to receive him; drive in his advanced-posts with impetuosity: such are the duties which this body may in turn be called on to perform.

269. The first of these duties, that of learning the whereabouts of an enemy, is intrusted to individuals, or to parties of more or less strength, as the occasion may require; light cavalry being usually selected, in preference to any other arm, for this service.

270. *Head of Advanced-Guard.* A head or leading detachment of some force, composed usually of both cavalry and infantry, and if requisite some pioneers, forms the advance of the main-body of the advanced-guard; for the purpose of searching all the ground within a dangerous proximity; and of clearing the way for the advancing columns. Through this detachment a communication is kept up with the flankers; and all the ground is thus hemmed in around the advancing column, by which an enemy might approach it.

271. The strength of the leading detachment will depend greatly upon the character of the country; and upon the state of the weather and season being more or less favorable to the unobserved approach of an enemy. A leading detachment of one-fourth the total strength of the advanced-guard; two flank detachments, to act as flankers, of one-eighth; and a rear detachment, acting as a rear-guard, also of one-eighth; taking, in all, one-half the total strength of the advanced-guard, is considered, under ordinary circumstances, a good distribution for the duties to be performed.

272. All the ground, within the proximity of the advanced-guard, must be carefully searched by it. No invariable rule can be laid down on this subject, everything depending on the character of the coun

9

try; the state of the weather; and the march being by day or night, as to the more or less dispersed order that can be adopted for examining the ground.

273. The leading detachment, and those on the flanks, should keep in a position, with respect to each other, that will admit of prompt mutual support, and guarding against the approach of an enemy unperceived. The flank detachments, for this purpose, keeping somewhat to the rear of the leading one. The most advanced portions of these troops should be of cavalry, unless the country be mountainous, or very thickly wooded, in which cases infantry is the best arm for the duty.

274. The distance that should be left between the leading detachment and the principal body of the advanced-guard, will depend upon the more or less of necessary precaution already alluded to. An interval of from a thousand to two thousand paces may be left between the leading detachment and the main-portion; the small detachments thrown forward from the leading detachment may precede it from two hundred to six hundred paces; whilst the leading men, who form, as it were, the apex of this disposition, precede the last about one hundred paces.

275. *Dispositions of Advanced-Guard.* From these indications of the manner of distributing the troops of the advanced-guard, the following general dispositions, adapted to ordinary circumstances of locality, may be gathered. The apex, or most advanced point, may be formed of a staff, or other intelligent officer, under the escort of a few horsemen; in his rear follow small detachments of horse, preceded by a line of horsemen, as skirmishers, in dispersed order, thrown out from them; this line of small detachments and their men may embrace a fron

See Plate III. for Articles 275, 285.

of a thousand or more paces, according to the face of the country. On each flank of the detachments, from which the skirmishers are thrown forward, march small detachments of both horse and foot, as supports of the line. In the rear of this line, at a hundred paces or so, may be placed a small detachment, charged with patrolling either on the front or flanks. Finally, at some sixty paces in rear of .he detachment for patrols, follows the remaining portion of the horse and foot, composing the leading detachment. The main-body of the advanced-guard, following some hundred paces farther to the rear; and the rear of its march, being closed by the small rear detachment already mentioned.

It will be seen, by comparing this disposition of the troops of an advanced-guard in march, with the one adopted for the advanced-posts at a halt, that they are analogous, and differ in no material respect, as their object in each case is the same.

276. In a forward movement, this general disposition of the troops of the leading detachment should be adhered to, as far as the features of the ground will permit. Whenever these features become such that a concentration on the centre is rendered necessary, a proper order should be temporarily taken, to enable the troops promptly to resume their original order, so soon as the ground opens. The leading line of skirmishers will carefully examine all the ground over which they pass; and observe all that occurs around them. The men, for this purpose, keeping in pairs; and taking all suitable precautions not to place themselves in positions favorable to being seen from a distance.

277. If the enemy is met, dispositions are immediately taken to receive him. The line of skirmishers is strengthened; the supports brought up;

and if there is any artillery, it takes position on the road, to sweep it. In this order, the whole of the leading detachment falls back slowly upon the main-body of the advanced-guard; and further dispositions are made according to the exigency of the case.

278. The general order of march of an advanced-guard remains the same in all circumstances of ground; the position of the troops alone varying with changes of its features. In broken ground, for instance, the line of skirmishers of the leading detachment would be of infantry, and this line would be supported by some cavalry.

279. A strict observance of good order, particularly among the troops of the leading detachment, is of the first importance; nothing should therefore be permitted which might either withdraw their attention from their chief duty of watching; or which might give warning to an enemy of their approach. They should especially guard against being drawn into the use of their fire-arms, short of an actual surprise.

280. On a night-march the precautions should be redoubled. The leading detachment will be more concentrated, keeping mostly to the road. If the enemy is seen, word will be sent at once to the rear, for a halt, and the suitable dispositions will be taken, as noiselessly as practicable.

281. All defiles met with of any length should be examined carefully by some scouts, before any number of troops venture into them; and then proper measures should be taken for securing them from an attack, until the troops are all clear of them. All woods that can be easily gone round should be made the circuit of by some horse, before passing through them. Thick forests should be carefully

examined, a hundred or more paces on each side of the road. And in all cases any doubtful ground must be first searched, by the leading troops, before any large body approaches within musket-range of it.

282. *Flank Patrols.* Besides the flankers proper, which constitute a part of the movable advanced-posts, detachments of an independent character are sent out to patrol along the flanks of the main-column. These should keep themselves in communication, by suitable dispositions of vedettes, with the flankers.

283. As the flank patrols are frequently beyond direct supporting distance, they must adopt all the necessary dispositions against surprise of any other body marching independently; having their advanced-guard, &c., &c.

284. These patrols keep on a level with their column; and particularly secure all lateral roads, or defiles, by which it might be suddenly attacked, until the column is beyond danger. Great activity, watchfulness, and caution, should characterize this service. The officer in command of a flank patrol must use his discretion, in meeting an enemy, whether to attack him, or to let him pass, if he has not himself been observed.

285. *Rear-Guard.* The duties of a rear-guard, in retreat, will depend upon the more or less of activity and vigor shown by the enemy in pursuit. If the enemy is enterprising, then it will require all the sagacity of the commanding-officer; all the firmness of the soldiers; to cover and defend the rear of the column, and to guard against demonstrations upon its flanks. To hold the enemy in check, just the time necessary to enable the retreating column to extricate itself from unfavorable ground; and then to withdraw from the fight, without being too

far compromised; to prevent the enemy from pressing on so hotly as to force the main-body of the rear guard upon the tail of the column whose retreat is to be secured, are problems of no easy solution; and call for all the best military qualities, both in the officer and the troops to whom the solution is assigned.

286. In mutual support among all the arms; aptitude for turning to advantage all variations in the features of the ground; and tenacity in keeping every advantage offered until the last safe moment; reside the excellence of a rear-guard. In interdicting by the fire of its skirmishers all approach to its covers; in occasional bold manoeuvres of its light-artillery, when the enemy's columns are open to its fire; in daring rapid charges of its cavalry, when the enemy presses forward to gain some critical point; a rear-guard may give an enemy such lessons as will force him to adopt that prudential course, on which its own safety, and that of its column, alone depend. .

287. As the march of a rear-guard is an almost continual running fight, its dispositions should be taken for this phase of its duties. Its rear should accordingly be closed by a line of skirmishers, properly supported by the other arms. This line must equally exhibit caution, coolness and firmness; giving way to no hasty movements; and reserving its fire until it can be thrown in with murderous effect. If forced back by superior numbers, the skirmishers should concentrate on the flanks of the other troops, leaving the road clear, either for the fire of the artillery, or for the action of cavalry, or of infantry in mass.

288. In all its actions, the rear-guard should never lose sight of the danger it continually runs of

being surrounded, or cut off, by a movement on its
flanks, or rear. Against this, its only course is to
push out flank patrols, as far as they can safely
venture; restricting these to the duties of conveying
timely warning, to the main-body of the rear-guard,
of any appearance of a movement of the kind referred to; and of preventing it, if attempted, by a
bold stand, either defensive, or offensive, as circumstances may demand.

289. *Advanced-Posts in Cantonments.* As cantonments are taken up either during seasons when
operations cannot be well carried on ; or to give the
troops some extraordinary repose, after a harassing
campaign; more advanced-posts will generally be
necessary than under ordinary circumstances; and
to fulfil their end they ought to be placed on ground
favorable to a strong resistance; in order to give
the separated corps time to concentrate against an
earnest attack of the enemy.

290. A good disposition of stations for out-posts,
from which the enemy can be seen at a distance;
a line of supports placed on strong ground in the
rear; easy communications for concentration on
the main-body; active and vigilant patrols, kept
moving not only along the front, but penetrating on
the flanks, and rear of the enemy, to get wind of
his strategical plans: such are the general precautions demanded of its advanced-posts, by an army in
station for some time.

291. In the disposition of the main force, to concur with the preceding, one precaution should not be
omitted in a stay of any duration; and that is, not to
allow any one body to remain long enough in a
village, or inhabited place, to become in a degree
domesticated. Nothing is more likely than this to
injure the *morale* of the best troops. The seductions

of otherwise harmless pleasures, may lead to fatal habits of remissness in duty ; and the officer quietly indulging in his game at cards, in a family circle, may receive his summons for surrender, as he is gathering up his last trick.

CHAPTER V.

292. There are no more important duties, which an officer may be called upon to perform, than those of collecting and arranging the information upon which either the general, or daily operations of a campaign must be based. For the proper performance of the former, acquirements of a very high order, in the departments of geography and statistics, are indispensable requisites; to which must be added a minute acquaintance with topography, and a good *coup d'œil militaire* for that of the latter.

293. However detailed and perfect may be a map, it can never convey all the information that will enable an officer to plan, even an ordinary march, with safety; still less, operations that necessarily depend, for their success, upon a far greater number of contingencies. To supply these deficiencies of maps, an examination of the ground must be made by the eye; and verbal information be gained, on all the points connected with the operation over this ground. This examination and collection of facts is termed a *Reconnaissance.*

294. From the services demanded of a reconnoitring officer, it is, in the first place, evident, that he should possess acquirements of no ordinary character; but in addition to these he should be gifted by nature with certain traits, without which his acquisitions would be of little account, in the discharge of the responsible duty in question.

295. With clear and specific information before

him, one-half of a general's difficulties, in planning his measures, are dissipated. In a letter from General Washington to Major Tallmadge, now to be seen framed in the office of the Commissary-General of New York, he remarks, in relation to reports made to him, on a certain occasion: "But these things, not being delivered with certainty, rather perplex than form the judgment." It is in truth this feeling of certainty that constitutes all the difference; having it, the general makes his dispositions with confidence; without it, he acts hesitatingly; and thus communicates to others that want of confidence felt in his own mind.

296. An officer then, selected for the duty in question, should be known to be cool-headed and *truthful*; one who sees things as they are, and tells clearly and precisely what he has seen. In making his report, whether verbally or in writing, the officer should study conciseness and precision of language. He must carefully separate what he knows, from his own observation, from that which he has learned from others; and add all the circumstances of place, and time, with accuracy.

297. *Duties of Reconnoitring Officer.* The first thing to be done by an officer, selected for a reconnaissance, is to ascertain *precisely* the duty required of him; and what further should be done in case of certain contingencies that may, from the nature of the duty, be naturally looked for. In the performance of the duty assigned him, and in making his report, the officer should keep always in mind the specific character of his mission, as his guide in both points.

298. As the need of a reconnaissance supposes a deficiency in information upon the features of the country, the officer, detailed to make one, should

provide himself with maps, a good telescope, such simple aids for judging of distances, and ascertaining the relative positions of objects, as he can himself readily make; writing materials; one or more good guides; and gain all the knowledge he can, from the inhabitants at hand, bearing upon his mission.

299. The talent of judging of distances, and of the connection between the various features of a country within the field of vision, is partly a natural and partly an acquired one. Some individuals can never be brought to have any confidence in their own judgment on these points; others have a natural aptitude for them, which requires but little practice for their perfect development. The powers of the eye vary so greatly among civilized persons, that no general rules can be laid down, as a guide for the matter in question. Among uncivilized hordes, used to a roaming life, there are found standards which are well understood by all,—the Arab, for instance, calling that distance a mile, at which a man is no longer distinguishable from a woman — growing out of their habits.

300. The first thing then to be done by an officer, in acquiring the *coup d'œil militaire*, is to learn, both from books and on the field, what space is taken up by a battalion and its intervals, by a squadron, and by a battery when in order of battle; how much when in column of march; and the average time required for certain movements, under given circumstances of the ground. This acquirement he may make by adopting some standard of his own; his ordinary pace, and that of a horse, serving for computing time and distance reciprocally. The next step is to acquire the habit of estimating, by the appearances of these different objects, from various

points of view, how far off they are. This must be done practically. A very simple aid to it is the following:—Upon the stem of a lead-pencil, cut square, and held out at a uniform arm's length from the eye, by means of a thread attached to it and fastened to the top button-hole, let the officer mark off, on one of the edges, the length seen on it by holding the pencil upright between the eye, and a man placed successively at different distances from it, as 100, 150—1000 yards. This will give one rough standard for practice. Another may be made by first ascertaining the average height of certain cultivated trees, as the apple, &c.

301. For getting relative positions, a contrivance for measuring angles roughly must be used. This is done by first folding a leaf of paper across, and then doubling it along the folded edge, as if to divide it into four equal parts. The angle between the edge of the first fold and that of the second will be a tolerably accurate right angle. Now, by cutting off carefully along the fold, one of the pieces, we obtain a quadrant, or 90°; then folding this at the angle, so that the two edges will exactly coincide, we get the half of a quadrant or 45°; and so on, by successive bisections, we can mark off smaller angles. Then making a pen or pencil-mark along each of the folds, and numbering the angles successively from 0 to 90°, we have a rough *protractor*, that can be used both for measuring angles and setting them off on a sketch. To measure vertical angles, a thread with a light plummet, must be attached to the angular point. If the object is above the horizon of the eye, we hold the protractor *with the angular point from the eye*, so that the plumb-line will fall along the face of the paper just touching it; then directing the top edge of the protractor

on the object, so that it is just seen by the eye-sighting along the edge, the angle formed between the plumb-line and the other edge, will be the same as the angle between the line of sight and the horizon of the eye.

If the object is below the horizon of the eye, the angular point *is placed towards the eye;* the same series of operations will give the angle below the eye's horizon.

302. *Guides.* Trustworthy guides are invaluable, but most rare, in an enemy's country. The best, from the information they acquire by their habits of life, are to be found among those classes whose avocations keep them much abroad, going from place to place within a certain sphere constantly; such as common carriers, hunters, smugglers, &c. Among the first thing to be attended to by an officer, in taking post at any point, is to find out persons of this class, and to ascertain their whereabout when wanted. Kind treatment, *dou-ceurs,* and promises, should not be spared, to enlist either their good will or their interests; and, if policy requires it, they may openly be treated with apparent harshness, to screen them from odium among their neighbors.

303. If none of this class can be found, then resort must be had to a higher; local authorities being in preference selected, and if necessary forced to act. Here very careful treatment is requisite; when the necessity of the case is admitted by them, much may be gleaned by kindness, courtesy, and a certain deference, from such persons, that cannot be looked for from their inferiors.

304. Before starting on his mission, the officer should question his guide thoroughly; and if he has several, question each apart; like precautions

should be taken with respect to other inhabitants
'Care must be had to find out the usual beats of one
taken as a guide, so as not to take him out of his
own neighborhood. In all cases, the guide must
be well watched, however trustworthy he may
seem. If unwilling, or sulky, he must, if needs be,
be tied, and attached to a strong man, with a rope
round his middle; being first strictly searched for
any cutting instrument about him.

305. Should there be but one guide, he must necessarily be placed with the most advanced portion
of the detachment accompanying the officer. If
there are several, one must be there also; the one
apparently the most intelligent with the officer, who
should ply him with questions; and the others in
the rear strictly guarded.

306. It may be well to remark, that guides are
useful even in a country of easy communications;
as, in case of a rencontre, they may point out bye-
ways convenient for retreat, if necessary.

307. *Reconnaissance.* To designate all the objects to be embraced in a reconnaissance, would
lead farther than the limits of this little work will
allow; some general heads, which will serve as
guides in all cases, will therefore be alone noticed.

308. A general view of the ground to be examined must first be taken in, so as to obtain some
notion of the forms of the parts, their connection, and
relations to each other, before going into a detailed
examination. To one possessed of some topographical knowledge, this study of what is before him
will not demand much time. A level country, for
example, he knows is usually well cultivated, and
therefore has plenty of hedges, ditches, &c., which
lend themselves well to affairs of light troops;—may
be not a little inconvenient to manœuvres of artil-

ıery ;—and frequently bring up cavalry very unex
pectedly in full career. In a mountainous one,
dangerous passes, narrow roads, torrents with
rough beds, ugly sudden turns, &c., will necessarily be met with. Each and all of these demand a
particular examination, and in his report their advantages and disadvantages should be clearly
pointed out by the officer.

309. If the reconnaissance is for an onward
movement; the distances from halt to halt, as well
as all others, should be estimated in *hours of march;*
the nature of the roads, and the obstacles along
them be carefully detailed ; the means that may be
gathered along the line to facilitate the movement,
as vehicles, men and materials for removing obstacles, &c. The points where cross-roads are
found, must be specified ; the direction of these
roads ; their uses, &c.

310. All local objects along the line, as villages,
farm-houses, &c., should be carefully designated,
both as to their position on the line, or on either side
of it ; and also as to their form, and color, &c., as
" square white house on the right ;" " round gray
stone tower on hill to left."

311. The names of localities, in the way in which
the inhabitants pronounce them, should be carefully
written, and called over several times, so as to be
sure to get them as nearly as practicable right in
sound ; then the names, as written by an intelligent
inhabitant, should be added.

312. All halting points must be well looked to ;
their military capabilities, in case of attack ; as
well as their resources for accommodating the
troops, be thoroughly gone into.

If the halt is to take position for some time, to
await or watch the enemy , then more care must be

taken, the whole site be well studied as to its fulfill
ing the proposed end; the points of support on the
flanks be designated, as well as others in front and
rear, that may require to be occupied; the suitable
localities to be chosen for parks, hospital, &c.; the
communications to be opened or repaired, pointed
out; and all the facilities either for an advance or
a retrograde movement, be laid down.

313. *Armed Reconnaissance.* Reconnaissances,
made in the neighborhood of an enemy, require to
be done under the protection of a proper detachment; the strength and composition of which will
depend on the object to be attained.

314. If the object be to gain secretly a knowledge
of the enemy's whereabout and strength, then a
detachment of light cavalry, conducted by a trusty
guide, through circuitous bye-ways, and moving
with celerity, but with proper precautions against
falling into an ambush, or having its retreat cut off,
is usually resorted to. The details for this will be
found under the head Patrols.

315. When an enemy's position is to be recon-
noitred, with a view to force him to show his hand,
by causing him to call out all his troops; then a
large detachment of all arms, adequate to the task
of pressing the enemy vigorously, and also of withdrawing with safety when pressed in turn, must be
thrown forward.

316. Under the shelter of either of these forces,
the officer, charged with the reconnaissance, takes
the best moment, and best point of view, for carefully ascertaining the dispositions made by the
enemy. A good time will be at early dawn, when
troops, in most services, are all made to stand to
their arms. The points which the officer must ex
hibit most attention in finding out, are those occu-

pied by the batteries, and all those in any way intrenched.

317. *Patrols.* Patrols are of two classes, from
the different objects had in view. The first are
those made with a view of insuring greater security
from the enemy's attempts to pass, or force the line
of out-posts, and may therefore be termed *defensive
patrols.* They consist usually of three or four men,
who go the rounds, along the chain of sentinels and
between the posts; seldom venturing farther than
a few hundred paces beyond the sentinel's chain;
the object being to search points which might present a cover to the enemy's scouts, and to keep the
sentinels on the alert.

318. The second class are those made exterior
to the line of out-posts, with a view of gaining intelligence of the enemy's whereabouts; and may
therefore be termed *offensive patrols.* They are
composed of larger bodies of men than the first
class, the number being proportioned both to the
distance to be gone over, and the extent of front to
be examined. In a position, presenting but few
cross-roads, and sparsely settled, a patrol of ten or
twenty horsemen, may be found ample, to search,
with all desirable thoroughness, from twenty to forty
miles in advance of the position, along the principal
avenues to it; whereas, with a more extended front,
presenting many lateral avenues, double this number might be required for the same duty. From the
information obtained, through the ordinary channels
of maps, and by questioning the inhabitants at hand,
the commanding-officer can usually settle, with sufficient accuracy, the strength of a patrol.

319. From the duties to be performed by patrols,
cavalry are usually employed alone; in cases of
very broken country, infantry may be necessary

but they should always be accompanied by some
norse, if for no other purpose than to transmit intel
ligence promptly to the rear.

320. The main duties of a patrol are to find the
enemy if in the neighborhood; gain a good idea of
his position and strength; to make out his movements, and to bring in an accurate account of his
distance from the out-posts of their own force; and
the character of the ground between the position
occupied by the respective forces.

321. From the nature of these duties, it is evident
that both officers and men, for a patrol, should be
selected with especial reference to their activity, intelligence, and the aptitude they may possess, from
previous habits of life, for a service requiring a
union of courage, prudence, and discriminating observation—usually to be met with only in individuals who have been thrown very much upon
their own resources. When the character of the
country admits of it, the employment of such individuals, singly, or in very small bodies, as scouts,
is one of the most available means of gaining intelligence of an enemy, without betraying the secret
of our own whereabout.

322. *Duties of Officer in command of a Patrol.*
In conducting a patrol, the commanding-officer
should provide himself with a good map, telescope,
and guides; and gain all the information he can
before starting, by questioning persons in the neighborhood. Nothing should escape his eye along his
line of search; and he should particularly note
points which might be favorable to his defence, if
driven back by the enemy; or by which his retreat
might be endangered.

323. The order of march of the patrol will be
regulated by the circumstances of its strength, kind

of troops employed, the character of the country passed over, the hour of the day, and the particular object in view. The intelligence and judgment of the officer in command will have sufficient exercise on these points; as he will be continually called upon to vary his dispositions. The general and obvious rule of keeping a look-out on all sides, will prompt the general disposition of an advanced-guard, rear-guard, and flankers, according to the circumstances of the case, however small his command. The sole object being to carry back intelligence of the enemy, no precautions should be omitted to cover and secure his line of march, without making, however, too great a subdivision of his force.

324. Too much circumspection cannot be shown in approaching points favorable to ambuscades; as woods, ravines, defiles, inclosures, farm-houses, villages, &c. The main-body should always be halted, in a good position beyond musket-shot, or where cover can be obtained, whilst a few men proceed cautiously forward, following at some distance in the rear of, but never losing sight of each other, to examine the suspected spot. If the officer deem it necessary, at any point, to detach from his command smaller patrols, to examine points at some distance on his flanks, he should halt the rest, at the point where they separate, until the detachments come in and report; or, if he decides to move forward, he should leave three or four men at the spot, to convey intelligence promptly to the rear, if anything is discovered, as well as to himself.

325. It may frequently be found that some eminence on the flanks may present a good view of the surrounding country, in which case, if it be decided to use it, two or three men ought to be detached for the purpose, with orders to keep in sight of each

other, but far enough apart to guard against a surprise of the whole.

326. When the officer finds himself in the presence of the enemy, he should halt his command at a convenient spot, where they will be screened from the enemy's view; and, having made his dispositions against a surprise, he will proceed with a few picked men to the most favorable point from which he can obtain a good look-out, to reconnoitre the position occupied, and the other points of interest. If he deem it advisable to keep his position, or change it for some other point more favorable, he will first transmit a report to the rear of what he has observed.

327. When the patrol moves by night, the ordinary precautions must be redoubled. Signals must be agreed upon to avoid danger, should any of the party become separated from the main body. Careful attention must be given to everything passing around; as the barking of dogs, noises, fires, &c. On approaching any inhabited spot, the command should be brought to a halt, whilst a few picked men move noiselessly forward, and if practicable, by stealing up to the windows, learn the character of the inmates.

328. It cannot be too strongly impressed upon the mind of the officer in command of a patrol, that he must be all ears and eyes; that he will be called upon in turn, to exercise great boldness, caution, presence of mind and good judgment, in accomplishing a mission where the enemy must be seen but not encountered; and such roads and halting points be selected, both in moving forward and returning, as shall be most favorable to his movements, and least liable to expose him to a surprise or a disadvantageous collision with the enemy.

CHAPTER VI.

DETACHMENTS.

329. Detachments consist of small bodies of troops, composed of one, or several arms, to which are intrusted some mission connected with the operations of the main-body, but, for the most part, performed beyond the sphere of its support; such, for example, as the occupation of some post, or defile, which is to be held temporarily, as necessary to the movements of the main-body; the surprise of a post held by the enemy; the seizure of a convoy, &c.

330. The composition of a detachment will depend upon the nature of the duty to be performed; the character of the country in which it is to operate; the distance of the point to be reached; and the more or less celerity required in the operation. As a general rule, detachments should be formed only of light troops, well acquainted with their duties; and, in every case where it can be done, they should consist of a proper proportion of each arm of the service, if the duty upon which they are sent is at all of an important character. By this combination each arm is enabled to act with more boldness and vigor, from the support with which it will meet in the others; and can better select its moment for action, according to the character of the ground on which it finds itself.

331. The combats of detachments will be mostly restricted to firing, and the skilful employment of skirmishers. The troops must be kept perfectly in hand for mutual support, the artillery keeping near

the infantry, and the cavalry, whenever the opportunity is presented, hazarding only short but vigorous charges against the enemy.

332. The officer placed in command of a detachment, should be thoroughly conversant with the handling of troops; so as to insure constant reciprocity of support; and to be able to seize upon those opportunities of bringing the proper arm into action, and for passing from the defensive to the offensive, which combats between small bodies of troops so frequently present.

333. *March of Detachments.* As a detachment must rely mainly on its own resources, the *person-n l* end *matériel* of the troops should be rigidly inspected before marching; to see that the men and horses are in a sound state; that nothing is wanting in their equipments; that the gun and other carriages are in good travelling order; and that the necessary amount of ammunition, provisions, and forage have been provided for the expedition.

334. Every source of information should be consulted with respect to the nature of the roads, and the country over which the column is to march; and good maps, telescopes, and guides should be provided. If a reconnaissance of the line of march has been directed, it should be placed in charge of a well informed staff, or other officer, conversant with the duties required of him; so that the commander of the detachment may be accurately informed of the state of the roads, as to their practicability for men, horses, and carriages; particularly the number of hours of march from station to station; and the character of the obstacles with which he may be liable to meet, from the state of the bridges, the nature of the water-courses, and the defiles along the route.

335. In order to avoid being anticipated in our object by the enemy, every attention should be paid to preserve strict order among the troops, and to advance with celerity; so that secrecy may be kept until the detachment reaches its destination. The troops, for this purpose, should be kept as closely together as the character of the ground will permit; and when guides are employed, they must be strictly watched, and not be dismissed until the march is completed.

336. The distribution of troops, or the *order of march*, will mainly depend upon the character of the country; the general rule to be followed is so to place each arm in the column, that the troops may be formed for action by the most prompt and simple movements. In a very open country, the greater part of the cavalry will be at the head of the column; where it is somewhat broken, half of the cavalry may be in front, and the remainder in the rear; and in a very difficult country the infantry will lead. The artillery may be placed in the intervals of the column where the country is not difficult; in the contrary case it will be in the rear, but covered by a small detachment which it precedes.

337. The column must be secured from a sudden attack of the enemy by an advanced-guard, flankers, and a rear-guard. The advanced-guard will be composed of cavalry or infantry, or of the two combined, according to the character of the country. In some cases it may be well to have two or three light pieces with the advanced-guard. The strength of the advanced-guard, for detachments not over two thousand men, need not be greater than one-fifth of the whole; for larger bodies it may be be-

See Plate V. for Articles 336, 375.

tween a fourth and a third, according to the degree of resistance it may be required to offer.

338. The advanced-guard of a detachment should seldom leave a wider interval than about a thousand paces between it and the main-body. In a broken country, when this force consists of infantry alone, the distance should be less, to avoid an ambush. The main-body of the advanced-guard should always be preceded a few hundred paces by a strong patrol of cavalry or infantry, to search the ground and secure the advanced-guard from falling into an ambush, or from a sudden attack.

339. The flankers will consist mainly of a few detachments, which march parallel to the column and a few hundred paces from it, according to the character of the ground; these will throw out a few men, from a hundred to a hundred and fifty paces, on their exposed flank, to keep a vigilant look-out, in that direction, for the enemy. Occasional patrols may also be sent out on the flanks, when it is deemed necessary to push an examination to some distant point, or to gain a height offering a commanding view of the country. As the object of the flankers is rather to give timely notice to the main-body of an enemy's approach, than to offer any serious resistance, the detachments of which they are composed need only consist of a few men.

340. The rear-guard, except in a very broken or mountainous country, which would offer facilities to the enemy for slipping to the rear, need only be a small detachment, placed more to prevent stragglers from falling to the rear than for any other object.

341. Night marches should not be made, except in case of necessity. When their object is to surprise an enemy, if there be an advanced-guard, it

should be kept near the head of the column. Patrols should be sent forward, with orders to advance with great caution, and not push on too far. Flying patrols may, if requisite, be kept up on the flanks. The most exact order and silence should be maintained, and extreme vigilance be exercised to avoid placing the enemy on the alert.

342. The following remarks, on the subject of marches, are taken from a little work, " *On the Duties of Troops composing the Advanced Corps of an Army*," by Lieut.-Col. Leach, of the British Army ; a work which, for its sound practical views, made in the vein of a judicious, well-informed soldier, who has seen service, commends itself to the *juniors* of the profession generally.

" At the time the following orders were first issued for the march of the light-division, in the summer of 1809, on its route from Lisbon to Talavera, the troops moved off by whole or half sections, according to the width of the road ; but, at a later period, a general order appeared, which directed that the infantry should march by threes.

" The division having formed in rear of the leading battalion, at whole, half, or quarter distance, or in close column, and the baggage being assembled in rear of it, the march was commenced with precisely the same regularity as would be observed by a regiment or regiments moving in or out of a garrison town; the bands playing, the light-infantry with arms sloped, and those of the riflemen slung over the shoulder, the officers with swords drawn, and exact wheeling distances of the sections preserved, and perfect silence observed.

" After having proceeded a short distance in this manner, the word of command, ' March at ease,' was given by the general at the head of the leading

mistaken, and this was passed quickly on to the rear
from company to company. The captains, instead
of continuing at the head of their companies, drop-
ped back to the rear of them: the reasons for allowing this station to them was, that they might see
any men of their respective companies who attempted to leave the ranks without leave. The
officers and non-commissioned officers preserved the
wheeling distances. The soldiers now carried their
arms in any manner most convenient. Some slung
them over their shoulders, most of them, indeed,
preferred this mode as the least fatiguing,) others
sloped them, and many trailed them, and they constantly changed from the right hand or right shoulder to the left. Whilst some lighted their short
black pipes, others sung or amused their comrades
with stories and jests, as is usual on those occasions.
Although allowed to prosecute the march in this
easy and unrestrained manner, a heavy penalty,
nevertheless, awaited the man who quitted the
ranks without permission from the captain or officer
commanding his company. The captains were always provided with tickets bearing their own signa-
ture, on each of which was written, 'The bearer
has my permission to fall out of the ranks, being
unable to proceed with the regiment.' Any soldier
found on the line of march by the rear-guard, without a ticket, was liable to be punished for disobe-
dience of orders ; and, as no difficulty was ever experienced by men who were sick, or knocked up, in
procuring this certificate of inability to keep up with
their regiments, such offenders certainly merited
punishment.

" If a soldier wanted to fall out of the ranks for a
few minutes only, he was required to ask leave of
the captain to do so, and, moreover, to take off his

knapsack, and to give it, together with his musket, in charge of the men of his own section, to be carried by them until he rejoined them. This was an admirable order, and it operated in two ways; first, the soldier was enabled, not being encumbered with either knapsack or musket, more speedily to overtake the column on its march; and secondly, if he loitered unnecessarily on the way to rejoin his comrades, who were doubly burdened with his arms and pack, he would be certain to incur their displeasure.

"About once in every hour and a quarter or half, a halt was ordered, and ten or twelve minutes allowed for the men to rest. When practicable, this was done on ground near which there was water; but it is almost unnecessary to add, that very frequently it was not possible to find such favorable spots.

"Preparatory to those temporary halts, the word of command, 'Attention!' was given at the head of the leading regiment, and passed on rapidly (as already stated) from company to company. Upon this, the captains moved quickly from the rear of their companies to the front; the arms of the soldiers were regularly shouldered or slung; perfect silence was observed; the pipes were instantaneously put out of sight, either in the haversacks or elsewhere; the dressing and the wheeling distances of the sections were correctly kept; and in an instant there was a magical change from apparent irregularity to most perfect discipline and order.

"On resuming the march after those halts, the troops observed the same extreme regularity during the first hundred or two of yards, as I have already described. The words 'March at ease' being again given, they returned to the song, the story, and the tobacco-pipe.

"On approaching rivulets or shallow pieces of water, wnich it was necessary should be passed, neither officers nor soldiers were allowed to pick their way through, nor was the smallest break or irregularity permitted to exist in the ranks; but the column marched through by half sections, sections, or subdivisions, (according to the width of the ford,) preserving the same order as if moving along a road.

"That this regulation was, on some occasions, too rigidly enforced, I have never heard disputed; still, the object at which it aimed, viz. that of expending as little time as possible on each day's march, so as to give the soldiers time to take their rest, to construct huts in the bivouac, to wash their linen, to mend their clothes or shoes, to draw their rations, and to cook their meals, that they might be fresh for whatever fatigues happened to be in store for them, was indisputably a most desirable one.

"Those who have campaigned know, that in advancing to attack an enemy, or in retiring before one, the passage of rivers in the line of march, even if so deep as to reach their middles, and under the fire of an enemy also, are expected to be crossed by the troops without a greater derangement taking place in their order of march than the obstacles which they are in the act of encountering, must necessarily produce in a greater or less degree.

"With a detachment consisting of a few hundred men, at a distance from an enemy, and with ample time before them to get over their day's march, it would appear that this order might well be dispensed with; but with a division of four or five thousand men, the case is widely different.

" Let it be supposed that it has arrived at a
stream which admits of being passed by sections,
subdivisions, or even by companies; and that, instead of proceeding straight through it in this manner, every soldier is permitted to pick his way across
in any manner he may think proper, and to break
off from his place in the ranks,—what a vast loss
of time would this occasion ! When would the
rear of the column have effected its passage ?
Surely the patience of those belonging to the front,
centre, and rear of this body of four thousand soldiers, would be pretty well exhausted long before
the opposite bank was gained by the whole, and
the march resumed.   •

" In the rugged and mountainous districts which
the army so frequently traversed in the Peninsula,
it encountered various defiles and other obstacles,
which precluded the possibility of their being passed
except by a very small number of men at a time;
and the following mode was therefore adopted by
each company in making its way along. The first
company of the leading battalion, as soon as it had
disentangled itself from the defile, or broken ground,
was directed to march forward, perhaps about a
quarter of a mile ; there to pile arms, and the men
to rest. The head of the next company, when it
had cleared the defile, halted about thirty or forty
yards on the other side, until all the men belonging
to it came up in succession. This done, the captain moved it forward independently until it joined
the leading company, where it piled arms. Thus,
each company, as soon as it had cleared the obstacles, was brought up en masse, and at a regular
pace, without reference to those in its rear. By
those means that most unmilitary exhibition of file

11*

after file running on, like a string of wild geese, to catch those in their front, was entirely avoided.

"Few things tend so effectually to fatigue and irritate soldiers who are already jaded, as that of trotting on, bending under the weight of pack, belts, and musket, to overtake those who continue to march on in their front.

343. "When the division was about to perform a march not in the immediate vicinity of an enemy, the following arrangements were made either for bivouacking or quartering it, (as the case might be,) so that no time should be lost after it had reached its destination.

"A staff-officer, accompanied by the quartermasters of the division, or (if other duties at that moment were required to be performed by the quartermasters) by a subaltern of each regiment, preceded the troops on horseback, so as to arrive long before them at the ground on which they were to halt for the day, or at the town or village in which it was intended they should be quartered.

"A whole street, or part of one, (as circumstances admitted,) was allotted by the staff-officer to the quartermasters for each of their regiments, who immediately divided the street into equal portions for the different companies, reserving a house or two for the staff of the regiment.

"A sergeant of every company of the division being sent forward so as to arrive long before the troops, and being told by his quartermaster how many and what buildings were set apart for his own people, again subdivided the houses into four equal parts for each of the sections.

"In the event of any noise or disturbance taking place, whether by day or by night, the probabilities were, that the officers belonging to the companies

where such irregularities were going on, would certainly hear it, and as instantaneously put an end
to it.

" If, then, the division marched into a town, each
company was by its sergeant conducted to the
houses allotted to it; in which they were established in a very few minutes. It rarely happened,
therefore, that the soldiers were kept waiting in the
streets for any length of time, as has too often been
the case.

" Should it, on the other hand, have been intended
to bivouac the division, instead of putting it into
houses, arrangements of a similar nature were
adopted, by sending forward officers and sergeants
to take up the ground ; by which means each company marched at once up to its own sergeant, on
whom they formed in open column.

" The rolls were immediately called ; the men
first for duty were warned for guards, (also in-
lying and outlying pickets, if near the enemy,) for
fatigue duties, to draw the rations, to procure
wood for cooking if none was near at hand, to go
for water if no river flowed near the encampment,
&c. &c.

" This done, and the alarm-post, or place of general assembly, having been pointed out to every
one, the men were dismissed; the arms piled, the
cooking immediately commenced, and all further
parades were dispensed with for the day, except a
roll-call about sunset.

" Parties to procure forage, whether green or
dry, were sent out in charge of an officer as soon
as the troops were dismissed.

344. " Amongst the various regulations laid down
for the light-division, I must not omit to mention
what were termed mule-guards.

"A corporal and three privates of every company, mounted guard at nightfall, whenever the division was encamped. The particular duty expected from the sentinels of these company guards was to keep an eye to the baggage animals belonging to their officers, (which were picketed to the trees or fastened in some other manner,) and to prevent them from breaking loose.

"After the establishment of those little guards, but few instances occurred of whole troops of noisy mules, horses, and asses, chasing each other round and through the camp or bivouac, and galloping over the faces and bodies of the soldiers whilst they were asleep.

"Independent of their utility in this way, every company in the division, having its own sentinel, was sure to be instantly apprized of any alarm during the night from the pickets in front; and they were enabled, also, to communicate to their respective companies, without the least delay, any orders arriving at the camp.

"Those only who have witnessed it can thoroughly understand with what uncommon facility and dispatch the division could suddenly get under arms, form in column of march, load the baggage, and proceed on the route chalked out for it."

345. *Defensive measures of Detachments.* In the combats of detachments, whether offensive or defensive, as the employment of skirmishers is the principal means resorted to, and the troops, but in rare cases, act in mass against the enemy, positions should be chosen which will be favorable for this kind of combat. It but seldom happens, in selecting a position for the defensive, that strong points can be found to secure the wings from an attack; but no position should be taken up which

does not present covers for the infantry; good points for the action of the artillery, where it will be but little exposed; as well as shelters where the cavalry may be kept at hand, ready for any emergency, and unexposed to the fire of the enemy's artillery.

346. The natural features of the position will necessarily determine the dispositions for the defence. It must, however, be borne in mind that, as it is essential to keep the troops well in hand for mutual support, they must not be too much dispersed; and that a position which requires this cannot be vigorously defended. The artillery should be kept within a hundred paces of the main-body of the infantry; and the cavalry at about two hundred paces. Offensive movements will be mostly left to the cavalry; which should be held in reserve as long as possible, in order that it may act with the more effect upon the enemy when he is weakened. The infantry should only resort to the bayonet under very favorable circumstances; as, when acting in mass, it will be more exposed to the enemy's fire, and be more in danger of being surrounded.

347. Defiles in the rear of a position do not present the same dangers to small as they do to large bodies of troops, and may indeed be very favorable to the defence in a retreat; but a position should not be taken up too far in advance of a defile, as it might give the enemy an opportunity of cutting off the retreat of the detachment. Whenever this danger is to be apprehended, it must be guarded against by flankers; whose duty it will be to give timely warning to the main-body of any movement of the enemy to gain their rear.

348. If the detachment is forced to retreat, the

greatest attention must be given to keep the troops
well together, and to inspire them with confidence
in their mutual support. Every advantage should
be taken of the strong features of the ground for
checking the enemy, by occupying it with skir
mishers. A portion of the cavalry should be always
at hand, to act offensively when occasion offers.
The artillery will retire by half batteries, or sections, for the purpose of taking up successive posi
tions to secure the retreat of the main-body. When
ever a defile is met on the line of retreat, the entrance to it should be timely secured, by occupying
every strong point near it, to cover the retreating
column. If the defile is of a character that admits
of interior defence, some men should be sent in advance to raise, at suitable points, barriers, or any
other obstacles that will serve as shelters from
which the enemy can be held in check.

349. *Defence of Defiles.* The term defile is applied to any narrow passage through which troops
can only pass in column, or by a flank; such, for
example, as roads confined between mountains,
causeways through marshes, a bridge, &c.

350. Defiles are occupied either to secure them
for our own purposes, or to prevent an enemy from
passing them. In either case, the position taken
up by the troops, whether in advance of, or in the
rear of the defile, to hold it, will depend upon its
length and the features of the ground at its outlets.
If the ground in advance is open to the enemy's
fire, the entrance to the defile cannot be defended
with any chance of success. In like manner, if
the ground in the rear is of the same character,
and within range of the enemy's fire, it will not be
practicable to prevent the enemy from *débouching*
If in sufficient force.

351. When the defile is to be secured for our own use, the ground in advance must be occupied, by taking advantage of all the natural features favorable to the defence. The flanks of the position should, if practicable, rest upon points that the enemy will not be able to turn. The entrance will be guarded by a strong detachment; and if there are points within the defile which would be favorable for checking the enemy, in case of retreat, they should be prepared for defence, by using such means as may be found at hand for strengthening them.

352. If it be deemed advisable to take position in rear of the defile rather than in front, the entrance to it should be occupied by a small detachment, for the purpose of observing the enemy; and if there are points on the flanks of the defile which, if in possession of the enemy, would render him master of it, they must be strongly guarded.

353. The detachment for the defence of a defile will be composed of one or several arms, according to the character of the ground. Each arm will be posted on the points most favorable to its action, and for mutual support. If the position taken up be in rear of the defile, the artillery should be placed at three or four hundred paces in the rear, so as to command by its fire the interior and outlet. The cavalry should be at some two hundred paces back, ready to charge the enemy in flank as he *débouches*. The skirmishers should seize upon every point near the outlet from which the enemy can be reached, both within the defile and as he *débouches* from it; whilst the main-body of the infantry will be posted on the right and left of the outlet, in the best positions for throwing in a heavy fire, and then driving back the enemy with the bayonet.

354. When a position taken in advance of a defile is likely to be forced, the retreat should be commenced by sending all the artillery except two pieces to the rear, to take a position to secure the outlet. A portion of the cavalry will next retire, the rest remaining with the rear-guard, to check by its charges the enemy, should he press on with vigor to seize the entrance. The main-body of the infantry will next retire by the usual movements, either from the centre or the wings, as the case may require. The rear-guard, having secured the entrance until the main-body is far enough to the rear to be out of danger, will retire; the cavalry, or the infantry leading, as the defile may present features most favorable to the action of the one or the other arm. As the troops successively clear the outlet, they will take position to receive the enemy should he attempt to force a passage.

355. In mountainous passes, where the flanks of the defile can be attained by the heights falling into the hands of the enemy's skirmishers, these points must be occupied by detachments, as well as all paths, or roads leading to the flanks, or to the rear of the defile. The reserves of the detachments should occupy in preference points where cross-roads meet. The communications between the detachments and the main-body must be well preserved; and if the detachments are driven in, they must fall back on their supports, and occupy other points on the flanks previously designated. A retreat, under such circumstances, will demand the greatest circumspection, and great unity of action. To secure the retreat of the rear-guard, the lateral issues should be well guarded by detachments.

356. Bridges and dikes are defended in the same manner as other defiles. A bridge in an open

133

country, particularly one over a small water course, is not susceptible of a good defence, and the best thing to be done, to render the passage useless to the enemy, is to destroy it. If the country on the side towards the enemy is open, whilst on the opposite side it is broken so as to present good covers for the troops, a position may be taken up behind the bridge, and the defence be conducted in the usual manner. If, on the enemy's side, the ground is broken, whilst the other side is open, a defence can only be attempted at great risk; as, in case of being forced to retreat, the movement must be made under strong disadvantages, arising from the exposed position of the flanks of the retreating force, whilst on the bridge, to fire, as well as that of the position which must be taken up on the opposite side, if an attempt is made to arrest the enemy at the outlet of the bridge. When both ends of the bridge are favorable to defence, the side towards the enemy may be occupied by a detachment whilst the main-body takes position on the opposite side.

357. Fords can only be defended with safety by taking up a position behind them when the ground presents good covers, near enough to the point of crossing, to bring a strong fire on the enemy whilst passing. Fords are usually the more difficult of defence, as several are frequently found in the same vicinity. The best plan to be resorted to generally, is to endeavor to obstruct them by any means at hand.

358. *Villages, &c.* Villages which are accessible on all sides should not be occupied by a detachment which is obliged to rely only on its own resources; but when they are so situated that they can be approached by the enemy only in front, having their flanks covered by natural obstacles

and the ground in their rear being favorable to a movement of retreat, they may be defended with success, provided they are not commanded by the ground in advance, within the range of fire-arms, and that the approaches to them can be swept by the fire of the defence.

359. On occupying a village, the commanding-officer should immediately make himself acquainted with the environs to at least within the range of fire-arms ; and lose no time in erecting such obstacles, as barricades across the streets, abatis, &c., as the means at his disposal will permit.

360. The defence will mainly fall upon the infantry, which should be divided into three parties for this object ; the one will occupy all favorable points where cover can be obtained on the outskirts of the village, such as ditches, inclosures, &c.; another, divided into a suitable number of detachments, will be posted, under cover, on the most accessible avenues to the position occupied by the first, of which they will form the supports ; the third will form one or more reserves, according to the extent of ground taken up, and will be posted at some central point most convenient to act, according as circumstances may demand.

361. The artillery will be placed at those points where it can best sweep the ground over which the enemy must approach to attack the weak points of the position. It should be covered by an epaulment, and be masked until it is necessary to open its fire.

362. Cavalry can aid but little in the interior defence of a village ; if it form a part of the detachment, it may take post so as to secure the flanks of the village, if they are not well covered ; otherwise a position should be taken by it in rear, to be ready

to cover the retreat, if the other troops should be driven out by the enemy.

363. In the defence of a village, the detachment, unless it should find itself decidedly superior to the enemy, will rely mainly upon the effects of its fire. Sorties may be attempted, if the enemy commits any blunder; such as exposing himself to a flank attack, or not supporting well his advanced line. When a sortie is decided upon, the point from which it is made should be strongly occupied, to cover the party sallying out in case of a repulse. The party for the sortie should attack with vigor, but with due precautions against being cut off; and if they succeed in driving back the enemy, they must not engage in a headlong pursuit, but fall back under cover of the party holding the point from which they sallied.

364. If the troops occupying the exterior line are in danger of being turned by a flank attack, they must retire upon the village, and take up positions previously designated for this contingency. To insure good order and steadiness in this movement, the supports should hold the enemy in check by a sortie on his flank.

365. When it is found that the village must be evacuated, the supports will act with the line of skirmishers, to delay the progress of the enemy, by disputing every favorable point, in order that the reserves may have time to retire and take up a position in the rear, to secure the retreat of the troops still engaged.

In the retreat, the troops falling back on their supports, or reserves, should be careful not to place themselves so as to obstruct either their movements, or their fire upon the enemy.

366. *Inclosures and Houses.* In the defence of

posts, it frequently becomes necessary to occupy isolated houses and strong farm-yard inclosures, to prevent the approach of the enemy on some point In such cases the doors and windows, through which an enemy might force his way in, must be strongly barricaded; those from which a good fire can be brought to bear upon the enemy, should be arranged to give the men secure shelter whilst firing; loop-holes must also be made through the walls to give more fire. If circumstances require that the house be held to the last extremity, the arrangements in the interior must be made to defend it story by story, until the object to be attained is accomplished.

367. The distribution of the troops will depend on the character of the inclosure. When it is spacious and open, the usual distribution of a line of troops around the walls, with supports and a reserve, will be made. In a house, the troops will be divided into several parties, each under the command of a subaltern, or non-commissioned officer, who will direct the defence of their respective stories. When there are men enough, two should be placed at each loop-hole, and a small reserve be kept in the most sheltered spot at hand. The main reserve will occupy the point most convenient to fall upon the enemy should he force his way in. The men at the loop-holes should be cautioned not to throw away their fire, and at suitable intervals they should be relieved by men from the reserve.

368. It is but seldom that artillery can be used in these cases. Some pieces may be posted with advantage in inclosures. Cavalry can be of no service, except it can act in ambush from some point where it may fall on the enemy's flank.

369. *General Measures for the Attack.* The dis-

positions made for the attack by the commanding officer of a detachment, will necessarily be based upon the defensive measures of the enemy. Therefore, in the first place, a correct knowledge should be gained of the position taken up by the enemy, and the manner in which his troops are distributed for its defence. The points to which attention will be directed in these respects, are, *first*, the natural features of the position as adapted to a good defence; and *second*, the distribution of the troops.

370. On the first point, the character of the ground in front of the enemy's position, as to its capabilities for the effective action of infantry, cavalry, and artillery, must be carefully examined; the flanks of the position, as to the practicability of turning them; finally, its rear, as offering a secure retreat to the enemy.

371. On the second point, we must endeavor to ascertain whether the enemy, in posting his troops, has taken advantage of the features of ground in his front, by placing each arm on those points most favorable to its action; whether the extent of ground taken up by the enemy is susceptible of a strong defence by the troops which occupy it; whether the different arms are so posted as to give a mutual support; whether the enemy has neglected to give proper supports and reserves, or to place them within suitable distances; whether he has crowded too many troops upon one point, or has posted too few on another; whether the points occupied by any portion of the troops, particularly by the artillery, or cavalry, are exposed to an enfilading fire of our own artillery; whether his flanks are assailable; whether there are defiles to his rear which he has omitted to occupy; finally, whether he has neglected

to guard avenues by which either his flanks or rea may be reached.

372. If the enemy's troops are well posted in front, occupying all the advantageous points presented by the ground, and well supported, we must look to see what can be done by operating on his flanks, or by turning his position and gaining his rear, whilst a feigned attack is made on his front. If the extent of his position is too great, and his troops too much dispersed, his flanks may be menaced whilst a serious attack is made on his front.

373. Attacks on the flanks by a portion of the troops are very favorable against an enemy not prompt at manœuvring; but, when made against a skilful active enemy, we expose ourselves to the same attack that we attempt against him, besides weakening our front.

374. In moving forward to the attack, the troops should be kept well in hand for mutual support. The artillery and cavalry should avail themselves of all covers presented by the ground, to avoid exposure to the enemy's artillery. The artillery should reserve its fire until it can open with a decided effect to clear the way for the action of the main-body; leaving to the skirmishers to push forward, and by their fire drive the enemy from his covers. If, however, there are points from which the enemy cannot be well dislodged without the aid of artillery, it should be brought early into action, to avoid the blood-shed of unavailing attacks of the infantry. In no case should the artillery be isolated, but always covered by a strong escort; otherwise it might at any moment fall into the enemy's hands.

375. In attacks of the character in question, where the skirmishers play so important a part, they will be required to resort frequently to the

bayonet, to dislodge the enemy fully from his covers whenever an opportunity offers, some cavalry should be at hand to take advantage of the retreat of the enemy when driven from such points.

376. The cavalry in its charges, however dashingly made, should use due circumspection, and not venture too far in a headlong pursuit, for fear of being brought up suddenly by the enemy, advantageously posted to profit by such faults.

377. The infantry will only act in mass and with the bayonet when the enemy has been well wearied by the fire of its skirmishers and artillery; if, when driven from his position, the enemy can be forced upon a defile, a few rounds of grape followed up by the bayonet can seldom fail of completing his destruction.

378. *Attack of Defiles.* The length of a defile, and the circumstance of its being prepared by barricades within it, to protract the defence, are points of grave importance in planning an attack. When the length is so great that the outlet is beyond the range of our cannon, the troops will not be able to pass it, except under the most favorable circumstances, as the enemy can make the best dispositions at a short distance from the outlet, to crush the troops which first attempt to *débouche.* If the defile is barricaded, the barricades should not be attacked in front, except for very grave reasons, as, if skilfully defended, they can only be carried at great cost of life.

379. In attacking the entrance of a defile, the troops should approach along the most convenient and best sheltered avenues, and deploy when a little beyond musket range. The skirmishers and the artillery should profit by the ground, in taking positions favorable both for shelter, and to reach

with their fire the enemy's troops Skirmishers should be directed to close in, particularly on the obstacles by which the flanks of the enemy's position are strengthened, and endeavor to dislodge his troops from them. The main-body, held in reserve to carry the entrance with the bayonet, so soon as it is seen that a serious impression has been made by the fire, should be kept under cover, and as near at hand as the ground will permit. If the enemy gives way, the main-body should make a vigorous attack in mass with the bayonet; and, following up closely the retreating troops, endeavor to secure the outlet by *débouching* from it before the front is so far unmasked by the retreating troops as to enable those, in position for its defence, to act with freedom. As fast as the troops *débouche*, they must occupy the ground in front of the outlet strongly, leaving a sufficient force for the immediate defence of the outlet. The reserve should remain at the other extremity of the defile to act as circumstances may require. So soon as we find ourselves in secure possession of the defile, a part of the reserve, with all the cavalry, should pass and take positions indicated on the opposite side. The greater part of the artillery follows, and takes position on the flanks to open its fire on the retiring enemy.

380. If the attack on the entrance to the defile is unsuccessful, the troops will retire behind their reserves, the latter covering this movement, and holding the enemy in check should he attempt a pursuit. If a renewed attack is ordered, the troops first in action will form a reserve for the fresh troops thrown forward.

381. When it is found impracticable to force the entrance by a direct attack, resort must be had to

stratagem, by pushing forward a few troops to act
on the enemy's flanks, and try to dislodge him from
the obstacles by which they are covered. If this
attempt is successful, the troops in action must be
gradually reinforced to gain supports for the flanks
of the column of attack in its advance movement.
As the column penetrates the defile, ground must
be gradually gained by throwing forward fresh
troops which dislodge the enemy, secure the issues
in case of retreat, and hold the points of support
of the flanks.

382. In the attack of defiles forming mountainous passes, the column of attack must be well covered on the flanks, by detachments which make a
simultaneous attack on the enemy's posts on the
heights, to prevent the one from affording support
to the other. These detachments should be strong
enough for the duty assigned, so that should any
post offer a vigorous resistance, they may be enabled to renew their attacks with fresh troops.

383. Two-thirds of the detachments will act as
skirmishers, the other third will be held in reserve.
So soon as any post is carried, the reserves will
occupy it. When the skirmishers move forward,
a portion or the whole of the reserve will follow,
as circumstances may demand. There should be
no intermission in the attacks when once commenced, but the enemy be driven by alternate attacks of fire and the bayonet, from point to point,
to enable the detachments gradually to gain the
immediate borders of the defile, so as to reach the
rear of the enemy's troops, and force them to retire. The main-body, in the meantime, should occupy the enemy in front, to prevent him from sending succor to the posts that secure his rear and
flanks.

384. *Attacks of Villages, &c.* As villages, when occupied with a view to defence, are usually prepared for it by the addition of artificial obstacles to those which the position naturally presents, an open attack upon them should, when practicable, be avoided, as it can only succeed, if the assailed perform their duty, at great loss of life to the assailant. In any case, whether made openly or otherwise, attacks of this kind ought not to be hazarded except with superior numbers, unless the enemy be very inferior in discipline.

385. In conducting the attack of a village, the troops should endeavor to approach their points of attack by avenues which will afford them cover from the enemy's fire until they arrive near them, and should particularly try to gain any commanding points from which a plunging fire may be brought to bear on the enemy's covered defences.

386. The most favorable points of attack are those which are salient; as they are naturally weak; those where there are no prepared defences, or where they are but slight; and the flanks and rear, when they are accessible, or are not well secured by troops so posted as to cover them.

387. The attack will mainly devolve upon the infantry. The artillery, by taking suitable positions either to enfilade any part of the enemy's line which lies exposed to its fire, to dismount the enemy's guns, or to throw shells from its howitzers into inclosures, will prepare the way for the infantry. The cavalry can only act as a reserve, to cover the infantry if repulsed, and to secure the flanks from an offensive movement against them.

388. The infantry will be divided into three parties for the attack; one, which will display as skir

mishers, may be a sixth of the whole; another which will act as the supports of the first, may be about the one-half of the whole; and the remaining third will form the reserve. The party in advance, in dispersed order, will get over the ground as rapidly as possible, and endeavor to close with the enemy's skirmishers; relying almost exclusively on the bayonet. Their supports will follow in line, at from one hundred to one hundred and fifty paces in their rear; the reserves at about the same distance in rear of the supports, taking advantage of the ground to screen themselves from the enemy's fire. If the advanced party succeeds in its attack upon the interior defences, they will follow up the enemy closely, and give him no opportunity to halt and make a stand; the supports will advance and clear the streets with the bayonet. Should the enemy form across a wide street to stop the advance, the skirmishers will move forward in open order, taking advantage of any shelters to cover themselves, and by their fire force the enemy to deliver his, and the supports and reserve in mass will attack with the bayonet. So soon as an entrance is secured, the skirmishers and supports will drive the enemy from the interior defences in their front, whilst the reserve will push forward to the central point, to attack his reserve if posted there, and to be in readiness to support the advanced parties at any point where succor may be necessary.

389. Whenever they can be procured, a party of well-trained sappers should be sent forward with the advance, to clear any obstacles by which their progress might be impeded. If this description of troops is not to be obtained, a few active men, used

to handling the axe and pick, should be detailed for this necessary duty.

390. In case of the repulse of the advance, they will fall back to the nearest cover from which they can open a fire on the enemy, and after being joined by their supports will renew the attack.

391. *Handling of Skirmishers.* Skirmishers play so important a part in all affairs of detachments, as well as in engagements of larger bodies, the circumstances being rare, either in the attack or defence, where they cannot be employed with considerable effect, either to harass or occupy the enemy, that a few words may be here especially given to the manner of handling them; even at the risk of repeating what has been already laid down.

392. The number of skirmishers employed will greatly depend on the features of the ground, as being more or less favorable to the action of cavalry, or of infantry in mass. In no case, however, should the main-body be unduly weakened by detaching too many skirmishers. A third of the entire force is the most that can be safely thrown forward for this duty; and, if it be found that they are unable to maintain their ground in the presence of the enemy, it will be safer to cause them to fall back and reinforce the main-body, by forming on the flanks, or any previously designated point, than to detach from the main-body for their support.

393. The manner of forming a line of skirmishers, and posting their supports and reserves, with the other ordinary manœuvres for extending, advancing, retiring, &c., belong to elementary tactics, and require no comment here. A few precepts, however, may be mentioned, as connected with this subject. The line of skirmishers should not be pushed so far in advance of the main-body that the

latter will not be able to come to their aid in time if
they should be vigorously pressed by the enemy;
or be able to profit by any advantages obtained by
them. The reserves to support the line should in
all cases be near enough for this object; and, as
far as practicable, be posted where they can readily
find cover from the enemy's fire; taking advantage,
for this purpose, of any irregularities of ground or
shelters, like walls, hedges, ditches, &c. The reserves may be of less strength in broken than in
open ground; being, however, never less than a
fourth in the former, nor a third in the latter case.

394. The position of skirmishers in advance of
the main-body will depend on the natural features
of the ground. As a general rule, they ought to
cover both the front and flanks of the main-body,
extending far enough beyond each flank for the
latter purpose; and, in all manœuvres of the main-
body in the face of the enemy, it should be protected
by skirmishers until the new position is taken up.

395. It is seldom necessary to throw forward the
skirmishers before the main-body is ready to commence the action. They should deploy and extend
oefore coming within reach of the enemy's musketry; and, when the lines are near enough to engage, they should retire to the positions previously
assigned them.

396. A quick eye, presence of mind, and good
judgment in taking up ground are indispensable to
an officer in command of skirmishers, to enable
him to keep his troops easily in hand; preventing
them from rushing on headlong in the pursuit, when
any success is gained; and directing them to seize
upon every cover, either in advancing or retiring,
from which they can with advantage annoy the
enemy or hold him in check.

13

397. The accuracy of aim, upon which the good effects to be obtained by skirmishers depends, requires that the men should be kept cool and in good order. All hurried and violent movements, by which the men may lose breath and become exhausted, should be avoided; and they should be frequently cautioned against rapid firing, which soon impairs the aim, and be directed never to raise the piece until they feel sure of their shot.

398. In an advance movement of skirmishers, their line will necessarily have to conform to the features of the ground; when this is open, the alignment should, as far as practicable, be preserved; and when broken, the officers should see that mutual support is given throughout between the detached portions; and that those on the flanks be particularly cautioned not to suffer their attention to be so much taken up by the enemy in front as to neglect securing the flanks from any attempt upon them, either openly or by ambush.

399. Wherever an open portion of ground occurs, it should be gotten rapidly over, so that the men shall be exposed as little as may be; and, if there is any apprehension from the enemy's cavalry in such cases, the men should be kept well together, or even be rallied on the reserves, until the character of the ground will enable them to deploy with safety.

400. If the more advanced portions come upon the enemy in force, they should halt and occupy him in front; whilst a portion may try to turn him, or to annoy his flanks. In like manner, in a successful attack on the enemy's out-posts, the skir mishers should endeavor to maintain their ground when they come upon his main-body, by occupying its attention until their own main force can come up.

401. In the attack upon all covered positions held by the enemy, skirmishes play the most important part ; and, although it may require the action of masses to dislodge the enemy under some circumstances, there are but few in which, by a judicious selection of ground, skirmishers may not greatly bother him. The broken features presented by wooded and rocky ravines, or the beds of small fordable streams, from the opposite side of which an enemy must be rooted out before ground can be gained forward, are ugly circumstances in an advance movement ; and great skill and patience are requisite on the part of both officers and men to accomplish their object. Points which afford a good cover for a few men, or from which a commanding or a flanking view of the enemy's line can be obtained, should be sought for ; and, where the men would be much exposed in gaining such points, from the open character of the intervening ground, they should be sent forward singly, with directions as to the best probable manner of attaining their object, and be particularly cautioned against exposing themselves in little knots of three or four together, as the chances of casualties will be thereby increased. If the crest of a hill intervenes in a pursuit, it should be gained with great caution, for fear of coming suddenly upon the enemy in force on the opposite side.

402. When the enemy occupies strong artificial obstacles, as palisades, an abatis, yards, of which the walls are loop-holed, &c., an attempt should be made to dislodge him by shells from howitzers ; the troops for the assault may then be advanced as skirmishers, and when within about two hundred paces, should clear the intervening ground at full speed, in closing.

403. In attacks upon forests, the intervening open ground must be cleared in a similar style; and after the enemy has been dislodged from the skirts, the further advance should be cautiously made; attention being paid to preserving the general alignment; the men taking care to avoid leaving any considerable gaps between them, or of losing sight of each other. A vigilant eye should be kept upon securing the communications to the rear by the reserves, in case of being forced to retire; and, before passing cross-roads, it should be well ascertained that they do not offer any facilities for an offensive movement of the enemy.

404. Whenever a defile is met with, which is not strongly guarded, some of the line of skirmishers may enter it boldly, relying on the bayonet, whilst others take up points from which they can enfilade it; but if the enemy makes a show of a vigorous resistance, the skirmishers should seize upon the best points on its flanks from which a warm steady fire can be kept up on it, and hold them until their reserves, or if necessary the main-body, can come up and force their way with the bayonet. When the defile is carried, the reserves follow the onward movement of the line of skirmishers, leaving it to be held, if it be thought necessary, by a detachment from the main-body.

405. Skirmishers necessarily play a very important part in mountainous warfare, as the broken character of the ground presents many points from which it may become exceedingly difficult to dislodge an enemy thoroughly conversant, from some days' occupancy, with all its resources. In such attacks, as the valley-passes will usually be occupied by the strength of the enemy, the skirmishers must try to gain successively the heights on the flanks of

the main position; care being taken that no party gets too much in advance of the other. If the enemy retires, a portion of the skirmishers should follow closely upon his rear, whilst others occupy commanding points from which they can keep up a well-directed fire on him. If, in the pursuit, paths should be found leading to the flanks, or rear of the enemy's main-position, some detachments may be pushed forward in these directions, to bother the enemy, whilst the rest join in the main attack.

406. If a vigorous resistance is offered by the enemy, it will be necessary to employ a number of small detachments to dislodge him from every cover. These should advance along the most advantageous paths, proceeding with great caution, and leaving no suspicious points to the rear, until they are thoroughly searched and their character ascertained. The communications to the rear, by which the skirmishers will have to retire if repulsed, must be well secured by the reserves, who will usually take post at the junction of cross-roads, or in other positions favorable to receiving the skirmishers and covering their retreat.

407. If an isolated post of the enemy is met with, every point around it, from which a fire can be brought to bear, should be occupied by skirmishers; and a steady unintermitted fire be kept up against it until he is dislodged, or driven from it by an attack with the bayonet by the reserves.

408. In the retreat, every advantageous point which offers cover to skirmishers, should be seized on by them, to hold the enemy in check, and thus give time to the main-body to retire in good order. The skirmishers, however, should not fall too far to rear, so as not to compromise their own safety; whenever obliged to this, a part of the reserves

may be thrown forward, to reinforce the line, and give more vigor to its fire; but a part should always be kept in reserve to be ready for any emergency. If the retreat be through a defile, and the enemy's pursuit is feeble, it will usually be only necessary to deploy the reserves of the skirmishers on such ground, on the right and left of the entrance to it, as may be favorable to bringing a good fire to bear on the enemy. As soon as the main-body has cleared the defile, or is sufficiently beyond the reach of an active pursuit, the skirmishers and their reserves retire by sections; keeping at from two to three hundred paces in the rear of the main-body. In case the enemy should push forward with vigor, the skirmishers adopt the same measures; but the additional precaution should be taken of holding the outlet of the defile, by a detachment posted advantageously for that object, until all the skirmishers have cleared it.

409. In all positions taken up for the defensive in mountainous, or broken ground, whether the valleys or the heights be occupied, those points from which the troops might be annoyed by the enemy's skirmishers should be guarded by our own, as well as all pathways leading to them; attention should be given so to post our skirmishers as to take the enemy in flank in his assault upon the front of the position.

410. The safety of the communications must be carefully looked to in a retreat; and for this object the position of the reserves should be judiciously selected; taking them at those points where the enemy would be met, should he take paths or cross-roads, passing beyond the flanks of the line occupied by the skirmishers, to gain their rear The skirmishers themselves should not hold pos

session too long of any point, in order not to have
their safety compromised, by leaving too wide an
interval between themselves and the main-body;
and whenever they are thrown into inclosures,
they should see that easy communications are
opened to the rear for a timely exit.

411. Although skirmishers should rely mainly
on a steady, well-directed fire, for the attainment
of their ends, still a resort to the bayonet by the
reserves should not be overlooked; as, by a judi
cious combination of caution with boldness, the
enemy may not only be held in check, and be con-
strained to a very circumspect course, but may be
frequently so forced back as to enable the skirmishers, if it be advisable, to recover lost ground.

412. The fact should never be lost sight of, that
a line of skirmishers is weak in itself; and even
powerless when exposed to the attack of cavalry,
or that of infantry in mass. It offers but a bad
mark to the enemy's round shot in front, but it
may be greatly damaged from an enfilading position; and care should therefore be taken not to
post a line behind any obstacle which, like a hedge,
or ditch, may so present itself to the enemy's batteries. The line may also greatly suffer when,
manœuvring in open ground, it comes within short
range of the grape and canister of the enemy. The
true tactics, therefore, of skirmishers, is to avoid
open ground, and to throw themselves into that
which presents obstacles to the enemy's movements, and affords covers not exposed to enfilading
views of his batteries; to seek for positions from
which their fire will annoy the enemy both in front
and flank, occupying him in front whilst ground is
gained on the flank; and in all changes of position,
whether advancing or retiring, to move from one to

the other, both with celerity and by an orderly simultaneous movement.

413. *Escalading.* This is a means of attack upon which our English friends rather pique themselves; in spite of some signal failures during the Peninsular campaigns, and some successes in which as much seems to have been owing to chance as to any other cause; as the reader, who may look over *Jones's Journal of the Sieges* carried on in these campaigns, will find. Since that time it has been successfully used in the attacks made on the *stockade forts* in India. How far it might succeed against ourselves, we have no means of judging; as in the attempts by our friends on our slight field-works, during the last war, very few of them had an opportunity of getting further than the ditch, under the deadly fire of our well-practised citizens. It is a resource, however, when others fail; and, in a favorable moment, may succeed, either through the surprise, or cowardice of the assailed.

414. In a little work, on the *Attack of Military Posts, &c.*, by Captain, now, we believe, Colonel Jebb, of the Royal Engineers,—which, as well as his Defence of Out-posts, is cordially commended to the perusal of our young officers, for its practical details and capital common-sense views; maugre its slap-dash flippancy of style, with which the *Juniors* of the British line, it seems, must be indulged, to cheat them into a little study of their art,—the manner of conducting an assault by escalade is given with some detail. Whether the groups termed *rallying columns* by the author, would act more harmoniously towards the attainment of the main object, than the groups of another more celebrated system, also brought together by their attractional sympathies, experiment alone can determine

415. The following is the outline of the method of escalade, proposed by Colonel Jebb in the work referred to. Ladders of suitable length for the enterprise are to be provided for scaling the scarp; the one proposed is three feet longer than the height of the scarp; so that, the foot of the ladder being planted a pace or two from the bottom of the wall, the top may project far enough above the wall to enable the men to step from the ladder with ease, in an upright position. An allowance of one ladder is made for every five feet of the face to be scaled; one hundred feet, for example, requiring twenty ladders.

416. To each ladder, from four to six men are assigned, according to its length. The ladders are borne, in the usual manner, on the shoulders of the men; two or three being placed on each side for this purpose.

The ladders for scaling the scarp are assigned to the advance. A second set of less dimensions, for descending into the ditch only, are assigned to the support. The scarp ladders are placed on the ground in line, at some suitable point, with the proper intervals between them; the men to carry them, properly "told off," are drawn up in rear of them; and, at the proper commands, are marched to their places at the sides of the ladders, and raise them ready for the forward movement. Similar dispositions are made for the counterscarp ladders, which are placed in line, from 100 to 150 yards in rear of the others.

417. At a given signal, the whole are to move forward; covered by an advanced firing party, to keep down the fire of the work, and followed by a reserve.

The scarp ladders are let down into the ditch,

the men descend, carry them across it, plant them against the scarp, and mount to the top. The top of the parapet gained, the men are to group themselves rapidly in *rallying-columns;* and proceed to clear the parapet by charging the assailed in flank.

418. The support and reserve, in the meantime, are to follow on without loss of time, to take their share in the action.

CHAPTER VII.

419. To conduct a convoy in safety through an nemy's territory, where it is exposed to attacks either of regular, or of partisan troops, is one of the most hazardous operations of war; owing to the ease with which a very inferior force may take the escort at disadvantage in defiles, or other positions favorable to an ambuscade, or surprise, and to the difficulty of securing a long column, like that presented by a convoy, from a sudden attack.

420. The escort should be of sufficient strength to beat off any presumed force that the enemy can bring against it. A weak escort will only hold out a temptation to the enemy to attack the convoy. When the convoy is of very great importance, it may be necessary, besides giving it a strong escort, to throw out detachments between its line of march and the enemy; and when there are posts occupied by our troops along this line, they should keep up a vigilant system of patrols, pushing them as far out as practicable, so that the escort may receive aid and timely notice of any hostile movement.

The escort, when it is deemed necessary, should be composed of all arms; but always of both infantry and cavalry, as, from the necessity of gaining timely information of the enemy's approach, patrols of cavalry must be pushed out to some distance, both in front and on the flanks.

421. As the convoy must be perfectly hemmed in and guarded on all points by its escort, the latter is

usually divided into five principal portions with this object; an advanced-guard, which is preceded by a small detachment to scour and search the ground in front of the line of march; a rear-guard; flankers; and the main-body. For the purpose of presenting a sufficient force upon those points of the convoy that will probably be assailed, the main-body is subdivided into four unequal portions; one-half of it will constitute a reserve; one-fourth will form a guard for the centre of the convoy; and the remaining fourth will be divided into two equal portions, one of which will march directly at the head of the convoy, and the other close in its rear. This subdivision of the main-body is made on the supposition that the enemy will attack the convoy either at the centre, or in the front, or rear. If the attack is made upon either of the two last points, the divisions for their protection can be readily reinforced by the advanced, or the rear-guard. As the reserve must be in readiness to reinforce any point menaced, and to offer a vigorous resistance, its strength should be greater than either of the other divisions.

422. The order of march of the escort will be regulated mainly by the natural features of the ground passed over. The advanced-guard will precede the convoy about a thousand paces. The detachment by which it is preceded, and which should consist of cavalry, will push forward as far as it can with safety, taking care to scour thoroughly all the ground passed over. The flankers, which will also usually be composed of cavalry, will be divided into platoons, and be thrown out as far as circumstances will permit. Each platoon will throw out a small detachment, on its outer flank, which last will furnish vedettes to move along

the outward flank of the detachment. The reserve will usually occupy some point near the centre of the convoy. The rear-guard will leave about 1000 paces between it and the tail of the column. The divisions immediately at the head and tail of the train will keep close to the convoy. The centre division will usually be divided into two portions, one being on each flank of the convoy; a space of eight or ten paces being left in the centre of the train, for these portions to pass to either flank, as circumstances may require.

423. The convoy is placed under the orders of an officer, subordinate to the commandant of the escort, who is charged with everything appertaining to its police, &c. A detachment of pioneers, or sappers, should precede the convoy, to repair the roads and bridges, &c. A few wagons, with all the necessary implements for the sappers, should accompany the convoy; and it is also recommended to carry with it a few *chevaux-de-frise*, the lances of which are of iron, and connected with the bodies by hinges, to pack conveniently, in order to form a temporary obstacle against the enemy's cavalry, when the convoy parks for the night, or when threatened with an attack.

424. When a part of the convoy consists of bat-horses, or mules, they should be placed at the head of the column of wagons, as they are found to travel better in this position than when in the rear.

425. *Distribution of the Train.* The train is usually divided into four sections. If money or powder form a part of the train, it should occupy the centre of the second section, as this point is usually best protected. The provisions and other munitions will be distributed equally among the other sections; so that, should any one be cut off

14

by the enemy, a portion of each kind may be saved in the remainder.

426. As it takes some time to set the whole column in motion, the horses are harnessed and hitched to successively, by sections. The second section will not commence to harness until the first is ready to move off, and so on in succession. The time for this operation will be ascertained by the officer in charge of the convoy; so that each section may be notified of the proper moment to prepare for the march. This should be done in order not to fatigue the horses unnecessarily, by keeping them standing in harness.

427. *March of Train.* The convoy will march in single or double files, according to the state of the roads. The files should not be doubled unless the road is wide enough for three files; and also when the train can march in this order at least an hour; otherwise there will be too great inconvenience and loss of time in changing the order of march. To pass from single to double file, the hindmost wagons of the first and third sections will lead off to the side of the road; and so on each in succession to the one at the head. The leading wagons of the second and fourth sections move briskly on in their new line of direction, followed by those in their rear. until they come up with the leading wagons of the other two sections. An interval of four paces should be preserved between the files. To change from double to single file, the first section quickens its pace, and when its last wagon has passed the leading one of the second section, this and the rest of the section follow in the new line.

428. The greatest attention should be paid to preserve regularity and good order in the march. For

this purpose small detachments of infantry, taken
from the centre division of the escort, should march
at intervals on the flanks of the train. When the
number of men will admit of it, each wagon should
be under the guard of a soldier, or at least of one
man to three wagons. If neither of these arrangements can be made, each section may be placed
under the charge of four or five horsemen, who will
keep in constant motion along the line, to see that
all goes on well. If, for any purpose, a wagon is
obliged to halt, it must fall out of the line, and not
be allowed to enter it until the rear wagon of its
section has passed. The line should be kept well
closed up; the leading wagons slackening their
pace, to allow the others to come up, if retarded by
any obstacle.

429. *Halt of Train.* When from any cause the
convoy is forced to halt for some time, as for the
repair of a bridge, the passage of a defile, &c., the
wagons should be parked either in lines of sections,
or as many in line as the character of the ground
will admit of. An interval of about twenty paces
may be left between each line. If there is any apprehension of an attack under these circumstances,
the lines may close to within fifteen paces; the
openings on the flanks being covered by wagons
placed across them.

430. *Parking of Train.* When the convoy halts
to park for the night, a strong position should be
chosen, offering only one side, if practicable, to an
attack. The park may be formed by lines of sections or in squares, as may be deemed most advisable. The faces of the park should be flanked by
some pieces of artillery, and the angles be covered
by any temporary obstacle, as a chevaux-de-frise,
a slight abatis, &c. The different portions of the

escort will take position around the park, to cover it from the enemy's approach; those divisions, which march with the convoy, being posted behind the wagons, and the obstacles which cover them. The usual dispositions of out-posts and patrols will be made, to guard against a surprise. It is not safe to park in villages, nor even to pass through them on a march, when powder forms a part of the convoy.

431. When the park is formed as a temporary intrenchment, to cover the escort against an attack, an open portion of ground should be selected, which offers no covers for the enemy to approach within musket-range. The wagons may be placed in one line, or in two if their number is sufficient to inclose the necessary ground for the troops, &c., so as to form a square, rectangular, or circular figure, as the locality may require. When the inclosure is formed of a single line of wagons, they are placed wheel to wheel, with an outlet of three or four feet between every six wagons; a wagon being placed, six paces to the rear of the line, behind each outlet to close it. If the inclosure is a double line, the wagons are placed end to end, and wheel to wheel, outlets, as in the preceding case, being left between every four wagons, and closed as before. The poles of four-wheel carriages are placed outwards; the shafts of the two-wheel inwards; the horses picketed opposite their wagons. The wagons that contain ammunition, or valuables, are placed within the inclosure, at the point regarded as least exposed. If the convoy is surprised on a march, and have not time to park in square, the files should be rapidly doubled if moving in single file, the heads of the horses be turned towards the centre of the road, so as nearly to touch each other, and the wagons be brought as closely together as practicable.

432. *Duties of Escort.* All the usual precautions, to guard a column in march against a surprise, should be redoubled in cases of convoys. The patrols on the flanks and in front should push as far out as practicable; so that the convoy may have timely warning of an enemy's approach; in order to park, according to circumstances, before an attack can be made. With drivers accustomed to their business, half an hour at least will be required for this operation. The advanced-guard should be particularly careful to occupy by detachments any lateral roads which might offer the enemy a favorable point of attack on the convoy. These detachments will keep their posts until the convoy has passed; and they will join the rear-guard as it comes up.

433. The officer in command of the head-division, marching with the convoy, will see that his detachment moves on regularly, as the pace of the convoy will be regulated by it; and, from time to time, he will bring it to a halt, to allow the carriages to close up; this precaution must be carefully attended to when near an enemy.

434. If menaced with an attack, the divisions at the head and tail of the convoy will keep their positions and repel the enemy by their fire should he attack; the centre division will move to the flank menaced, and take position to cover the two centre sections of the convoy; the reserve will move towards the point threatened; the advanced and rear-guards and flankers will close upon the convoy to be in readiness to act as circumstances may require.

435. Before entering a defile, a detachment from the reserve should be sent forward to secure its flanks and outlet, and then send out patrols in all directions to examine the ground in front, and as

that all is safe. As the convoy comes up to a point
designated in rear of the defile, it is parked in lines
of sections. The centre division of the escort will
join the advanced-guard to cover the front; the rear-
guard will take position to cover the rear; the
flankers on the flanks; and the reserve in a central
position to advance upon the point which may be
attacked. When the patrols report all safe, the advanced-guard and centre division pass the defile,
and proceed far enough beyond it to cover the
ground where the convoy will park as it reaches
the other side; the reserve and flankers will cover
the flanks of the convoy as it moves to its new position, and will then take post as before; the rear-
guard joined by any detachments left to secure particular points on the flanks of the defile, will follow
so soon as the convoy and the rest of the troops are
in position. When all the troops have passed, strong
detachments are sent forward, in all directions, at
least one hour before the convoy is again put in
motion.

436. When the escort takes position at night,
within the park, for defence, the reserve will be
posted in the centre, and the divisions that march
with the convoy in rear of their respective sections.
The advanced and rear-guards and the flankers will
take post without, and establish their out-posts and
sentinels in the usual way for safety. The cannon,
placed at the angles of the park, will be supported
by detachments of infantry and cavalry in their
rear. The different divisions will throw forward
skirmishers to meet the enemy if he attacks; whilst
others will occupy the wagons from which they can
fire. Should the enemy not be beaten off by the fire
of these troops, the reserve will sally out and attack
with the bayonet.

437. *Attack of Convoy.* An attack upon a convoy is a comparatively easy and safe operation, and may be made with a force quite inferior to the escort; as the latter is obliged, for the security of the convoy, to keep on the defensive.

It will usually be best to attempt a surprise, choosing points which are favorable to ambuscades. The manner of conducting the attack will depend upon its object, whether it be to capture the entire convoy, to cut off a part of it, or simply to delay its march. In the first case, the escort must be beaten and dispersed, whilst a detachment is sent to secure the convoy. In the second, an attack may be made on one point with the view of drawing the main-body of the escort to the defence of that point, whilst a detachment atte npts to cut off the part of the convoy from which tne escort has been withdrawn. In the last case the convoy will be frequently menaced with an attack, to force it to halt and park for defence; the roads will be obstructed, bridges broken down, &c.

438. If the attack is successful, the main-body of the troops should be kept together in position, to cover the captured convoy, whilst the detachment sent to secure, or destroy it, is performing its duty. The cavalry will endeavor to disperse the escort, and bring in all the horses that may have been cut loose from the convoy. The precaution should be taken of having spare horses in harness, in readiness to take the places of those which the escort may have cut loose, or maimed, to prevent the wagons from being carried off. For the attack of a convoy parked for defence, some pieces of artillery will be necessary, and howitzers will be found particularly useful. Without the aid of this arm it will be very difficult to force a defensive park with infantry, un less the escort is very feeble, or the position chosen for the park presents covers within the effective range of musketry, from which, after keeping up a well-directed fire, a rush may be made on the park.

CHAPTER VIII.

439. These two classes of operations depend for their success upon the same point, that of being able to attack the enemy suddenly when he is not prepared to resist. The term *surprise* is applied to unexpected attacks upon an enemy's position; that of *ambuscade* where a position is taken for the purpose of falling suddenly upon the enemy when he reaches it. Secrecy, good troops, and a thorough knowledge of the localities, are indispensable to the success of either of these operations.

440. *Surprise.* In planning a surprise, the officer must spare no pains in ascertaining the face of the country leading to and in the immediate vicinity of the enemy's position; the character and disposition of his troops; and the state of preparation of the defences of the position. Information may be obtained on these points from spies, deserters, inhabitants of the locality occupied by the enemy, good maps, &c.

441. The troops to be employed in the expedition, as well as the other necessary arrangements, will depend upon the information gained on these points. If the position be an intrenched one, infantry will constitute the main force; cavalry and artillery can be of little other use than to cover the retreat of the infantry, and to make prisoners of those who may escape from the position. A body of engineer troops or of picked men used to handling tools, will accompany the infantry, carrying with them such implements as may be requisite from the character of the defences, as axes, saws, crowbars, small scaling ladders, &c.

442. If the position be not intrenched, as an open village, &c., cavalry may perform a very important part, by a sudden dash among the enemy, in creating confusion and alarm.

443. As the success of the affair will greatly depend upon the secrecy with which these preparations are made, and the celerity with which it is conducted, all orders for collecting the necessary implements and assembling the troops, should be given at the shortest notice; no more troops should be taken than are indispensably necessary; and they should carry nothing with them but their arms, and the requisite amount of ammunition.

444. Midnight is the best hour for small bodies of troops to carry out such enterprises; as they must effect all they desire to do and be off before daybreak. A few hours before daylight is the best time for large expeditions; as the dawn of day will be favorable to their retreat, by which time they will have been able to effect their purposes. The season of the year and the state of the weather should be taken advantage of. Winter and bad weather are most favorable, as the enemy's sentinels and out-posts will then, in all probability, be less on the alert, and more disposed to keep under such shelters as they can procure.

445. As our purpose may be divined by the enemy, measures should be taken against such a contingency. These will mainly consist, in securing by detachments all defiles and roads by which our retreat might be cut off; and by designating a rallying point, on which our force will fall back, if repulsed, which should be strongly occupied by

cavalry and artillery, if they constitute a part of
the force.

446. In conducting the march, the troops will be
kept well together; the greatest order and silence
be observed. Instead of the ordinary precautions of
an advanced-guard and flankers, reliance should
rather be placed upon a few active and intelligent
scouts, to gain timely notice of any movement on
the part of the enemy.

447. Concerted attacks upon several points are
good means of creating confusion and paralyzing
the enemy's efforts, when they can be successfully
carried out; but, as they may require some of the
detachments to make considerable circuits to reach
their points, much will depend upon chance as to
their success. In such cases, some signal must be
agreed upon, to let the detachments, already in position, know when those, which are likeliest to reach
theirs latest, are ready; but this may have the inconvenience of giving the alarm to the enemy. Rockets
may be used for this purpose, and also to give notice
to the troops to retire together.

448. The retreat after a successful issue should
be conducted with the same promptitude as the advance. Time must not be lost in waiting too long
for all the detachments to come in at the rallying
point, as the safety of the whole command might
be compromised.

449. *Ambuscade.* In planning an ambuscade,
we should be well acquainted with the enemy's
force, and the state of discipline shown by it. The
position chosen for the attempt must be favorable to
the concealment of troops, and if practicable it should
be reached by night, every precaution being taken to
insure secrecy. The best positions are those where
the enemy is inclosed in a defile, or village, and has

not taken the proper precautions to secure himself from an attack. By seizing the outlets of the defile by infantry, in such cases, and making an impetuous charge of cavalry into it, the enemy may be completely routed.

450. Ambuscades may frequently be attempted with success in the affairs of advanced and rear-guards; by pushing the enemy vigorously and then falling back, if he offers a strong resistance, so as to draw him upon a point where troops are posted in force to receive him.

451. To trace anything more than a mere outline, as a guide in operations of this kind, which depend upon so many fortuitous circumstances, would serve but little useful purpose. An active, intelligent officer, with an imagination fertile in the expedients of his profession, will seldom be at a loss as to his best course when the occasion offers; to one without these qualities, opportunities present themselves in vain.

CHAPTER IX.

452. *Definitions.*—In tracing out the movements of ancient armies, as far as we have the
means of doing so, from the often very obscure
narratives of historians, it will be observed that
in some features they conform very closely to
those of modern armies, whilst in others they
differ essentially from them. Those in which
this conformity is seen, and which pertain only
to the general operations of a campaign, belong
to that branch of the military art which has
received the appellation of *strategy.* Whilst those
in which a marked difference is noticeable, such
as the manner of conducting marches, dispositions for battle, the arrangements of encamp-
ments, etc., belong to the domain of *tactics.* For
example, the famous expeditions of Hannibal
and Napoleon over the Alps present more than
one point of resemblance in their general features; whilst the battles and combats which
afterwards followed have no points of comparison. The reason of this is, that general
operations are controlled by the topographical
features of the seat of war; whilst those of a
partial character, mere evolutions, or, in a word,
tactical combinations, depend solely upon the
weapons with which troops have been armed at
different epochs. The study of military history
thus becomes very instructive in a strategical
point of view, whilst, on the other hand, in en-

15

deavoring to apply the notions, gleaned from the same source, on the tactics of the ancients, to our modern armies, errors of the gravest character might be committed. Every servile imitation in this latter case—an error which more than one man of talent has fallen into, from not having sufficiently weighed the enormous difference that exists between what are known, in the present day, as firearms, and the weapons for like purposes used by the ancients, and the consequences which must necessarily ensue from this cause in the arrangement of troops for combat—is greatly to be deprecated.

453. From the foregoing remarks, it will be inferred that strategy is, in a peculiar sense, the science of generals in command of armies; whilst tactics, in all its ramifications, from the elementary drill of the soldier to orders of battle, from the *bivouac* of an outpost to the encampment of an army, belongs to officers of all grades. Still, with these marked differences, it is sheer pedantry to pretend to define the precise limits of these two prominent branches of the military art, as they present a multitude of exceptions in which they approach and run into each other.

Tactics, if we restrict its meaning to the evolutions and manoeuvres of troops on the field of battle, may be taught with mathematical exactness, because every movement is accurately prescribed, and the more so the lower we descend the scale of this branch of military knowledge. But this is far from being true of strategy, because, in the calculations involved in its operations, a great many considerations enter which do not admit of exact computation, and upon which success or failure essentially depend: as

171

time, the character of the roads over which the
army has to move, the nature of the obstacles
which lie between it and the enemy, the moral
qualities and activity of the enemy's forces, etc.,
etc. For example, a general might commit a
gross mistake by supposing that the position A,
Pl. VII., Fig. 14, would be protected by an
army at M, from the attempts of an enemy's
force at N, which lies outside of the arc of a
circle described from A as a centre with the
radius AM. For, even on the supposition that
the line of march of the two opposing armies
upon A is equally favorable, and therefore that
the army M might reach A before that from N
could, still A might not the less be compromised,
for the enemy at N, although having the longer
march to make, might, by taking the initiative,
gain the advance before the army M was apprised
of it, and, reaching a point, say P, within the
arc, before the army had got in motion, could
reach A first, having the shorter distance to
march, before the army M could. It is not therefore by the actual distances that the advantages
of the positions of two armies are to be estimated, but by the time that may be requisite to
inform one of the movements of another; and
it is this element of time that in war gives that
party so greatly the advantage over the other
which understandingly assumes the initiative
and follows it up with activity and vigor. If to
these considerations the character of the roads,
defiles, rivers, etc., which an army may have to
traverse, be joined, it will be seen that, these
circumstances not being the same on both sides,
the problem of reciprocal positions becomes still
more complicated and less subject to geometrical
combinations.

Having shown in what sense the words strategy and tactics should be received, terms upon the precise definition of which too much stress, perhaps, has been laid within a recent period, that which is the real gist of the matter under consideration may be entered upon.

454. In all military operations of a general character, and which come under the head of strategy, three principal things are noticeable and demand consideration; these are the line from which the army starts in commencing its onward movements; the point which it aims to attain; and the line which it is obliged to pass over to reach this point.

455. The first of these is termed the *base of operations;* the second the *objective* or *objective point;* the third the *line of operations.* When maintaining a strictly defensive attitude, the base of operations becomes what is termed the *line of defence,* and in a backward movement the line of operations becomes the *line of retreat.*

To take a recent example in our own history, the Potomac was for a time the base of operations for our army having in view the capture of Richmond; this city was the objective point; and the roads leading to it from the Potomac the line of operations. More recently the roads between Richmond and the Potomac became our line of retreat, and the Rappahannock and the Potomac successively our lines of defence.

456. *Bases of Operations.*—The base of operations should be a series of points having the properties of military strength, as the supplies of the army for its onward movements are collected upon it; and it should have commodious lines of communication leading from it to the

objective. If these strong points lie upon any
natural obstacle, as a river without fords, a
rugged mountainous chain, swamps, or thick
primeval forests, and have an easy communication between them, the base is all the better,
from the difficulties which a line of this character offers to the enterprises of the enemy in case
of being thrown on the defensive.

457. A base of some extent is better than a
short one, because more latitude is given to operate against the enemy, and, if obliged to retire
upon it, there is less chance of being separated
from it by the enemy gaining our rear. Should
it consist of a single city, for example, with but
one line of operations from it, by seizing on this
line the enemy might cut off the army from all
supplies and reinforcements.

458. The outline which the base assumes is
far from being a matter of indifference. If it is
concave towards the enemy, or has its two ends
resting upon any natural impassable obstacle
lying in advance of the general line, the army
moving from it will find greater security for its
wings than in a case where the base is either
generally convex towards the enemy, or presents
a salient point to him.

459. When an army moves to a considerable
distance beyond its base, it will become necessary to take up a new base in advance of the
primitive one, in order to have its depôts, from
which it has to draw its supplies of every description, nearer at hand. This new line is
termed a *secondary base of operations.* It should
possess the same military properties as the primitive base, and art should supply whatever
nature may be found deficient in for this purpose,

15*

in order that every thing collected for the army on it may be secure.

460. If prudence points out the necessity of taking up new bases as the army advances further into an enemy's country, it does not follow that the army should be detained to organize them on a suitable footing. This task is devolved on a body of troops left behind for this purpose, who, with the reinforcements sent forward, occupy the fortified places on the new line, erect new field works, establish magazines, &c., whilst the army pursues its march to profit by its first successes.

461. When the secondary base is not parallel to the primitive one, that end of it which is most advanced should be strengthened by every accessory means, as it is the one most exposed to the enemy's attacks. The other end, though less exposed, from its retired position, also affords less support to the army in advance.

462. An oblique base affords the advantage of threatening the communications and base of the enemy without exposing our own. For example: the army M, Pl. VII., fig. 15, whose primitive base is R S, parallel to P Q, the primitive base of the enemy, and whose natural line of operations is the line A B, perpendicular to R S and P Q, cannot move against the left wing of the army N without running the risk of having its communications with its own base interrupted, unless it has established a secondary base X Y, oblique to the line A B; for the military conditions of the problem are reciprocal: if, under like circumstances, we cut the enemy's communications he may do the same with respect to ours which have been left exposed. But with

the new base x y, the operation supposed is no
longer imprudent, since there is a direct and
secure line of retreat on the extremity y of the
new base, which is near enough to afford support in case of need.

463. The example just cited is analogous to
that of the concave base which has already been
alluded to. When the concave form of the base
is very marked, it affords the facility of changing the line of operations at pleasure, without
losing the support of a good base. For example: let R s T, Pl. VII., Fig. 16, be the general outline of the base: the army, M, which, at the outset
of the campaign, has been operating on the line
A B against the army, N, having P Q for its base,
will be able, if compelled by necessity, or
prompted by some obvious advantage to be
gained, to change its line of operations to B C,
resting on the portion of the base s T.

464. When this change in the line of operations is made just at the moment of delivering
a great battle, it may be attended with signal
results, as the enemy's plans may be completely
foiled by it. Great generals alone have shown
themselves capable of such attempts.

465. As to the army at X, which has the base
P Q only in rear of its line of operations, A B, its
movements are controlled by the connexion:
for to cover P Q it must assume a position across
A B, and nearly perpendicular to it. This is a
rule which cannot be violated, even with the
superiority in numbers, without great risk.

466. When we are complete master of the sea
between our own and the enemy's coast, we
may choose our base upon any point of the coast
which offers the means of subsisting an army,

and from which good communications lead into the interior of the enemy's country. A good seaport under such circumstances is a sufficient base for an invasion. This was experienced by the United States in its recent war with Mexico, and English history furnishes many like examples.

467. *Lines of Operation.*—All lines of communication leading towards an enemy's base do not offer equal advantages to an army acting on the offensive. Some lead more directly and offer more security than others in an advance on the enemy; some may offer greater advantages than others when our superiority lies either in infantry or in cavalry; some are more favorable as to subsisting an army, or affording it more convenient transportation, or in enabling us to turn the enemy's position; others again receive better support from the base of operations, &c. The talent of a commanding general is chiefly shown in weighing the advantages and defects of each of these circumstances, and selecting from them the best.

468. A line of operations is said to be *simple* when the army corps moving against the enemy are kept together, or at least are not so far separated as to be beyond mutual supporting distances. These corps consequently must all move on roads nearly parallel, and not too far apart, and without any impassable obstructions between them.

469. A line of operations is said to be *double* when an army divided into two parts follows two sensibly parallel roads which are so far asunder that the two portions cannot be reunited upon the same day on the same field of battle.

470. Unless we are superior to the enemy on each line, both in numbers and the moral qualities of our troops, a double line of operations is purely disadvantageous to us; and particularly so if the two lines diverge as we advance; for the enemy, by throwing himself between the two fractions of our army, may beat each of them separately, and find himself in an attitude to intercept our communications. The more rapidly the double lines diverge, the greater will be the danger to us and the certainty of success to the enemy.

471. Here we find a marked difference between what may be termed a strategical and a tactical operation. In the latter the greatest danger that an army can run is to be surrounded on the field of battle; whereas an army that throws itself by a strategical movement, between several fractions of an enemy's army beyond supporting distance of each other, may, by superior activity, defeat them all in succession.

472. The only case in which—the armies on the two sides being sensibly of equal strength, and controlling reasons calling for it—a double line can be followed, in the face of a general of respectable abilities, is when the latter has also adopted double divergent lines, or lines very far asunder. But in this case our double line must be an *interior* one, or lie between those of the enemy, so that our two fractions м,м', Pl. VII., Fig. 17, may, in case of need, support each other if attacked; or be suddenly concentrated so as to attack one of the fractions on the enemy's exterior line, the other in this case being beyond supporting distance of the one attacked. This principle of interior lines, particularly when they

converge as we advance, is, at bottom, only a modification of the one of a single line. It amounts to keeping the fractions of our army in such distances from each other that they are nearer together than those of the enemy, and can be concentrated on any one of his before it can be reinforced by the others. Still, it must be observed, that it is always safer to manœuvre on a single line than upon two, although they may be interior.

473. It is important not to confound double, or multiple lines, with the various lines of communication over which fractions of an army are necessarily marched, in order to concentrate on a particular point. In this case the movements of all concur to the same end; the army corps are momentarily separated only to march with greater convenience and rapidity; to reconnoitre the ground more thoroughly over which they move; and to subsist more comfortably. This momentary separation of our forces, to be again united at the moment of battle, when well executed, is the very acmé of good generalship. It is one of the best means of keeping the enemy for a long time uncertain of our real intentions as to the point of attack. To know when, in turn, to scatter our forces to embrace a greater extent of country, when circumstances permit or call for it, and then to concentrate them, in order to strike a decisive blow, is one of the most marked features in the qualities of a great captain. No general of modern times has shown this trait in as high a degree as Napoleon.

474. When, by the eventualities of a campaign, we find ourselves forced to abandon our primitive line of operations and take up a new

one, the latter receives the appellation of an *accidental line of operations.* This term is not properly applicable to a line voluntarily taken up, to march upon a point which the enemy may have weakened by withdrawing from it troops, under the apprehension that he was threatened on some other. This change of line, so far from being an accident, is the legitimate fruit of profound combinations, and may be the cause of important successes. The primitive line was, to some extent, a feint; and the line apparently but secondary the true one; it cannot therefore be termed accidental; it will be thus simply the *new line of operations.*

475. In like manner in a retrograde movement an army may abandon its natural line of retreat and take up another, leading off laterally from it, for the purpose of enticing the enemy into a district of country less favorable to him, and to throw him further off from his main object. The line of retreat in this case will be sensibly parallel to our own frontier instead of being, as it is generally, perpendicular to it. This new line of retreat also cannot be classed under the head of accidental lines, since it is one voluntarily adopted, and presents advantages over the natural line of retreat. It has received the name of the *parallel retreat,* a term sufficiently expressive of the thing itself. To be successfully executed the retreating army should not be too inferior in force to the enemy, and should run no risk in being cut off from its own frontier by moving too far from it. The local features are particularly to be taken into consideration in such operations. If they are of a broken character, the movement will be the less perilous; if, on the

contrary, the country is open, and without strong natural points of defence, the safest plan will be to regain our frontier by the shortest line.

476. When a choice between several lines of operation is offered, it will be best to adopt the one where the army can be most easily subsisted, and in which, according to the kind of troops of which it is composed, the army will be most secure from the enemy's enterprises. If the army is superior to the enemy in cavalry, it will naturally prefer to move over an open district of country; if, on the contrary, its main strength lies in its infantry, it will prefer to skirt along the foot of a mountainous range, or to march through a broken country. A line of operations parallel and near to a river presents the advantage of having its wing nearest the water course secure from attack, whilst the river itself furnishes an excellent communication for bringing forward supplies. The defensive position taken up by the enemy also has great weight in determining the direction of the line of operations. If he occupies cantonments extending over a considerable line, the most natural line will be the one by which the army can throw itself into the centre of the enemy's isolated corps, and thus separate them and beat them in detail. By attacking one wing of a position of this kind we should, in all likelihood, force back one corps after another upon the neighboring one, until, in the end, the whole would, in this way, be concentrated in their natural order of retreat. If, on the contrary, the enemy's corps are in supporting distance of each other, the natural point of attack is one of his wings, provided that, in making this movement,

the line of operations of our own army is not
left exposed; for the first of all necessities is
never to place either our base or our line of
operations in jeopardy. The choice to be made
will also depend upon the characters and military
talents of the enemy's generals, the quality of
his forces, their moral condition, &c., &c.; these
are points which carry such great weight with
able commanders that they have often been
known to have adopted plans the very reverse
of what they would have done under contrary
circumstances, according to their being in front
of one or another general. Turenne, having for
his opponent Condé, did not allow himself to do
things which seemed to him as easy and a matter of course before the Archduke. On one occasion, in 1654, he lost some men whilst passing
within the range of grape in front of the Spanish
lines, which called forth remarks from some of
the officers accompanying him. To these he replied: "The march we are making would be
very imprudent before Condé's position; but it
is very important that I should examine thoroughly this position; and I am so well acquainted with the Spanish service, that I feel
assured that before the Archduke has been informed of it, has sent word to Condé, and called
together his council, I shall have completed it
and returned to camp." "See," said that captain
who more than other was capable of pronounc-
ing a judgment on such points, "here is something that pertains to the divine portion of the
art." In truth, military genius manifests itself in
just such subtle distinctions and delicate shades.

477. As has been laid down, our line of operations should be directed on one wing of the
16

enemy when his forces are concentrated, if it can
be done without compromising our line of
retreat. Now this is seldom possible, for the
party that attempts to turn another is necessarily
exposed to the same danger. This is rigorously
so, in an operation of this kind in a perfectly unobstructed country, when the bases of the two
armies are sensibly parallel and of equal extent.
For example, an army M, Pl. VII., Fig. 18, can
move upon the line of communications of the opposing army, N, only by taking up a line of operations, S,B, oblique to its base, R,S, and resting on
its extremity; but, in doing so, the central line
of operations, A,B, and the one leading from the
other extremity of the base, are left uncovered;
and we thus deprive ourselves of the advantages
of an extended base, as, from our line, B,S, we can
only retire on the point S in case of reverse. It
is only therefore in cases where from the obstructed character of the ground we are enabled
to defend, with comparatively small corps, the
lines B R and B A, against the enemy's attempts
to seize them, that we may with some safety and
probability of success direct our principal line
upon the enemy's wing; as by throwing forward
the two small corps, m and m', we cover our own
base, and give the alarm to the enemy on his
centre and right. It may therefore be safely
laid down as a principle, that it is only under
cover of natural obstacles that we can with safety
direct our principal operation against the enemy's
wing when his forces are in supporting distances
of each other. The influence of the natural features of the country over which operations are
carried on is continually felt in all warlike plans;
a careful study of the bearing of these features is

therefore of the highest importance to officers of all grades; but particularly for those upon whom rest the responsibilities of high command.

478. A line of operations which has too great a length, with respect to that of its base, loses somewhat of its positive value, as it offers more chances to the enemy to cut it. Owing to this, we are therefore under the necessity of adopting secondary bases, in proportion as our line of operations is prolonged. But to undertake to establish anything like mathematical proportions between these bases and the line of operations itself would be simply pedantic and absurd. The triangle, of which the army is the apex and the base of operations the base, may vary under a thousand circumstances. Its form and dimensions are seldom if ever subject to arbitrary rules. All that can be said is that the greater the extent of the lines, the further advanced may be the apex, without uncovering the communications; like a pyramid, which, without losing anything of its solidity and stability, may be the more elevated as its base is made broader.

479. *Strategical Points.*—The points of operation are also termed *strat-gical points;* and under this appellation are comprised not only those which may be regarded as the chief end to be attained, but also those by the occupation of which the army will receive incontestable advantages.

480. The capital city of a country is in Europe regarded as a strategical point of great importance, chiefly from political considerations, arising from the influence which the seat of government exercises over the whole country. This, to a certain extent, is true of our own country; for

although Washington city, in a military point of view, might have but little influence on the results of a war, and has no controlling influence over public opinion at home, still its loss would be regarded by Europeans in a European point of view, and its possession, whether by a foreign or domestic enemy, would have a damaging effect abroad, besides exercising a certain moral one at home.

481. A point is strategical that gives us the control of several important roads, the course of a river, or which guards some important passage

482. In a flat country there are usually few strategical points. Those which hold this position usually owe it to fortifications by which they are surrounded, and by the various resources for military purposes which they can furnish. Wooded, hilly, and well watered regions present many such points.

483. In high mountain ranges, strategical points are very restricted in number, but are usually of a very decided character. They are met with behind the narrow mountain passes at the points of junction of several valleys along which roads have been made. They are also found at elevated points where the ridges of several chains seem to come together. Troops occupying such points can choose the roads by which they think best to descend from; their movements, in such a case, are from the centre towards the circumference, whilst those of an opponent can only be made, with a prospect of success, by making wide circuits, to turn the spurs which obstruct any lateral movement. Having entered one of the valleys leading to the top, an enemy is obliged to follow it up, as he

cannot without great difficulty cross from one to another, whilst the body of troops holding the elevated point of junction of the valleys can do so with comparative facility and promptness.

484. *Plan of Campaign.*—Before undertaking any military operation, great or small, we should first settle down upon some decided end to be gained; determine upon beforehand, as far as practicable, the steps to be taken to attain our object. In one word, we should clearly see what we propose to accomplish, in order that we may not go blindly to work and leave anything to chance. The mental process by which all that is here supposed is elaborated is termed *the laying out the plan of campaign.*

485. In the first place, it stands to reason that this plan should be so limited as to comprise only the leading strategical dispositions, thus presenting only the outline features, within which the meshwork of the minor operations is to be confined; thus leaving ample latitude for all movements of detail and their execution. Nothing could be more absurd than to pretend to dictate to the commanding general what he shall do from day to day; yet this has been done, and with but few exceptions, with disastrous results. Once within the sphere of the enemy's operations, a commanding general is no longer at liberty to do what he wishes, but what he best can. Marches, manœuvres, combats, depend on circumstances for the most part imperative; decisions arrived at are often sudden, and brought about by the attitude, resources, strength, and the *morale* of the enemy. The commanding general should have *carte blanche* for carrying

out the details of the campaign, the plan of which may have been decided upon by a council, but even this is far better left in the hands of him who has the whole responsibility of its execution on his shoulders, and has the greatest interest in its success.

486. It is with the aid of the general maps of a country, made to a small scale, as embracing a wider territory, that the general plan of campaign is marked out. All that is wanted for this object is that the map should contain the exact positions of the places upon it; the water courses, the mountain crests, the principal lines of communication, and the political and geographical boundaries. The less detail on such maps the better they are for this purpose, as the mind is not distracted by them from the main features. For all points of detail topographical maps, on a large scale, are necessary. To these we have recourse when it is a question to choose an encampment; to decide upon a military position; to dispose an order of battle, &c.

487. The plan of campaign lays down the points where the troops are to be assembled, the base and line of operations, and the strategical points to be attained.

The choice of the positions where the troops are to be assembled is not only dictated by the facility of subsisting them, although this is a point of great importance; but by their suitableness to deceive the enemy as to the point on which we intend to make an advance, so that we may take the initiative and follow up our blow with crushing effect. The distances of these points should be so regulated, with respect to the one at which the army is to be concentrated for

187

action, that all the corps may reach this last point at a designated moment.

488. The base of operations can seldom be a subject of doubt in a foreign war, as it necessarily lies on that portion of the frontier next to the enemy. The only question that can arise is at what point of the frontier it will be best to advance against the enemy. It is here that a consideration of the general outline of the base comes up. Is it concave, or makes to some extent a re-entering angle, the army then in advancing will find both its rear and wings securely supported. Is it strongly convex, or offers a salient angle, it has the advantage, by assembling our army towards the apex of the angle, of keeping the enemy in doubt as to which side we will adopt for our base, and thus forcing him to distribute his forces on an arc of which we occupy the centre. But even should he concentrate on one point, we have still the resource of threatening him on one side, so as to draw his attention there, whilst by the shortest line we throw ourselves on the opposite one. This convex form is then decidedly advantageous on the opening of a campaign; but, in case of reverse, it may lead to our separation from our base. The inverse holds for the concave base.

489. There can seldom, if ever, be an equality of choice between two frontiers as a base of operations; one will necessarily offer preponderating advantages over the other, which will cause its adoption, and it is upon this one that all our means of attack must be brought together It is a grave fault to pursue a double offensive, in starting at the same time from two bases. It is much better to stand strictly on the defensive

on one of the frontiers, so that by accumulating more troops on the other we may increase our chances of success. It is a rare thing that we arrive at a satisfactory result by dividing our forces; and the same reasons which render double lines of operation dangerous are equally against attempting a double offensive. We should, on the contrary, concentrate our efforts as much as we can, in order that the advantages we obtain may be decisive; and they must always be more so on the preponderating frontier than on the other; it is upon the former, therefore, that we should act with the most vigor, holding back from the other all that is not indispensable to the defensive; as upon the field of battle we refuse one wing, drawing from it troops to strengthen the one engaged, and upon which we count for victory.

490. A thorough discussion of the different lines of operations is the essential part of the plan of campaign. There are so many considerations attendant upon it, so many points to be carefully weighed, that the choice of the best line is always a matter of great delicacy, and it is here that the real general shows his capaci'y. No other rules can be well laid down than those previously given in treating of lines of operation. It may be further added, that in comparing several lines, the effective distances, or the time which it will take troops to traverse them, are alone to be considered, and not the distances upon the map which by measurement are the shortest. We may decide on taking the best made road when urgent motives are not against our doing so; for troops will march more rapidly and with more convenience upon wide and com-

modious roads than upon narrow and obstructed byways. The nature of towns or defiles to be traversed may force us to leave them on one side to take byways, although bad; for we overcome with less difficulty material obstacles on our line of march than we can towns and defiles well defended. When an army can, in its onward movement, rest one wing upon a natural obstacle to an enemy, it will be well for it to keep as near that obstacle as practicable; because it will be better covered by the army, the front of which during the march occupies always several miles in extent; at least so long as a battle is not imminent. When the two wings of the army are not supported in this way, the line of operations should cut the middle of the front of the army, in order that it may be equally well covered on each side. There is one general rule both on the march and for battle, which is, never to expose your line of operations; every disposition, on the contrary, should be taken to cover it and defend it in the best possible manner.

491. *Defensive Plan.* The plan of campaign for the defensive is usually termed the *defensive plan.* It chiefly consists in deciding upon the character of the warfare to be adopted; one which will depend upon national traits, the resources, topography, and climate of the country. The French, for example, make a defensive warfare by assailing their enemies; the Germans, on the contrary, carry on patiently a methodical defensive behind their own frontiers; the Spaniards have been seen to carry on an exterminating war of detail; whilst the Russians, under like circumstances, have laid waste whole pro-

vinces, and destroyed by fire their capital city, to deprive their invaders of every material resource. A brave people, but not habituated to privations, will not drag out a war by patient endurance, but will endeavor to bring it speedily to a close by a few brilliant actions; its preferences will be for sledge-hammer blows, preferring the hazard of a great decisive battle, in which it may fall with glory, to a series of petty combats which only serve to exhaust the resources of the country without bringing about any decisive results.

492. Carrying the war into the heart of the assailant's country, or that of his allies, is the surest plan of making him share its burdens and foiling his plans. The courage and conduct of troops are improved in this way, and the chances in their favor increased. But to be successful, the party adopting it must not be too inferior in strength, and the nature of the frontiers should favor it; as there would be too great a risk under less favorable circumstances, and in these even it would not be prudent to advance too far beyond our own frontier. The army will chiefly depend for the supply of its wants upon the zone of territory adjacent to the frontier, and this should be desperately disputed, by uniting all its forces against the enemy's invading corps. If this succeeds, from the defensive the army can assume the offensive. If unsuccessful, nothing remains to be done but to concentrate all the troops possible and fall back upon positions selected beforehand, either of great natural or artificial strength; as rivers, mountain-passes, fortresses, etc. In this manner the enemy is drawn forward into a region

the devastations of which are upon his shoulders. The skilful Montecuculi, in his memoirs, argues strongly for the adoption of such a plan of defensive measures; remarking that upon the territory of our enemy we arouse the discontented, whilst the fountains of men, money, and whatever else war calls for, are only disordered and fail in this portion in which the war rages.

493. In fighting on our own soil we have much to suffer, it is true, but the dangers are less; the home population are for us; they act as our spies, and lend us every assistance practicable; we fight in positions chosen beforehand, and, in some cases, strongly intrenched in time; and when the enemy is compelled to advance to attack us, we can move in any direction, because every portion of the territory, not occupied immediately by the enemy, can serve us as a base of operations; we have also great facilities for threatening his lines of communication, and in forcing him to detach largely to hold the places he may have taken possession of. These detachments of the enemy offer to us fair game, as we may attack them in detail, beat, or surround them. When fortune is favorable to the army acting on the defensive, victory is more decisive when gained within than beyond its own frontiers; because the enemy, being defeated, has defiles to traverse, and to make a retreat in the presence of and through an exasperated population, waiting but the opportunity to rise and throw themselves upon him.

494. A frontier convex towards the enemy is favorable to the defensive at the outset, and this may decide upon the kind of warfare to be adopted. For, from a central point, which we

hold in force, we overlook the surrounding periphery of the vulnerable frontiers of our enemy, and are ready to invade the one which offers the most favorable chances by the shortest line to it.

495. Having decided upon the general features of the defence, the details are next to be determined on, and in these consist, in fact, the *plan of defence.* The determination of the points on which resistance is to be made, those upon which we are to fall back in case of disaster, and the roads leading to these, in retreat; the dispositions of our forces at the outset so as to anticipate the enemy on every point; an indication of the points in rear of our frontier for concentration, so soon as the enemy has unmasked his projects; the mode of supporting our advanced corps and those of observation by central reserves; finally, the designation of the points to be fortified by art, bridges to be destroyed, roads to be repaired, etc., etc.: such are some of the objects upon which attention must be directed in any defensive plan.

496. The suitable military dispositions in all such plans will be controlled by the local topography; it is, therefore, impracticable to lay down invariable rules on this point; the most that can be said is, that too great a dissemination of our force is always dangerous; therefore that, so far from attempting to defend every pass some must be abandoned to their fate, in order to effectually guard those which are most important and the more directly threatened by the enemy. If, instead of moving upon the latter, the enemy makes a show of gaining the former, he must be met by analogous movements, and our task

should be to be in readiness to meet him by whatever route he may arrive; and also with the most troops we can concentrate. It is from this cause that the configuration of frontiers, and the direction and nature of the roads by which they are approached, have so great an influence upon the defensive measures against invasion. If these last are such as to permit our moving on right lines, from a centre, upon the enemy manœuvring on the periphery, every advantage of mobility is on our side, and we ought to reach any point before the enemy. But, in any case, it is next to impossible to close every pass. To do so would require a continuous line of troops, which, from its extent alone, would be weak at all points, and which an enterprising enemy would easily pierce at any one. Instead of attempting any such impracticable plan it would be better to place a considerable force at some one favorable point in rear of our frontier, and, from there, take the chances of anticipating the enemy on any point he may threaten by moving on him promptly. In advance of this central force, and upon its front and flanks, small bodies can be thrown forward to occupy the principal passes momentarily and give warning of the enemy's movements. These detachments, by retiring slowly and holding the enemy in check, will give the main body time to make its dispositions, either to advance or to receive the enemy at any point further back. With these precautions the main body will be secured from surprise, and all the troops can be kept near enough to concentrate for battle. Such are the general defensive dispositions recommended by the highest military authority. It is readily seen

that great discretion is necessarily left to the
commanding general, and that his measures
should lend themselves to the local features of
his line of defence. All that is requisite that
these should be good is that they should be based
upon the simple idea of concentration. This is
always preferable to a feeble continuous line,
with separated bodies that cannot afford mutual
support; which are too far removed from the
supervision of the commanding general, who
cannot be everywhere, and which, owing to the
distances between them, cannot be rallied and
concentrated in time when the line is pierced at
any point.

497. With the foregoing dispositions there
should be combined some suitable system of signals, or other means of transmitting intelligence
promptly from the interior line of detachments
to the main body. No pains should be spared to
have this system as perfect as practicable, and not
liable to mistakes.

498. A position chosen on the direct road that
the enemy must follow is not always the best to
check with advantage his onward march; flank
positions can also often be found of superior advantage for this purpose, from which the enemy's
line of operations can be threatened if he persists
in neglecting this position. This is particularly
the case if the force thrown on the flank is of
such strength that the enemy dare not leave it
in his rear, and therefore must attack and drive
it back so that he may not expose himself to be
separated from his base. In this manner the
enemy is forced to a battle on ground of our own
choice, and where we will have had time to make
every defensive disposition. The searching out

and establishing, on sound principles, flank positions for concentration of troops, forms an essential feature in laying down any plan of defence.

499. Having decided upon the most advanced positions to be occupied, attention should next be directed to those of a secondary character, which will naturally be controlled by the water courses and mountain chains in rear of the first line. These will demand in their selection very careful study. The best of this class are those which have their wings or extremities resting upon natural obstacles that an enemy cannot turn—as the sea, lakes, unfordable rivers, which, in some respects, overlook the lines of approach on them; are accessible from the front only by a few practicable roads which can be easily guarded; the general outline of the position being convex towards the enemy, and in rear having good roads leading to all points of it, along which troops can be rapidly moved to any point in danger.

500. Fortified places on a frontier will, of course, play an important part in any defensive plan; even open towns, by properly covering them with field works, may give the means of effective resistance to any usual mode of attack. When these places lie upon a river, which is itself a line of defence, particularly when they occupy both banks of it, they afford great facilities for the operation of an army which can manœuvre on either shore with safety, so long as the place itself is not invested. Fortifications so placed completely prevent the enemy from using the river as a means of transportation, whilst they assist us in so using them; and, in

most cases, they would therefore force an enemy
to take all the known measures for giving possession of them before he would dare to pass
beyond them. In whatever way a river may
lie, which has fortified points on it, the disadvantages to an invading force are necessarily
great. If parallel to our line of frontier an
enemy cannot cross the river, leaving these occupied in his rear, without running the risk of a
great disaster. If perpendicular, he cannot with
safety divide his forces to operate on both banks
at once, as we have, by means of the fortified
points, the facility of concentrating on either side
at pleasure. Without such strong points on it,
a river, on the contrary, might be a positive advantage to the enemy, by allowing him to secure one of his wings from attack by resting it
upon the river, whilst he would also thus facilitate his own means of transportation.

501. As to military positions, properly so
called, that is localities favorable to accepting
battle, great care should be taken in designating
them on the plan of defence, and in preparing
them beforehand for every eventuality, by field
works, lines of retreat, the removal of all obstructions between the points of the position,
&c. In every plan of defence, particular care
should be taken in pointing out what roads
should be carefully preserved, and which, in any
emergency, may be broken up, or otherwise obstructed. These measures of destruction are
almost always put off so late as to become impracticable at the moment of need. Nothing is
more common in war than to hear that some
advantage has been lost or gained, through the
neglect of securing or destroying some bridge or

road, in time. All roads connecting points along the line of defence, or which run parallel to it, ought to be kept in perfect order, so that assistance can be promptly carried from one point to another, or raids be organized upon the enemy by a rapid concentration of troops at any point.

502. The above are the main ·points in planning a defensive campaign, so far as the movement of troops is concerned. There are many others of not less importance which belong to the administrative functions of an army, as the commissariat, quartermaster's, medical and signal departments. Belonging to the plan of defence, they should be discussed with as much care as ·the purely military movements. Combats are comparatively of but rare occurrence, whilst these things are of every hour, and the health, safety, and comfort of the troops, upon which their fighting qualities so essentially depend, are due to the proper and efficient working of these semi-military departments.

503. *Strategical Operations.*—It is by preparatory movements, by marches skilfully conducted, so as to throw our forces on the vulnerable point of the enemy's line, that those grand results are obtained, which flow from a single victory. A battle gained is always a fine thing; but the consequences resulting from it may be very different, according as, by our previous measures, we are able to cut the enemy's line of communications; separate him from his base; disperse his forces, or simply force him to retreat without further loss than that on the battle-field. In the first case, victory is complete if the first success is promptly followed up. In the second, the enemy will soon be able to rally his forces, and

offer a new battle. Vigor on the field and rapidity of pursuit should go hand in hand for great success. The latter is of as great importance as the former. Marshal Saxe was so thoroughly pervaded with this conviction, that he laid it down as an axiom, that "*military success resided in the legs of the soldiers.*" A *dictum* that is ably enforced by all authentic military history.

504. A march, regarded as a strategical operation, may be either towards or from the enemy; either a *forward* movement, or one in *retreat.* In either case the army, if numerous, is necessarily divided into several corps, which move upon separate roads, either to subsist more easily, or to have all the space necessary for deployments, and the other preparatory movements for delivering battle. The different columns of march should be kept the closer together, as the enemy is known to be the more bold and active in his movements. If there is danger of an attack, the columns should be kept in supporting distances of each other, and they should not be thrown into any position where an obstacle might prevent their being brought together at any desirable moment on the field of battle. At the same time discretion must be shown, so that so simple a rule may not be pushed to an absurd extreme, by keeping the various columns so close to each other that parallel roads will have to be made for them with the axe and pick, when those already in use cannot be turned to account. Any attempt of this kind would, except in rare cases, so greatly retard our movements that the least enterprising enemy would take advantage of it. Military history offers epochs where this circum-

spect course was pursued by armies, but no
truly great general has ever submitted to such
trammels. So long as a march is not made
within cannon range of the enemy, more or less
interval can be left between the columns whilst
executing the marches which are to bring
them into position on the battle-field, according
to the nature of the locality. The only limit to
be fixed is, that the intervals shall not be so
great as to prevent any corps reaching the battle-
field on the day prescribed.

505. Each column should adopt all the usual
precautions to prevent a surprise. Neglect in
doing so has brought on some of the greatest
disasters recorded in history. Of all marches,
those which are most likely to produce the
most splendid results are the ones that are
concealed from the enemy, and therefore termed
secret marches. Well planned and executed,
they enable an army to throw itself unexpectedly on the enemy's flank, threaten his
base of operations, surprise his cantonments, etc.
A country cut up with forests, water courses,
and like natural obstacles, lends itself best to
the operations of a secret march; as these both
conceal the movements of troops, and lead the
enemy into fancied security from the character
of the locality, and cause him to neglect the
usual precautions to guard against a surprise. It
cannot be too strongly impressed upon every
soldier that, with patience and a determined
will, there is no natural obstacle that troops cannot overcome, when there is no enemy to interrupt our work. In this respect, in looking back
on military history, it may with truth be said
that nothing is impossible to a determined will.

506. Speed is one of the chief characteristics of strategical marches, as it is of the ordinary movements on the battle-field. In this one quality reside all the advantages that a fortunate initiative may have procured; and by it we gain in the pursuit all the results that a victory on the battle-field has placed in our hands. By rapidity of movement, we can, like the Romans, *make war feed war*, by remaining so short a period in any one spot as not to exhaust the resources around us, however unequal to a prolonged sojourn. By this means, we disembarrass ourselves of those immense trains which are otherwise indispensable for the ordinary daily wants of an army; we carry along with us only what is indispensable, obliging the soldier to keep himself always supplied with a few days' rations of bread in his knapsack, driving along with the army herds of cattle in sufficient numbers to furnish the meat ration. In this manner, an army, freed from all of the *impedimenta* that might retard its motions, will be able to accomplish the most stupendous labors in marching and fighting. No great success can be hoped for in war in which rapid movements do not enter as an element. Even the very elements of Nature seem to array themselves against the slow and over-prudent general. The chevalier Folard has very well remarked, "that the slow and heavy in war will partake of as little of the glory of this world, as the lukewarm will of that of the world to come."

507. In the preceding part of this subject the advantages of interior lines of operation were pointed out. Marches which lead to this result deserve the close study of the general. If the

enemy, for example, is moving on an extended front, upon our army, with the purpose of surrounding it, the true resource for safety is for us to move in mass upon some weak point of his centre, and, having thus separated his wings, beat them both in detail. In this manner we shall not only foil the enemy's plan, but scatter and force his forces on divergent lines of retreat; the more disastrous to him at the moment, and the less advantageous for his concentration later.

508. If the enemy's forces are concentrated, we may direct a movement of our army towards each of his flanks, so as to induce him to separate in his centre for the purpose of securing each of his flanks, when, having done so, we may reunite our separated forces and rapidly concentrate them on the one of his fractions the most accessible to us. A movement of this kind cannot be attempted with a prospect of success unless the topographical features are of such a character as to mask our movements. For example, supposing a river to lie between our force and that of the enemy, so as to prevent him from moving on our centre, we might direct two fractions on the extreme right and left of the enemy's position, and, if he weakens himself on his centre to reinforce his wings, we might take advantage of this to cross the river rapidly on his centre, everything having been prepared for it, and thus, holding a point between his wings, concentrate on either and overwhelm it before it could receive succor from the other. Here everything depends on rapidity of movement, and subsequent vigorous action. An hour's delay in such combinations may not only cause the failure of the best laid plan, but entail dis-

astrous results. A single hour may suffice for
the enemy to gain the strategical point and
overwhelm us with superior forces. If Fortune
is on the side of the heavy battalions, she also
frequently grants her favors to superior activity
and audacity.

509. From the preceding discussion, if based
on sound principles, and historical precedents
are strongly in its favor, it follows that to defend
with advantage a frontier menaced on several
points, the true rule is not to attempt to hold
every point in force, but to watch every outlet
by small corps, just of sufficient strength to check
and delay the enemy, and to hold the chief portion of our forces concentrated at some central
point, from which they can operate rapidly
against any considerable fraction of the enemy's
forces.

510. For example, let us suppose an army of
80,000 acting on the defensive against one of
120,000 separated into three corps of 40,000
each. To oppose to the enemy three corps of
equal strength we should have but about 26,000
in each, and consequently would find ourselves
inferior in numbers on all points. If, instead of
this, we opposed to each fraction of the enemy
a corps of from 12,000 to 15,000, it would be
sufficient to hold 40,000 in check, whilst our
main body, consisting of from 35,000 to 40,000,
holding a central position, could move on the
point first menaced, and, being joined by the
corps of observation, would offer to the enemy
an effective force of about 50,000 combatants,
which, all other things equal, should beat the
enemy.

511. The principle is not the less true, and

the rule the less imperative, even when the disparity of force is far greater. It may happen that, with every effort, we may not succeed in obtaining the preponderance in numbers on any point; still the only chance of success lies in concentrating all we can, and trusting to skill, promptitude, vigilance, and audacity, to do the rest. History furnishes brilliant examples of what a great general can accomplish, even under apparently the most discouraging state of things, by promptitude and rapidity of movement in throwing his reserves first on one and then on another of the enemy's fractions.

512. In marches in retreat, like those in advance, the same general rule holds of keeping to a single line, so as to have our fractions well in hand to oppose the greatest force possible to the enemy. Those retreats that are termed *divergent*, or *eccentric*, and which are made at the same time on divergent routes to deceive the enemy and render his pursuit uncertain, are extremely dangerous. In separating, to follow these divergent lines, we weaken ourselves on every point; the corps, being isolated, offer no mutual support; they are easily beaten, and, being forced upon any impassable obstacle, or surrounded, must be either annihilated or forced to surrender. The enemy, without allowing his attention to be drawn off from his object, will stick to one of these fractions until he has destroyed it, knowing that the others must fall an easy prey wherever they may be found; as from their dispersed condition they can offer no effectual resistance. Merely to keep them from reuniting will be enough for present purposes.

513. There is but one case in which our forces

can be dispersed with safety, and that is when we have just gained a decisive victory, and are in the presence of an enemy who, having lost his communications, is entirely disorganized and demoralized. In this position of affairs we have only to throw our force into the midst of these broken up fractions to determine them to fly. We may here attempt any blow ; no movements can fail to turn out well except those which are too slow and methodical. This exception only becomes legitimate under the supposition that the disorganization and demoralization of the defeated army are complete.

514. In a retreat, therefore, even more than in a forward movement, we must keep together, as the only means of safety. Keep up, as far as circumstances will permit, good order in the ranks, or, at least, march with some show of being united. Present an imposing front to the enemy, and, should he pursue with temerity, turn upon him and punish him for his want of prudence. Even dare to make an offensive return upon him when he attacks or approaches negligently. More honor may be gained in a well conducted retreat than in gaining a battle, where fortune frequently plays so conspicuous a part.

515 Great advantages sometimes arise in conducting a retreat parallel to our frontier, when the topography lends itself to this operation; as the enemy, in following us up, really gains but little ground in advance. A few words have already been said on this point, in speaking of accidental lines of operation. If a retreat of this kind, termed a *parallel retreat*, is made in the enemy's country, the army subsists at the

enemy's expense; the evils of war fall on him; and he is almost as badly off as if he had not the upper hand. If this retreat takes place within our own frontier we draw after us the victorious army; we force him to move onwards without gaining a foot of ground towards the interior; we abandon to him only our borders, whilst we force him to offer his flank to any force we may have in the interior. But, with all these obvious advantages, we must look out how we attempt anything of the kind in a territory which is open, and would give the enemy an easy means of cutting us off from our base. Such a retreat, therefore, requires to be covered by a river, a mountain chain, or some other obstacle that an enemy cannot cross with safety, to interrupt our communications to the interior.

516. If the parallel retreat is covered by a river, all bridges by which the enemy might intercept our communications, or attack in flank, should be timely destroyed, the fords obstructed and guarded. Like precautions are to be taken, when covered by a mountain chain, in occupying the main defiles, and obstructing other less important passes. Our troops should be so disposed as to fall in mass upon any corps of the enemy that attempts to force its way through; and we should not show too much anxiety respecting any weak body of troops that may have risked a raid upon our rear, as the peril is for it and not for our troops.

517. It will be readily seen that a parallel retreat can only be resorted to with effect along a frontier of some considerable extent. Although a frontier of this character is more difficult to guard than one more limited, it presents,

on the other hand, the advantages above pointed
out, and lends itself well to the *defensive—offensive* on our side, which of itself, in the hands of
an able general, is the surest means of success in
a defensive war.

518. In connexion with marches as strategical
movements, those operations, performed by *detachments*, made to favor some design of the
main-body, and termed *diversions*, find a place;
as the marches of the main body and of the detachment have, for the most part, to be co-
ordinated, forming what is termed *combined
marches*.

519. Diversions, and detachments made to aid
the operations of the main body, when they
have a long circuit to accomplish, are contrary
to sound strategical principles. In the first
place, the co-operation, at the desired moment,
with the main body, is extremely uncertain, and
the delay of an hour or two may thus change
what has every prospect of victory into irretrievable disaster. Military history has no
more striking lessons than are found in it on this
point.

520. Diversions are dangerous on other obvious grounds. The main-body is weakened by
the amount of force thus withdrawn from it.
The attention of the commanding general, which
should be concentrated on the principal field of
action, is necessarily distracted by any considerable diversions, as he is necessarily kept anxious
for their result, knowing by what slight causes
they may fail; besides the complications that
must attend affairs, from the employment of the
requisite intermediate links between the two
simultaneous operations. If the main body is

victorious, its advantages are seldom complete, for the want of the very troops that have been detached; if, on the contrary, it is defeated, it may result in disaster, as it can derive no succor from the detached corps.

521. In war, as in every other art based upon settled principles, there are exceptions to all general rules. It is in discerning these cases that the talent of the general is shown. Diversions belong to this class of exceptions. There are cases where they are not only called for but are imperative upon the general. As, for example, when there is some position held by the enemy that must be carried before any other step can be taken, a diversion may be made either to threaten his line of communications, or to seize some commanding point near his position which, by forcing him to detach to meet the danger to him, will so weaken him as to allow us to make our main attack with good prospects of success. Cases of this kind are of frequent occurrence in mountainous positions, where, in order to force the enemy from some vantage ground, a diversion on his flank or rear has to be made by a long circuit. Here the exception becomes the rule. Still, even in such cases, care should be taken to call in the detachment as soon as the result is obtained, and fall back upon the rule of concentration and unity of operations. Besides, diversions are less dangerous in countries broken by forests and mountains, as the enemy finds it more difficult to throw himself between the main body and the detachment than in a country which has but few such obstructions and masks. In a mountainous region, a small corps may find itself in a narrow valley,

208

where it can neither be turned by its rear nor by its flanks, and where a large body would not find room to fight. In such cases, the isolated corps need only be strong enough to defend themselves in front along the valleys they occupy. Here dissemination of our forces is only an apparent violation of the general principle; as, by falling back, each corps has still its line of retreat secure, and all can concentrate on some central point in rear of the mountain passes.

522. Another exception is found where our force is very superior to that of the enemy, and that we can better subsist our troops by separating them. Here, we but follow a rule of Napoleon, which he invariably put in practice; which is, *to disperse our force to subsist and to concentrate for battle.* However simple this rule may appear, none but an able general can carry it out successfully in practice; for it supposes a talent for military combinations possessed alone by generals of this class. When our superiority in strength and *morale* is decidedly superior to that of our adversary, we may then resort to diversions, to threaten his communications, to force him to abandon his fortified positions, to make raids into his territory, placing them under contribution, &c. All operations of this character, undertaken even under the most favorable circumstances, must be carried out with promptitude, vigor, and even audacity, to insure success. If made against a timid, irresolute commander, the chances of their success are still further increased. But unless such favorable circumstances co-operate, it will be safer not to risk them.

523. In condemning such diversions, the ob-

ject of which cannot be mistaken, it does not follow that all blows of this kind are to be avoided. There is a class which, if carried out to their legitimate ends, may change the entire aspect of a war; and those are where we abandon the portion of our territory invaded by an enemy to carry the war into his. This in no manner resembles those of which mention has been made. Here there is no division of our forces. The entire movable army strikes at the enemy in the heart of his own country. Such resolutions by great generals are stamped with the mark of true genius; when attempted to be carried out by feeble commanders the result is disaster. Such was the grand operation of Hannibal, when he invaded Italy; and such, but on a smaller scale and with a smaller object, was the last campaign of Turenne against Montecuculi, when, far from being intimidated by the offensive movement of this last general, in crossing the Rhine, he at another point crossed the same river, and, carrying the war into the enemy's territory, forced Montecuculi to leave France to follow him.

524. A combined march is undertaken for the purpose of reaching two points of an enemy's position; for example, to attack it in front and rear at once, or in front and on one flank. There is no operation, however, subject to so many failures as one of this kind, however well planned. A heavy rain, a river that suddenly rises, a guide that runs off, a mistake in a road, and hundreds of other petty causes, by bringing about the delay of an hour, may frustrate the best laid plan, and entail ruinous consequences. Besides these, the main army may have been

suddenly attacked and forced to retreat, leaving thus its detachment to find its way back to it as best it can. Even upon the field of battle, it is seldom that a considerable detachment can be risked to fall on the enemy's rear when he becomes engaged; but when, instead of a few miles' march, a long *détour* of several days has to be made, the fault committed is very much greater. History offers but too many examples to confirm this view of diversions. Still the temptation to cut the enemy off from his base, and to secure grand results, is so great, that generals are led into it, and some rare cases of success will outweigh both the force of examples and the cogency of reasons against the attempt.

525. *Pursuit.*—A victory, by which the enemy is only forced from the battle-field, is for the most part but a half success, as the losses under fire are but small compared to those arising from the demoralization of a broken and dispersed army. A prompt and vigorous *pursuit* is the only means of insuring complete success. Defeated and disorganized, the only hope that remains to the enemy is that he may have time to rally and concentrate his scattered troops. The only way to frustrate this hope is to pursue these disorganized masses, which are in no condition to resist a very inferior force if it assails them in good order. Under these circumstances we may separate our army into corps, forcing the enemy thus upon divergent lines of retreat, and preventing all coöperation between them. In doing this, we must, however, be very careful not to drive the enemy in such directions as will lead to his concentration on any one point.

526. If the enemy retires in good order,
covering his line of retreat from our attempts to
turn it, nothing remains to be done but to push
him back with our entire force; keeping close
upon his heels, and giving him no time to take
advantage of defiles or other strong points to
check us, so as to make us lose time, and give
the opportunity to him to receive reinforcements. When he attempts to do this, we
should hold him in check on the main road,
whilst we attempt to turn his flank, and endeavor to gain his rear. By this promptitude and
vigor of action our forces will hardly be retarded, but will be always in position to turn
any point upon which he attempts to make a
stand, and thus force him to fall back continually as we push forward.

527. When we have come up with the enemy,
we have one of two courses open to us: either
to throw ourselves across his line of retreat, or
else to leave this open to him, whilst we take a
position on his flank. This last course is usually
the more prudent, for, however weakened, it is
a very dangerous thing to reduce an enemy to
despair, and thus call forth heroic efforts, where
but a moment before there was nothing but discouragement and a willingness to get away at
any cost, even honor. With great superiority
of force, by barring the way to the rear, and
pressing on vigorously in front, we may hope
" to bag " the entire army; in all other cases, it
is more certain to limit ourselves to operating on
the flank, and thus secure a part, with but little
loss to ourselves, but with great demoralization
of the enemy

528. Having dispersed and demoralized the

enemy's forces, the more difficult problem remains of holding the conquered territory. This
becomes the more difficult when the enemy's
territory has no fortified places that we have
been able to seize, and thus hold as rallying
points for our own troops. All that remains
then to be done is to occupy strong strategical
and populated points, by detachments of sufficient strength to keep the enemy quiet. This
brings about numerous inconveniences: first, as
these points must be strengthened by field works,
and, in the second place, the main army must be
greatly weakened by the detachments that this
system renders necessary. In the mean time
the enemy's broken forces having retired towards the interior, are there reorganized, recruited, and concentrated, until, at last, an equilibrium between the two contending forces is
brought about, and the struggle is recommenced
to go, perhaps, through the same phases.

529. These inconveniences may, in a great degree, be avoided by having a *reserve* force in rear
of the movable army, charged with the sole duty
of holding the territory occupied. This reserve,
which should not be further than a few days'
march from the front of operations of the movable forces, should be dispersed over as great an
extent, parallel to this line as practicable; thus
enlarging the base of operations, collecting supplies on a greater extent, and keeping a larger
amount of population quiet. This reserve may
be composed of new levies, and, being held in all
points subordinate to the active army, it will be
ready to cöoperate with it in any way deemed
best. The main functions, however, of this reserve will be to relieve the active army from any

apprehensions respecting its supplies, the timely
arrival of reinforcements, and its line of retreat.
It will, therefore, take all the requisite measures
to secure these important objects, thus leaving
the active force free to fight at pleasure, and the
more vigorously as it knows its rear and all its
subsistence are free from danger.

530. Such dispositions suppose us to be superior to the enemy both in numbers and discipline.
Where this is not so we shall have to resort to
movable columns, which can be directed at any
moment upon any point where their presence is
needed. By great activity on the part of their
commanders, these columns seem almost to mul-
tiply themselves, in the eyes of the inhabitants,
by their marches and countermarches, and thus
inspire a salutary apprehension.

531. *Repose.*—When, after long fatigues, some
repose must be given to an army, it must be dispersed over a sufficient extent for subsistence.
This disposition of the troops is termed *canton-
ing*, and the camps occupied *cantonments*. This
state supposes that the enemy will not for some
time be in a condition to attack us. Still, even
this assurance should not induce any relaxation
of proper military precautions to prevent a surprise, and to enable us to concentrate on some
suitable point either for offensive or defensive
movements. The dispositions to be made for
this purpose resemble, in their principal features, those for one of advanced posts. Advanced
points are held by some of the troops where
there is no relaxation of discipline allowed; other
points, in their rear, are occupied as supports to
the first; and all are connected with some main
central position where the army is to be concen-

trated in case of need. The communications to
the rear, at least of all these detached portions,
should be kept in good travelling order, and no
obstruction to the free movements of the troops
be even for an hour allowed to exist.

532. When cantonments are taken up in winter they are termed *winter quarters*. They differ
from the preceding only in being often of greater
extent, and therefore, from their weakness, requiring all the additional means of defence at our
disposal, taking up our line in rear of some impassable natural obstruction, as a river for example.

Remarks.—From the preceding discussions we
gather what are the leading principles of strategy, and the objects that constitute the proper
application of them. In all ages professional
men have been met with who, animated alone
by the spirit of pedantry, have seized upon anything that has a novel aspect, and, to use a
vulgar phrase, have "run it into the ground;"
and, most frequently, have obscured what in
itself was simple and easily comprehended by
any sound mind, with a load of technical terms
and distinctions often too subtle for any one but
themselves to discover. Thiers, in his comments
upon the campaign of 1805, in speaking of the
battle of Austerlitz, has the following remarks.
"In the last century, after Frederick, at the battle of Leuthen, had destroyed the Austrian army
by attacking on one of its wings, persons in-
vented the theory of the oblique order of battle,
of which Frederick himself had never even
dreamed, and to this theory they attributed the
entire success of this great man. Subsequently,
when General Bonaparte had shown his great

superiority in those lofty military combinations,
by which he had so often surprised and surrounded the generals opposed to him; other
commentators of the same stamp discovered that
the whole art of war consisted alone in a certain
manœuvre, and they harped upon but the one
string, that of turning your enemy. To receive
implicitly their *dicta* they had discovered a new
science; and for it, accordingly, they had coined
a new word, STRATEGY; and, having done this,
each ran off to offer his aid to such sovereigns as
were willing to submit themselves to their teach-
ings." This little bit of not uncalled for satire,
from the great historian of the Consulate and the
Empire, must not lead us to suppose that he did
not believe in the settled principles of military
science, or was disposed in practice to under-
value them. On the contrary, in his comments
on the campaign of 1809, up to the taking of
Ratisbonne, he remarks: "If one dared to do so
we would add, that it was better that the triumphs gained were somewhat less, by acting in
conformity with the true principles of war—
which, after all, are only the *dicta* of good sense
—in running no perilous risks, than to have obtained more brilliant results in trusting too much
to mere chance. Napoleon would never have
fallen had his political measures been conducted
on this occasion as were those of his military
operations."

533. Men have been misled by the very simplicity of these almost self-evident principles,
and have felt disposed not to attribute to them
their just value, unless they were surrounded by
the verbiage of technicalities. Like the captain
of the Syrian host, they look for some great

thing from their prophet, forgetting upon what
a seemingly narrow basis the principles of almost
every science rest; whilst the developments to
which they lead, both in theory and practice,
have tasked the greatest mental powers of those
who have come after their discoverers. A La
Place condenses, in a short formula, the demonstration of the stability of the universe; whilst it
tasks the profound research and indomitable
industry of a Bowditch to point out to others the
steps by which he reached his sublime conclu-
sion.

534. To others again this very simplicity has
been a cause of more grievous error, leading
them to suppose that what was so clear to their
apprehension must be equally easy in practice.
Hence our large class of generals of the parlor,
the stock exchange, and the daily press, who,
with remorseless energy, without knowing how
to set up even a squad, murder the reputation
of truly able men, by their ceaseless, senseless
criticisms. How many men are there who can
demonstrate the most difficult proposition of
Newton's *Principia*, yet who would be puzzled
to apply the most simple law of statics to some
practical purpose. So is it in all the fixed
sciences. In them, however, the path once entered on and there is no way of straying from it.
How different in almost every military problem,
except in the bare mechanism of tactics. In almost every case, the *data* on which the solution
depends are wanting, or of such a character as
to render it very complicated, or even indeter-
minate. Too often the general has only conjec-
tures to go upon, and these based upon false pre-
mises. Even where he thinks he sees his way

clearly, he knows that the rules by which he must
be guided admit of many exceptions. That,
whilst he is deliberating, events are succeeding
each other with rapidity; that what is true now,
at the next moment may have no existence, or
exist in a contrary sense. All these considerations, and a thousand others that will present
themselves to any well constituted, reflecting
mind, will readily explain why history produces,
on its record, the names of so few great generals;
w iat real mental superiority it supposes even in
men of second-rate ability. For the first, as for
genius in every line, we have no standard.
Their failures are even grander than the successes of other men. For the second, whom we
always judge after the event, and most frequently without any knowledge of the circumstances
that led to it, let us exercise all the charity we
can. Let us assume the modesty of supposing, if our vanity ever disposes us to act otherwise, that had they known all that we have
since gathered, and had perceived as well as we
do what was best to be done, and still *have done
just the contrary*, they were impelled by circumstances over which they had no control.
How many great men have been struck down
by the hand of adverse fortune; and how much
of mediocrity has, by happy chance, been lifted
far above its true level.

535. It is in military history that we are to
look for the source of all military science. In it
we shall find those exemplifications of failure
and success by which alone the truth and value
of the rules of strategy can be tested. Geometrical diagrams may assist in fixing the attention,
and aiding by the eye the reasoning faculties;

but experience alone can fully satisfy the judgment, as to the correctness of its decisions, in problems of so mixed a character, into which so many heterogeneous elements enter. The greatest master of the art that the world has yet produced, Napoleon, recommends, as the best study and preparation of a commander, a minute acquaintance with the campaigns of Alexander, Hannibal, and Cæsar, among the ancients, and of Turenne, Frederick, and others, of modern times. A brief synopsis of some of the most marked of his own will alone be here attempted, as more immediately illustrative of the strategical principles above enumerated.

THE CAMPAIGNS OF 1796–97 IN ITALY.

536. *The Seat of War.*—Northern Italy, Pl. VIII., which has been the scene of some of the grandest military dramas, and was the theatre upon which the transcendent genius of Napoleon, as General Bonaparte, first manifested itself, as a great captain, is that singularly beautiful and rich portion of Italy which, bounded on the north and west by the lofty and rugged chain of the Alps, on the south by the lower crests of the Maritime Alps and the Apennines, and on the west by the Adriatic, is nearly equally divided by the river Po, which, having its sources in the Maritime Alps, flows nearly from west to east, emptying into the Adriatic, by several mouths, some thirty miles to the south of Venice. The Po receives a number of affluents from the Alps on the north and west, and from the Apennines on the south; the former of

which, from the greater extent of surface drained, and the greater slope of the water sheds, are by far the most considerable in size and velocity; and, on this account, present several strong defensive lines, which are nearly parallel, as the Ticino, the Adda, and the Mincio, against an enemy obliged to operate on the north of the Po; but which are easily turned by operating on the south side, as the affluents here, like the Trebia and others, present no serious obstacle; the only one being the Po itself. Besides these tributaries of the Po, there are several important streams on its north which, draining the valleys of the Tyrol, flow from north to south for the greater part of their course, and then trending east, empty into the Adriatic. The principal of these are the Brenta, which empties into the Gulf of Venice, and at the mouth of which is the city of Venice; and the Adige, upon which the strong fortified city of Verona lies. The upper portions of these streams are inclosed with steep banks, and their current is rapid; the lower portions wind their way sluggishly through a flat, and, in many parts, marshy country. From their natural features and from the position of their mouths, they present strong defensive lines, as they can be turned only by a *détour* towards their sources, through a broken difficult country, or by an enemy having control of the sea.

537. From the almost constant state of war to which Italy has been subjected, being drawn, in some manner, into almost every European struggle, many strongly fortified places have been built upon these streams; among the most important of which are Alexandria, on the Tanaro, a southern affluent of the Po; Pavia, on the Tici-

no; Placentia, on the Po; Peschiera and Mantua, on the Mincio; and Verona, on the Adige. To these may be added Genoa, at the head of the gulf of the same name, and at the foot of the northern point of the Apennines.

538. *Political Divisions of the Theatre of War.* —In 1797, as until a very recent period, Austria and Sardinia were the preponderating powers, both as military states and from the control they exercised over their neighbors, which, like Venice and its small continental territories, Modena, Parma, &c., existed, as independent principalities, only through the sufferance and jealousies of the ruling states. They were all hostile to France, not only from her politically aggressive course, but from their fears of social disturbances, growing out of the propagandist republican spirit which the French armies carried with them wherever they went. This hostile temper was most bitterly shown in the priesthood, and through them was communicated to the peasant class, more under their influence than any other, and who, from their position, could offer more annoyance than any other class to an invading army.

539. *Military Situation.*—The French army, commanded by Scherer, which in the preceding campaign (1795) had gained some advantages over the Austrians and Piedmontese, in the basin of the Loano, were distributed from the Col di Tende eastwardly along the Alps towards the Apennines. Its entire active force was not over 36,000 men, one division of which was on the north of the Apennines, observing the entrenched camp of the Piedmontese at Ceva; the greater portion, some 30,000, on the south side along the

coast. These troops, although greatly in want of almost every necessary, had still been inured to hardship in many fields, and were composed of admirable fighting material.

540. The Piedmontese, under Colli, in number about 20,000, were in nearly one body at Ceva, on the north slope of the Apennines; and the Austrians, numbering from 36,000 to 38,000, were advancing by several roads from Lombardy to Genoa.

541. *Plan of Campaign.*—Not satisfied with Scherer, and having conceived a high opinion of the military talents of Bonaparte, the French Directory decided to place the latter in chief command, having adopted his views of the coming campaign. This was a very simple one, but stamped with the genius of the future great captain. Several roads or passes lead from the coast, across the Alps and Apennines, into the basin of the Po. The principal of these are from Nice by the Col di Tende; from Savona by the Col di Montenotte; and from Genoa by the Bocchetta. Bonaparte resolved to throw himself into the midst of the enemy's forces, which were distributed over a long line, and not in supporting distances of each other, by the lowest of these passes, that of Montenotte, whilst he alarmed them for the safety of Genoa towards which he made a strong demonstration.

542. The opposing generals, Beaulieu and Colli, although their total available force was nearly 60,000 men, had each a separate interest to guard. Beaulieu wished to keep up his communications, through Genoa, with the English, whose fleet controlled the coast, whilst he covered Lombardy in his rear; whereas Colli desired to cover Turin, the capital of his own State.

543. Besides the inherent weakness of all plans based upon separate interests under the management of separate and independent heads, the military *status* of the allied forces was also inherently bad; not only as to the position of their forces, but as to their lines of retreat, which, from the points to be covered, threw them on divergent lines at the outset, and thus virtually dissolved all connexion between the two commanding generals. With Bonaparte matters stood just in the reverse order. There was but one head and but one interest to be guarded. His forces were concentrated; and, if thrown back, he covered by his front his base on the river Var, and his magazines which were in Provence.

544. With these advantages Bonaparte was very young, of prodigious mental activity, and of almost unparalleled physical endurance; whereas his opponents, Beaulieu in particular, were old men, though still vigorous, but trained in the methodical habits of military routine peculiar to the Austrians.

545. Almost unknown to the army when he took command of it, Bonaparte, to a superficial observer, had little physically to recommend him. His first address, however, to his army breathed that spirit of determination which ever finds its way to the heart of the true soldier, when emanating from one of the same stamp, "Soldiers," he said, "you are badly fed and are nearly naked. The government owes you much, but can do nothing for you. Your fortitude, your bravery do you honor, but have procured for you neither benefits nor glory. I am about to lead you into the most fertile plains of the

world; you will find there large cities, wealthy
provinces; you will find there honor, glory, and
riches. Soldiers of Italy, will you fail in courage?"

546. Without going into details, which, by
leading the mind off from the strategical features, might defeat the object of this summary,
it will be sufficient here to say that the French
and Austrians commenced their movements on
the same day, April 11, 1796. The Austrians
moved one column upon the French, along the
coast road from Genoa to Savona, whilst another
moved on Savona by Montenotte. At this last
spot an incident occurred which perhaps saved
the fortunes of the French, and is worthy of
mention, as showing how much depends on the
devotion of a few brave men. Colonel Rampon,
with 1200 men, held a redoubt which closed the
pass at Montenotte. Correctly estimating the
importance of his post, this hero not only resisted the efforts of the Austrians, but, under a
most murderous fire, he made his soldiers swear
that they would die before they would surrender. An oath which was faithfully kept until
relief came to them the following day, after a
night passed by all under arms.

547. Bonaparte retiring his right and pushing
his centre columns onwards, the Austrians were
driven back upon Dego, where they rallied.
Being now between the Austrians and Piedmontese, he attacks with impetuosity the former at
Dego, on his right, the latter at Millesimo on his
left. The results were that the Piedmontese
were forced back upon Ceva and Mondovi, and
the Austrians in the direction of Acqui.

548. It was on this occasion, when, at the

head of his army, looking over the plains of Italy stretching out before him, he exclaimed with emotion, "Hannibal crossed the Alps, but we, we have turned them." A phrase, as Thiers justly remarks, that explains the whole plan of campaign to every intelligent mind.

549. Following up the Piedmontese he attacks and defeats them at Mondovi, from which they retire on Cherasco, where an armistice was agreed upon, by which the strong places of Alexandria, Coni, and Tortona, are delivered into the possession of the French.

550. Having settled with the Piedmontese, Bonaparte prepares to follow up the Austrians, who, in the mean time, have seized the fortified town of Valencia on the Po, crossed the Po, and taken position at Valleggio, at the apex of the angle formed by the Po and Ticino. Making a feint of attempting to pass the Po at Valentia, Bonaparte descended the river rapidly, and, with a small force, crossed it at Placentia, where he disperses the enemy opposing him. Following rapidly in pursuit, he made the celebrated passage of the bridge of Lodi in the face of the Austrians on the opposite bank. It was here that he received the *sobriquet* of *Petit Caporal* from his soldiers.

551. Not having been able to intercept the Austrian line of retreat, by gaining their rear, Bonaparte takes possession of Milan, and, after some delay, moving on the Austrians, who had taken the Mincio as their line of defence, he makes a feint of attempting a passage at Peschiera, and forces one at Borghetto. At this stage of the campaign the Austrians retire into the Tyrol, by the roads leading north along the

Adige; having thrown a strong garrison into Mantua, which was not only strongly fortified but in the midst of a marsh, and, accessible only by narrow causeways, was considered impregnable, except to famine occasioned by a blockade.

552. Having driven the Austrians into the Tyrol, and closely invested Mantua, by seizing the ends of the causeways (June 14), which formed a kind of *tête de pont* for these communications, the north of Italy was literally conquered, and the task now before Bonaparte was to hold the country in his possession.

553. Attributing all the failures of the French, in their previous campaigns in this territory, to a faulty selection of their defensive lines, Bonaparte decided upon selecting the Adige for his defensive line, for the topographical reasons already stated, as the Mincio, though a shorter line, was at times fordable, and, besides, had the defect of emptying into the Po.

554. Having decided upon this important point, the next step was to distribute his forces so that he could observe the Austrians on every possible point of approach, and be able to concentrate in time to meet them upon any one on which they might appear in force. Three points of approach were accessible to the enemy. The *first*, leading from the Tyrol, crosses the Adige near Roveredo, somewhat above the upper end of Lake Guarda, and passing around it on the right, leads to Salo and Brescia in its rear. The *second*, also leading from the same point, crosses the river below Roveredo, and winding along the base of the heights between it and the lake, rises to the plateau of Rivoli, by a steep ascent, near this place, whence it reaches a point behind

the Adige, nearly midway between Verona and Peschiera, sending out a branch road to each of these places. The *third* leads from Roveredo to Verona along the left bank of the Adige. The two first, at this period, were rugged and hardly practicable for artillery through the mountainous portions; the last was the best, but, unlike the others, did not turn the Adige. With these favorable defensive topographical features, these lines were all easily guarded, and each could be defended for some time by a small force. To effect this, Bonaparte made the following disposition of his forces. At Salo, 3,000 men. At Corona and Rivoli, 12,000. Near Verona, 5,000. At Legnago, 8,000. At Castelnovo, where Bonaparte had his headquarters, the reserve of cavalry and horse artillery.

555. Wurmser, who commanded the Austrians, had his headquarters at Roveredo. His plan of campaign was offensive, whilst that of Bonaparte was, at the outset, necessarily defensive, but awaiting events to become also offensive. From his superiority of force, Wurmser designed to surround the French. For this purpose, he detached one column of 20,000 men to turn Lake Guarda, by Salo; whilst with one of 40,000 he followed the two other roads. On July 29, the French outposts were attacked and driven in, and the next day the French were driven from Salo, Corona, and Rivoli, and the Austrians were in march on Brescia.

556. At this stage of the operations, Bonaparte, coming to one of his rapid conclusions, decided on abandoning the siege of Mantua, as this place must eventually fall if he were victorious, and he accordingly destroyed all his siege

material, buried his guns, and withdrew the be-
sieging corps. He then concentrated rapidly on
Peschiera and Valeggio, on the Mincio, whilst
the Austrians, at the same time, had passed the
Adige and Mincio; Wurmser entering Mantua,
whilst a column of 25,000 had reached Lonato
and Castiglione.

557. Placing divisions at the bridges of San
Marco and Montechiaro, on the Chiese, and
ordering the Austrians to be held in check at
Salo, Bonaparte decided to attack the Austrians
at Lonato and Castiglione, before Wurmser, from
Mantua, could effect a junction with them.
Aug. 3, Bonaparte defeated the Austrians at
Lonato, and marched on Castiglione, where
Massena had also driven them back. During
these movements, Bonaparte, displayed an almost incredible activity, riding post haste from
one position to another of his forces, overseeing
and directing everything himself. It was on
this occasion that having only about 1,000 men
at hand, a large detachment of 4,000 of the
enemy coming upon him with his staff, at Lonato,
summoned him to surrender. Directing the officer to be blindfolded and led into the midst of
his staff, he reprimanded him for his temerity in
bringing such a message to a general in the
midst of his army, and sent him back demanding
a surrender of his own detachment, which was
speedily complied with. On Aug. 5, the battle
of Castiglione was fought, with considerable
odds against the French; the Austrians were
driven back, and Wurmser retired upon Corona
and Rivoli, whilst the column from Salo retreated
on Roveredo.

558. The results of this short campaign of a

week were most remarkable. The French, with not more than 30,000 men, placed 60,000 Austrians *hors de combat;* killing or wounding from 7,000 to 8,000, and taking from 12,000 to 13,000 prisoners.

559. After retiring into the Tyrol and having recruited his army to 50,000 men, Wurmser projected another campaign as follows. Leaving a force of 20,000 men to hold the upper Adige, with the rest of his army he proposed to descend the Brenta, and, marching on the Adige, force a passage at some point between Verona and Legnago.

560. Bonaparte, in the meantime, leaving sufficient forces to guard the principal points of the Adige, and blockade Mantua, ascended the Adige to search for Wurmser. Having united his forces at Torbolo, at the head of the lake, he in succession drove the Austrians from Mori, San Marco, Roveredo, and Calliano, and on Sept. 5, entered Trent. Leaving a sufficient force to hold the Austrians in check in the Tyrol, he moved Sept. 6, with 20,000 men, after Wurmser. Overtaking the Austrians, Sept. 7, at Primolano, he drove them before him and forced Wurmser, on Sept. 8, from Bassano on the Brenta. After a hasty flight, the Austrians succeeded in crossing the Adige at Legnago, Sept. 11, and on Sept. 13, Wurmser got into Mantua. In this brief campaign the Austrian loss was about 20,000, and that of the French 8,000.

561. After these events Bonaparte occupied himself with recruiting his army, which numbered nearly 38,000 men, dispersed over a much longer line than previously, occupying positions in the Tyrol in front of Trent, on the Brenta, on the Adige, and around Mantua.

562. Alvinzy, who now took command of the
Austrian forces in the field, crossed the Piava,
Nov. 1, and moved on the Brenta. The Austrian plan of campaign was, that one column
under Davidovitch should descend the two
roads along the Adige, and driving the French
before them unite with Alvinzy, who, with the
main force, was to march on Verona. From this
point, the two armies united were to march to
the relief of Wurmser, in Mantua.

563. Bonaparte, in the meantime, ordered
Vaubois to hold Davidovitch in check whilst he
marched on Alvinzy, whom he attacked, Nov. 6,
in a strong position between Carmignano and
Bassano. In this he was only partially successful, whilst Vaubois, owing to a panic in two of
his demi-brigades, was forced back on Corona
and Rivoli. Under these circumstances, Bonaparte retired, Nov. 7, into Verona, sent reinforcements to Vaubois, and went himself to see
that the troops were properly posted at these
important positions. The Austrians, in the
meantime, followed after Bonaparte with great
caution, and took position on the heights at Caldiero, not far from Verona. On Nov. 11, Bonaparte advanced on Caldiero and drove in the
Austrian advanced guard, but after an unsuccessful attack on the Austrian position, was obliged
to fall back upon Verona.

564. In this conjuncture of affairs, Bonaparte's
condition had become desperate; his force was
reduced to 15,000 men, whilst the Austrians had
45,000. With no chance of success, if he either
remained in Verona, or met the Austrians in a
field favorable to their superiority of force, he
was suddenly inspired by one of those impulses,

which men term an inspiration of genius, but which are given only to those who merit them by a thorough acquaintance with the resources of their profession, and which are only gained by painful and unremitted study. Between Verona and the village of Ronco, below it, the Adige spreads out into several arms, which embrace some small islands. Between this river and a small stream, termed the Alpon, the ground is low and marshy, and traversed only by narrow causeways. By descending the river to Ronco, and crossing it and the Alpon, at the village of Arcola, Bonaparte saw that he would gain the flank and rear of the Austrian position at Caldiero, and cut Alvinzi off from his base. This plan seemed feasible, even with his disparity of force, as the causeways lent themselves to an attack of a small force against superior numbers.

565. Leaving but a small garrison in Verona, Bonaparte left the city by night for Ronco. Passing the Adige and pushing forward columns, on Nov. 15, on the causeways leading to Caldiero and Arcola, the French, after severe fighting throughout the day, during which Bonaparte nearly lost his life whilst leading a charge, by being pushed over into the boggy marsh, failed to gain Arcola, and at night withdrew behind the Adige. On the following day, Nov. 16, the same harassing attacks were made on the Austrians, and the French again, at night, withdrew behind the Adige. On Nov. 17, the French again made their assaults on the dikes, whilst a column, descending to near Albaredo, crossed the Alpon there, and thus turned the bridge and village of Arcola. The Austrians, after their

heavy losses in the last three days, finding their position turned, fell back upon Vicenza. On the last day of this celebrated battle, Bonaparte resorted to a stratagem which produced great effect on the enemy. The Austrian left wing was covered by a marsh, having a thick undergrowth of brush and tall rushes. Bonaparte ordered an officer to take twenty-five horse and a number of trumpeters, and proceeding through this screen, fall upon the Austrian rear, with all the noise he could make. This was admirably done, and the enemy gave way.

566. In the meantime the corps at Rivoli held the Austrians in check, and finally driving them back into the Tyrol, reoccupied their former positions.

567. Both armies having been rested and recruited, the French having 45,000 and the Austrian 60,000, the Austrians again opened the campaign, Jan. 8, 1797, by driving in the French outposts.

568. The Austrian plan of campaign was, for Alvinzy, with a corps of 45,000 men, to move again by the upper Adige, whilst Provera, with another of 20,000, should move on the lower Adige, gain Mantua, and connect with the territory of Romagna and the army of the Pope.

569. On Jan. 12, the French were forced back at Rivoli, but Provera failed in his attempts both at Verona and Legnago. Having secured these two places from assault, Bonaparte turned all his attention to the position of Rivoli, so long the object of his study and care. This position is a plateau lying between a range of rugged heights, termed the Monte Baldo, which lie between, and border Lake Guarda and the Adige. The princi-

pal access to it is by the main road, which rises from the Adige to it at Incanale, by a steep, difficult ascent. Several small roads lead to it through the passes of the hills in its front, but are not practicable for artillery.

570. The Austrians were divided into three bodies to make their attack. One corps, composed of infantry, artillery, and cavalry, was to move on the main road by Incanale; a second of infantry was to assault in front, by the narrow roads leading to it; whilst a third was to pass between Monte Baldo and the lake, and gain the French rear. Still a fourth corps was to move towards Verona on the road on the left bank of the Adige.

571. The result was, that after heavy fighting on Jan. 14, the centre column of the Austrians was driven back into the hills; the right hurled down the road towards Incanale, in inextricable confusion, whilst the left, after coming on the French rear, was forced to surrender. It was on the occasion of this surrender that Bonaparte, although the fortunes of the day were undecided in his front, exclaimed, on seeing these troops in his rear, *Ceux-là sont à nous*, and that the soldiers inspired by a like confidence, said, *Ils sont à nous*.

572. Taking with him Massena's division, Bonaparte left Rivoli, Jan. 14, and marched all night upon Mantua, to prevent the junction of Provera's forces, who had passed the Adige above Legnago, with those of Wurmser. Continuing his march all the day of the 15th, and directing other troops on the same point, he made his dispositions for battle on the evening of the same day. On the 16th, he fought the battle of

La Favorita, in which Provera was taken prisoner with 6,000 men, and Wurmser forced back into Mantua. Alvinzy regained the Tyrol, after losing a large number of prisoners.

573. The brave old Wurmser held out in Mantu.t, although famine was ravaging the place. Having sent an officer to propose articles of capitulation, and who spoke in confident terms of the means they still had of holding out, Bonaparte, who, *incognito*, listened to the negotiations, stepped forward, and said, "See, Sir, here are the conditions that I will grant to your marshal. If he had provisions for only fifteen days and spoke of surrender he would not deserve an honorable capitulation. That you are here shows that he is reduced to extremity. I respect his age, his bravery, and his misfortunes. Bear to him the conditions I have granted; let him leave the place to-morrow, in one month, or in six, I shall offer him nothing better, nothing worse. He may remain as long as he thinks honor demands at his hands; his position shall in no respect be rendered the more aggravated."

574. Wurmser having surrendered as a prisoner of war, was allowed to leave the city with the honors of war on Feb. 2, 1797, which was the closing scene of this grand military drama.

575. *Résumé.*—The results of these campaigns were truly stupendous. The French, who entered upon them with about 30,000 men, and in all, did not receive more than 25,000 men as reinforcements, had, at the close, defeated 200,000 Austrians; had taken 80,000 prisoners; killed or wounded 20,000; had fought 12 pitched battles and more than 60 combats.

576. To what are we to attribute then such

20*

results? The Austrian troops were not wanting in soldierly qualities. Their leaders were men not deficient in capacity, in bravery, or in experience, yet they failed with such advantages in their favor. The French, although excellent soldiers, active, and confident in their leaders aud themselves, still had to contend against odds too great for success unless aided by extraordinary circumstances. These conditions were theirs. For leader, they had the greatest captain that the world had thus far seen. Grandly endowed by Nature, his great talent was to turn all his talents to the best account. Although he had had but little experience as a general, before taking command of the Army of Italy, he had pondered long and profoundly on his profession; he had stored his mind with all that others had treasured up. Whilst other officers were wasting their time in vain discussions, he was literally lying on his maps, and studying out the great problems then being solved under his eye, and giving his own solutions to them. When summoned to command he had but to apply what he had acquired. In after years, when looking back upon those scenes in his caged exile, he said: "My profession (*mon état*) is that of soldier. I have made myself acquainted with all that pertains to it. If I have need of gunpowder, I know how to conduct the manufacture of it. If I want shoes for my soldiers, I can give directions as to the manner in which they ought to be made." Men of ordinary capacities think they can neglect such things; and those who are ignorant of their importance, have sneered at Napoleon for bringing down his mind to attend to such minutiæ, but in this he has given a lesson that every young soldier should lay to heart.

577. The simple principles of the military art, so simple that all can see their bearing, but how few, alas! can rightly apply them, lay at the bottom of these great results; these were but a legitimate emanation from the former. Attacking first disconnected, dispersed corps on their centre, and driving them on divergent lines of retreat. Selecting a strong defensive line on the Adige, and holding his corps well in hand, for concentration at the most favorable central point, wherever the enemy might strike, but still observing him closely. Wonderful activity, aided by those sudden inspirations of genius, as they are termed, and a *coup d'œil* both for time and place never perhaps surpassed. And last, that electric spark which, unseen, flies from man to man, and which produces such heroic deeds on the battle-field. Such were the causes of success. These were but too well intensified by the faults of the Austrian generals, repeated over and over again, with hardly a variation, either in their strategical or tactical combinations. Dispersing their corps; operating on double lines, and dividing their forces on the battle-field, as at Rivoli, these men seemed stultified by routine, and unable to profit by any lesson. Add this to the spirit of the Austrian rule of that time, and although our wonder is not lessened, we can find something like adequate causes for the events that occurred.

CAMPAIGN OF 1805.

578. *Political Position.*—The campaign of 1805 grew out of what is known in French history as the third Coalition against France. After the rupture of the peace of Amiens, in 1803, and the annexation of Genoa to the French empire, England, but Austria in particular, felt the perilous position in which they were placed, and mainly through their agency, the coalition between them and Russia, Sweden, and Naples, was brought about, with a view of wresting from France the territories she had acquired beyond her ancient borders, during the wars of the Republic.

579. To this end Russia, England, and Sweden were to attack Holland and Belgium, by the way of Pomerania; Russia and Austria were to advance by the valley of the Danube; the Austrians were to attack Lombardy; and the Russians and English were to make a descent into Southern Italy, and being joined by the Neapolitans, were to expel the French from the Peninsula.

580. Formidable as was the coalition, and widespread the circle of its operations, it had the vice of all such projects, and carried within itself the seeds of its own destruction. At no period of his career was Napoleon in a more favorable position to meet the dangers that now threatened him. The large force which he had distributed, in six camps of instruction, from the Texel to Bayonne, for the invasion of England, had been, since 1803, under his own eye, preparing for every contingency of war. Devoting his

great administrative powers to perfecting it, he
had given it an organization that has since
served as a model to the world. In speaking of
the plan and the means at the disposal of Napoleon, to meet this formidable array against him,
Thiers says: "Never captain, either in ancient
or modern times, had conceived or executed
plans on such a scale. Also never had a spirit
more powerful, one of less unshackled will, and
having at its disposal more vast means, had so
extended a field for its operations. In truth
what spectacle, for the greater part, is presented
to our contemplation in like cases. Irresolute
governments which are deliberating when they
should be acting; short-sighted administrations,
which are only commencing to organize their
forces when they ought to be on the battle-field;
and subordinate to these, generals who are hardly
capable of manœuvring upon the restricted theatre of war assigned for their operations. Here,
on the contrary, genius, will, foresight, absolute
liberty of action, all concurred in the same man
to the same end." How true these reflections.
What a lesson does history here present us,
and how patiently and pointedly has she repeated
it, from age to age, and yet with how little
profit!

581. *Theatre of War.*—Looking around him,
from his central position, upon the wide circle
occupied by his opponents, Napoleon, with his
intuitive insight in military matters, decided at
once to strike a crushing blow upon the most
menacing point, judging that success there
would dissipate all danger at every other. Observing with sufficient forces only the minor
points, he determined to concentrate his main

efforts upon the line of the Danube, against the Austrians and Russians.

582. The basin of this celebrated river, Pl. IX., had been the scene of the great battles between France and Austria. Taking its rise in a rugged but not very elevated district, termed the Suabian Alps, and in the celebrated Black Forest, near the point where the Rhine at Basle abruptly changes its westwardly course to one nearly due north, the Danube soon commences to receive, from the south, a number of tributaries which have their sources in the Alps. The first of these is the Iller, then the Lech, the Isar, the Inn, &c. Skirting closely the base of the Suabian Alps, and that of the southern range of mountains by which Bohemia is encircled, it receives no tributary of importance except from the basins lying between the termination of the Suabian Alps and the hills of Franconia, and the territory of the Upper Palatinate lying between the same hills and the Bohemian mountains on the north-east.

583. The southern tributaries, on all of which are fortified points, being, for the most part, deep and rapid, having the Danube, into which they empty, on the north, and the Alps, in which they rise, on the south, have always been looked upon as strong defensive lines against an invasion from the side of France, and the more so, as in all their wars, the French had entered the valley of the Danube at its head, by crossing the Rhine between Strasburg and Lake Constance, and proceeding through the defiles of the Black Forest, or those of the hills separating the Rhine from the Danube.

584. The Black Forest, on the side of France,

was covered with a heavy forest growth, and had passing through it a number of defiles connecting the valleys of the Danube and Necker with that of the Rhine. The Suabian Alps, which is but a mountain spur, lying in a northeast direction, terminate near Nordlingen in a level country.

585. *Military Positions.*—Russia and Austria having to act along the line of the Danube, the Austrians, faithful to their military traditions, advanced to the Iller, as their defensive line, which they occupied from Memmingen to Ulm. The Russians had formed two corps; the one, under Kutusof, was marching through Moravia to join Mack, who commanded the Austrians at Ulm; the second, composed of the guards and the army of Buxhowden, was at Pulawi on the Vistula with the Emperor Alexander.

586. The army of Napoleon was distributed as follows: One corps in Hanover, under Bernadotte; one in Holland, under Marmont; the main body at Boulogne and its environs, from Montreuil to Ambleteuse.

587. *Plan of Campaign.*—The Austrians holding the strong position of Ulm, which they regarded as unassailable in front, were waiting for the Russians to join them before commencing offensive operations.

588. Napoleon, who calculated on the well known tardiness of the Russian movements, and the traditional military policy of the Austrians, based his plan on these two facts. It was simply to attack the Austrians before the Russians could come up, and, having beaten them, to beat the Russians in turn. But, not satisfied with the results of simple victories, Napoleon aimed

at a grand disaster for the Austrians at Ulm,
which he intended to accomplish by turning
their position below the Iller, cutting them off
from their line of retreat, and thus, hemmed in
by the Alps on the one hand, the Danube on the
other, and his own corps, to force them to surrender; thus, as Thiers says: "to make use of
a means very simple in theory, but very difficult
in the execution; that of beating one's opponents
in succession."

589. *Military Operations.*—Not the least remarkable features of this campaign were the
marches by which the troops were first concentrated, and then moved in concert on the Austrians. The army, which had been organized
into army corps, was composed as follows. The
first corps under Bernadotte, 17,000 men. The
second, under Marmont, 20,000. The third, under Davoust, 26,000. The fourth, under Soult,
40,000. The fifth, under Lannes, 18,000. The
sixth, under Ney, 24,000. The seventh, under
Augereau, 14,000. Besides these there was the
grand reserve of 22,000 cavalry and 1,000 horse
artillery, under Murat, and the general reserve
of 7,000 men and 24 guns of the imperial guard.
These last two corps being under the immediate
control of Napoleon. The first and second corps
received orders to concentrate at Wurtzburg on
the Main in Franconia; the third, fourth, fifth,
and sixth, with the reserves on the Rhine, between Manheim and Strasburg. The seventh
corps, which was at Brest and had the whole
breadth of France to traverse, was to form a kind
of reserve for recruits, &c., and to reach Strasburg after the others.

590. Acting with that profound secresy which

he carried into all his official acts, Napoleon had all his orders prepared by a confidential officer, ready on Aug. 26, and issued Aug. 27. The line of march of each corps was so chosen that it would meet with no hindrance to reach its destination on the day fixed upon. The first corps was to move Sept. 2, and reach Wurtzburg, Sept. 20. The second to move Sept. 1, reach Mayence, by the Rhine, on the 15th or 16th, and Wurtzburg on the 18th or 19th. The corps from Montreuil, Boulogne, and Ambleteuse, to move Aug. 29, and to reach the Rhine between the 21st and 24th of September. Each corps was to move in three divisions on three consecutive days. In the meantime Napoleon had used every stratagem to put the allies on the wrong scent, and had gathered all the information possible, through his aides-de-camp, of the roads leading from the Rhine to the Danube. He himself left Paris Sept. 24, and reached Strasburg Sept. 26.

591. Having concentrated his army at the points designated, Napoleon commenced his grand strategical march on the Austrians. Having thrown the corps of Lannes forward, in front of Strasburg towards Stuttgard, to cover in flank the movements of Ney, Soult, and Davoust, he ordered Murat to cross the Rhine at Strasburg, Sept. 25, and, with the reserve of cavalry, to penetrate the defiles through the Black Forest; and Lannes was ordered to support him with some battalions of grenadiers. This was done simply to mislead the Austrians as to the true movement on their flank and rear. Having ordered the corps of Ney, Soult, and Davoust to take four days' rations of bread in their knap-

sacks, and four days' provision of biscuit in wagons, in the event of a forced march, Napoleon crossed the Rhine with the guards, Oct. 1, having seen all his parks in motion.

592. Three roads lead from the Rhine to the Danube between Donauwirth and Ingolstadt on this last stream. First, the principal one passes through Pforsheim, Stuttgard, and Heidenheim, striking the Suabian Alps, and communicating by numerous defiles with the valley of the Danube, is the most exposed to an enemy on its flank. This road was taken by Murat, Lannes, Ney, and the guards. The second one, lower down the Rhine, and passing through Spire, Hall, and Ellwagen, was followed by Soult. The third, still lower down, from Manheim through Heidelburg, Neckar-Elz, Ingelfingen, and Oetlingen, was taken by Davoust, which brought him near those taken by Bernadotte and Marmont from Wurtzburg.

593. Napoleon designed that all these corps should *débouché*, between the 6th and 7th of October, upon the plain that lies between Nordlingen, Donauwerth, and Ingoldstadt, the movement pivoting upon the right wing. Having given time for the heads of the columns on his left to reach the same line, parallel to the Danube, as his own, he gave orders, Oct. 4, for his right to move by Stuttgard, sending Murat in advance, and ordering him to move rapidly and penetrate and hold each defile, in succession, on the flank, until the army was safely past it. This movement he supported by 50,000 men. The corps on the left were thus secured from danger, and within supporting distances of each other. The whole army of 180,000 men moved on a front of

about seventy miles, and in such order as to be able to concentrate 100,000 at any point in a few hours.

594. Having experienced the difficulty of divining the truth from the confused statements of persons witnessing such movement, Napoleon kept the Austrians ignorant of his true designs, by false reports, spies, deserters, &c., whilst Soult, on the 6th and 7th of October, surprises and seizes the bridges of Munster and Donauwerth; and Murat, crossing the Danube, seizes the bridge at Rains over the Lech. Napoleon, leaving Ney with 20,000 men on the left bank of the Danube, on the road to Wurtemburg, places Murat and Lannes between Augsburg and Ulm, at Burgau, with 40,000 men, leaving Soult at Augsburg with 30,000. Davoust was placed at Aichach, to hold the Austrian rearguard in check, and Bernadotte placed at Munich. To prevent the escape of the Austrians through the Tyrol, Napoleon pushed Soult forward to Memmingen, on their extreme left, giving him instructions to reach and secure his position by Oct. 13; having decided to carry Ulm by assault on the 14th. Ney, in the meantime, had crossed the Danube, driven the Austrians from the strong position of Elchingen, and gained possession of the heights of Michelsburg, on the left bank of the Danube, which completely command Ulm.

595. In this posture of affairs, completely hemmed in at Ulm, the Austrian commander had no alternative left but to attempt to cut his way through the French lines, or to surrender. On the evening of the 14th, the Archduke Ferdinand attempted this last course with success, taking with him a detachment of 6,000 or 7,000

cavalry, and a corps of infantry; but he was quickly followed by Murat, who, in a hot and incessant pursuit of four days, killed or captured the whole of this force, with the exception of 2,000 or 3,000 cavalry, who, with the Archduke, succeeded in gaining the road to Bohemia.

596. Napoleon, having summoned Mack to surrender, Oct. 16, this unfortunate general asked for eight days to wait for reinforcements to relieve him, on the non-arrival of which he agreed to surrender. Napoleon granted him six, and the place and army were given up Oct. 20.

597. Thus, to use the words of Thiers, "the plan of Napoleon was completely realised. In twenty days, without delivering a great battle, by a series of marches only, and a few combats, an army of 80,000 men was destroyed."

598. The facts of this campaign are their own best criticism. By marches profoundly combined and admirably executed, the French army was thrown upon the flank and rear of the Austrian, concentrated on the Iller; and which, if attacked in front, could, if beaten, have fallen back, each day bringing them nearer to the Russian army, then in its march to form a junction with it. Such a movement merited the success it obtained.

599. For both political and military reasons, Napoleon decided to hasten his march on Vienna. The Russians were in his front with about 70,000 men. The Austrian archdukes, Charles and John, were upon the right flank of his line of march; the former in Lombardy with 70,000 of the best troops; the latter in the Tyrol with 25,000 men.

600. Forced to march between the Danube

and the Alps, over a narrow and obstructed zone
of country, it was of the first importance for Napoleon to guard his exposed flank, by preventing
a junction of the two archdukes. For this purpose, he ordered Massena, who held the defensive line of the Adige, to keep closely on the
heels of the Archduke Charles, and detached Ney
into the Tyrol to secure that region of country.
Bernadotte was also destined to occupy the territory of Salsburg, through which the Salza river
flows to join the Danube. Without entering into the details of these movements, it is sufficient
to say that they were all carried out with complete success; the Russians, beaten in several
severe engagements, were forced across the
Danube at Krems, and finally fell back towards
Bohemia; and the movement, commenced Oct.
26th, ended in the occupation of Vienna before
the middle of November.

601. In connexion with these splendid operations, another branch of his profession, not less
important, though wanting the *éclat* that attends
marches and battles, occupied the profound attention of Napoleon; one which, as Thiers tells
us, "he was more and more occupied with as the
scale of his operations became the grander, and
in which he stands without an equal, for foresight and the activity of his oversight." Those
were the precautions necessary to keep his army
supplied with everything, and to recruit its
losses. This system of precautions had for its
object to furnish him with points of support,
whether he advanced, or felt himself under the
necessity of retiring. Besides a certain amount
of fortified strength, he brought together at
these points an immense quantity of supplies of

all kinds, for his army, with everything neccessary for the soldiers' comfort. For this purpose he selected Augsburg, on the Lech, as his grand depot; and ordered from Nuremburg, Ratisbonne and Munich every article they could furnish for his purposes.

602. Being in quiet possession of Vienna, Napoleon took immediate measures both to secure it from attack, and to follow up the Russians into Moravia, before they could effect a junction with the two archdukes, who, besides, would have to make a wide circuit through Hungary to reach each other. For the first purpose, he called back Marmont, who was at Leoben on the river Muhr, and placed him on the Styrian Alps, nearer to Vienna, to guard the grand route from Italy to this city. He brought Massena nearer to Marmont, and placed them in supporting distance of each other. The corps of Davoust was distributed around Vienna; one division being at Neustadt so as to support Marmont, another in the direction of Presburg to watch the defiles from Hungary, a third in front of Vienna on the road to Moravia. Two divisions were placed in Vienna. The corps of Soult, Lannes, and Murat marched towards Moravia; whilst Bernadotte, who had crossed the Danube at Krems, followed up the steps of Kutusof.

603. Thus, like a spider in the centre of his web, Napoleon, from Vienna, was ready for an enemy's approach on any side. Each corps was so placed, that, if attacked, it could hold out until supported by the others adjacent to it. To quote the words of Thiers again: "Napoleon thus fulfilled, in the most perfect manner, the conditions of that art of war, which, on a later

day, in conversation with his lieutenants, he defined in these terms: "THE ART OF SEPARATING TO SUBSIST AND OF CONCENTRATING TO FIGHT. Never were the precepts of this formidable art, by which empires are founded or destroyed, better defined, or better carried into practice."

604. After some combats with the Russians, the French corps entered Brunn, the capital of Moravia, Nov. 19, and Napoleon fixed there his headquarters on the 20th. In the meantime the Emperors of Austria and Russia met at Olmutz, where they had assembled about 75,000 Russians and 15,000 Austrians, or 90,000 men in all. After many discussions, which only served to display the weakness and folly of their plans, the allied sovereigns decided to march on Brunn, and attack the French. Their plan was to turn the position of Napoleon, in front of Brunn, by his right, and placing themselves on the road from Vienna to Brunn, cut off his line of retreat on Vienna, and either capture his army, or force him to retreat on Bohemia. Napoleon, who had thoroughly examined the country around Brunn, and had also divined the plan of the Allies, decided to take up a position where he could act defensively until the enemy had fallen into their own trap, and then, assuming the offensive, overwhelm them. For this purpose he selected the memorable battle-field of Austerlitz.

605. The village of Austerlitz, Pl. X., from which the battle takes its name, lies about twelve miles from Brunn, and a little to the south of east. Between these two places, several small streams run nearly north and south, which, taking their rise in a heavily timbered spur from the Bohemian range, that terminates

a little to the north of the road from Brunn to Olmutz, which here runs almost due east, are lost in several ponds about nine miles south of the road. The principal of these streams, termed the Goldbach, and which runs nearly due south, lies rather more than five miles from Brunn, and has along it several small villages, the principal of which are Schaplanitz on the north, and Sokolnitz, Telnitz, and Menitz on the south. Between the Goldbach and another small stream, a little to the west of Austerlitz, running in a southwest direction and emptying into the same ponds as the Goldbach, is the rising ground which forms the plateau of Pratzen. Towards Austerlitz, and to the north, the plateau is more or less undulating; but south and towards the Goldbach, the slopes are more steep, and cut up into ravines, which form hollow and somewhat intricate roads, leading to the villages. Such are the chief features of the position chosen by Napoleon to receive the attack of the Austro-Russian army. His own army was posted along the Goldbach, from a small eminence, termed the Santon—a little to the north of the road from Brunn to Olmutz—to Menitz. His cavalry on his left; the Santon occupied by a heavy battery; his main body and reserves nearly opposite the plateau of Pratzen; and the villages occupied by his infantry. Feeling that the enemy would attempt to turn his right, by the villages on it, to gain the road to Vienna, which runs nearly due south from Brunn, Napoleon decided to let them engage themselves fully in this, when, assuming the offensive, he would carry the heights of Pratzen, and thus, having pierced the enemy's centre, capture or destroy his left wing at least. Such was the simple plan of this decisive battle. It was fought almost as if he had decided upon the movements on each side. His own generals literally carried out his own plans, and the Allies committed the blunders he expected. Their left was literally captured or destroyed; many being drowned in the ponds, which, being frozen, they had ventured upon for escape. In the utter rout and consequent confusion of all, the two Emperors vainly attempted to stop and rally the mere mob into which their forces were now confounded. Their entreaties and commands were unheeded. The confused mass rolled slowly back, like a flock of sheep, but still, from their mere density impenetrable to the French cavalry and infantry, were literally pushed from the field. The two sovereigns were at length obliged to fly rapidly across the fields of Moravia, during profound darkness, separated from their military households, and exposed to the insults of their own licentious soldiery. Alexander, whom his wisest counsellors had entreated to remain at his capital, and not to move with the army, where his presence could only give rise to petty jealousies and intrigues, had here an occasion to see the wisdom of leaving military matters to men long trained to their profession; and, as Thiers remarks, "could now well perceive that, under the present circumstances, the presence of a sovereign was not worth that of a good general." A lesson that all governments might profit by.

606. Such was the great battle fought Dec. 2, 1805, and named by Napoleon *the day of Austerlitz,* in his admirable bulletin, dated from the battle-field. The Austro-Russian loss was 15,000

killed or wounded, 20,000 prisoners, 8 generals, and 10 colonels, 180 cannon, with an immense amount of warlike stores, and 40 standards, including those of the Russian imperial guard. The loss of the French was only from 7,000 to 8,000 killed and wounded.

607. The Austrian as well as the Russian soldiers fought with indomitable courage. Their disastrous defeat was the effect of bad generalship. Though greatly outnumbering the French their line was too extended, and their attack upon both wings by weakening their centre, gave Napoleon the opportunity he waited for. Besides this, their left wing, by which the decisive blow was to be struck, was entrusted to a man, General Buxhowden, vain, presumptuous, intemperate, and without military skill, who, when not a mere idle spectator, only added to the confusion of the moment. Added to this, the battle was planned and the general movements traced out by one of those pretenders who are the more confident as they are the more incapable of taking but one view of a case. This general, who, as a spectator of the scene avers, read his plan to the assembled generals the night before the battle, as a pedant might have done to a class of young pupils, when one of the number said: "all this is very well, general, but suppose the enemy should anticipate us, and make their attack near Pratzen, what shall we do then?" replied: "that is not a supposable case." In war he who does not foresee and provide for every supposable case, may, like Weirother, on this occasion find his Austerlitz.

CAMPAIGN OF 1814.

608. The opening of the campaign of 1796, and the subsequent operations, up to the defensive position taken up by Bonaparte behind the Adige, were strictly offensive; from this last period to the close of this brilliant series of military triumphs, Bonaparte acted on what may be termed the defensive-offensive; that is, he selected his positions, to observe and await the development of the enemy's plans, and, when he was fairly committed to them, he seized the opportune moment to foil him. In the campaign of 1805, become Emperor, and with no will but his own for a law, we find him pursue a like course to the one followed in 1796–97. Directing his admirably organized forces, by a series of combined marches, which will be a model to generals of all future times, so as to turn the enemy's position, and cut him off from his line of retreat, we see him, after his first overwhelming success, follow it up without a day's loss, driving before him the Russians, and capturing the capital of Austria. Here he pauses, only a moment, to look around him and judge of his position, whilst he at the same time applies his own simple maxim, to disperse his forces to subsist, and concentrate them to fight. Expecting to be attacked, with superior forces of the Allies in his front, he pushes before him those of his opponents who were within reach, and, stopping at Brunn, the capital of Moravia, he divines the enemy's projects, carefully selects his field, on which to fight a defensive-offensive battle, and at Austerlitz leaves

another imperishable record of his overshadowing genius.

609. In the campaign of 1814, that grand closing scene of the terrible drama of disasters which opened with the retreat from Russia, Napoleon had no choice. Nothing but the application of an energy and an audacity which he alone possessed here held out any hope of success, and these he displayed in a degree worthy of his best days; combining the lessons of experience of so many grand military events with the activity and fertility of imagination of his early youth.

610. *Military Situation.*—Towards the close of December, 1813, the Allied forces invaded the French empire. The Austrians and Russians, under Schwartzenberg, numbering 160,000 men, crossed the Rhine at Basle, Pl. XI., whilst the Prussians under Blucher, 60,000 strong, crossed it at Mayence. The intention of the first body was to advance on Paris, by Béfort and Langres, so as to descend along the Seine; whilst the Prussians, passing between the fortresses on the north-eastern frontier, were to strike the Marne, and finally concentrate with the Austro-Russians before Paris.

611. To oppose this formidable array Napoleon had within his reach only about 60,000 men under Marshals Marmont, Ney, Victor, and Mortier, and some troops that he was hastening forward from Spain, with such conscripts as could be got together and incorporated, whilst still undisciplined, in the old regiments, that still preserved a skeleton of their former selves.

612. *Theatre of War*—The approach of the Allies on Paris lay through what is known as

the basin of Paris; that sector, which, having
Paris for its apex, and the Vosges mountains, on:
the east, as its base, is watered by the Yonne,.
the Seine, the Aube, the Marne, the Aisne, and
the Oise, all of which flow towards the one remarkable centre, Paris and its environs. From.
the broken character of the country, it was very
favorable to the plan of Napoleon and his small.
disposable force.

613. *Plan of Campaign.*—The Allies had but
one objective point, Paris. This capital in their
possession, they knew they would be able to.
dictate a peace.

614. Having put everything in train at Paris,.
Napoleon proceeded to Chalons, on the Marne,.
where he arrived Jan. 25, 1814; his whole force
under his hand not exceeding 47,000 men.
Whilst all his generals saw nothing but disaster,
from the great disparity of the contending forces,
Napoleon endeavored to infuse hope and confidence into all. Looking at the great arc which
the Allies were dispersed over, from Belgium to.
Switzerland, and the consequent difficulty of
their being able to concentrate on any point, by
a given time, Napoleon, than whom none ever
weighed better the influences of the chances of
war, and the blunders of leaders, entertained
reasonable prospects of being able to take advantage of some of these necessary openings to success. Having at the outset placed the Marshals.
above named on the Vosges, between Epinal
and Langres, to observe and check the Austrians,
Napoleon intended to fall first upon Blucher, who
was advancing on the Marne, by St. Dizier, and,
having forced him back, to throw himself next
upon the Austro-Russians, under Schwartzen-

*berg, on his right, who were advancing on the Seine. To accomplish these ends, he adopted the Aube, from its central position with respect to the Seine and Marne, as his line of communi-cation with Paris; the main road passing through Ferté-sous-Jouarre, Sezanne, and Arcis and Brienne on the Aube. Upon this line he collected his supplies, ordering each dépôt to be strengthened with such resources as field fortifi-cations could supply.

615. *Active Operations.*—In pursuance of this plan, Napoleon moved on St. Dizier, Jan. 26, and drove the enemy from it, and, crossing from there to Brienne, he, on Jan. 29, attacked and drove Blucher from Brienne.

616. The Allies, from the dispersed state of their forces, were laboring under a considerable military disadvantage, as Blucher was obliged to keep up his connexion with the forces in Bel-gium, to march on Paris by Chalons, whilst Schwartzenberg directed his column on the same point, by Troyes on the Seine, to preserve his connexion with the forces in Switzerland. On January 30, however, the Allies had concen-trated around La Rothière, a little to the south of Brienne, a force of 170,000 men, whilst Na-poleon had only 30,000. With this force the Allies attacked Napoleon, who, after a desperate resistance, to avoid being forced into the Aube, retired towards Troyes, at which place he re-mained until Feb. 8, keeping all the while on the alert, to profit by any blunder of the enemy.

617. After the success of La Rothière, the Al-lied plan was, for Blucher to collect the forces coming from Belgium, and marching by the Marne, gain Napoleon's rear, whilst Schwartz-

enberg should move by the Seine, and Wittgenstein, with a considerable corps, mostly of cavalry, was to move along the Aube, keeping up thus a
connexion between Blucher and Schwartzenberg.

618. Blucher, with his usual impetuosity,
pushed forward rapidly on Meaux, driving the
French before him, but, at the same time, leaving his forces in a very scattered state, from
Chalons to Ferté, along the Marne, and also upon the Aube. Schwartzenberg, on the contrary,
moved slowly and timidly on Troyes, and re-
called even Wittgenstein from the Aube to cover
his flank.

619. Seeing this state of the Allies, Napoleon
covered Paris by a corps holding the bridges
over the Seine and Yonne; and pushing Marmont to Nogent, and then on Sezanne, giving
Ney orders to follow him, he, with Mortier, prepared to bring up the rear, thus concentrating
30,000 men, directed on Blucher's flank. From
Sezanne, Napoleon moved, Feb. 10, on Champaubert, where he disperses a Russian corps,
capturing the general and his staff; and, on the
11th, on Montmirail, in face of the Russians, defeating first Sacken with heavy losses, and next,
turning on Yorck, defeats and drives him
through Chateau-Thierry. Having accomplished this he returned towards Champaubert, near
which place Marmont had taken position, having
been forced back by Blucher and joining Marmont,
and assuming the offensive, he drives back the
Prussians on Etoges, from which they were driven during the night of Feb. 14. Thus, in these
four combats, without any general engagement,
Napoleon deprived the Allies, numbering 60,000
men, of 28,000, a large quantity of artillery, and
a number of flags.

620. In the meantime, Schwartzenberg moved forward, forcing some of the bridges over the Seine and Yonne, towards Fontainebleau, the French generals opposing him retreating behind the small river Yéres, and waiting for Napoleon's movement.

621. Leaving Marmont to watch and check Blucher should he advance, Napoleon, on Feb. 14, with a part of his guard, moved on Montmirail. Here two plans presented themselves to him. The one, with only 25,000 men at his disposal, to cross from the Marne, by cross roads, to the Seine, and attack the dispersed corps of the Austrians in flank. The other, to move by the road, through Meaux, on Fontenay, just south of it, near the Yéres, collect the corps of Victor and Oudinot by the way, which would swell his force to 60,000, and then attack the Austrians in front. He decided for the latter, as the cross roads were bad, and as on this last line he had an excellent highway, gained a large accession of strength, and had every prospect of throwing himself upon the rear of the more advanced of the enemy's corps, and thus cut them off.

622. Putting this resolution into immediate execution, Napoleon pushed forward his columns on Meaux, where he arrived in person, Feb. 15, and, on the 16th, joined Victor, and put his column in motion, on the 17th, from Guignes, a small place south of Meaux. Encountering the advanced guard of Wittgenstein at Mormant, he drives it from there, causing it considerable loss, and marches by Nangis upon the bridges over the Seine at Montereau, Bray, and Nogent, expecting, in this way, to cut the enemy's column. This well devised plan was defeated by the un-

seasonable delay of Victor at Nangis, as it enabled the enemy to take measures to dispute the passage of these bridges. The bridge of Montereau being finally forced, with considerable loss to both parties, Napoleon intended to recross the Seine at Méry, to the east of this last place, and then offer battle to the Allies in front of Troyes. Having, with much loss of time, crossed the Seine at Montereau, Napoleon, having now about 70,000 men, reached Nogent, Feb. 22.

623. Blucher, in the meantime, decided to move from the Marne to the Seine and join Schwartzenberg, and thus reached Méry Feb. 23, the point on which Napoleon was also moving. Schwartzenberg, however, had retired to Chaumont on the Marne, leaving a corps at Bar, on the Aube; and Blucher then took position at Méry and Arcis on the Aube, but, Feb. 24, passed the Aube at Anglure, and moved on Sezanne, to the north of it. Continuing this movement, he endeavored to cut off Marmont and Victor, who eluded him, and took up a strong position behind the Marne, and the Ourcq a small tributary of the Marne, which falls into it a little to the east of Meaux.

624. Napoleon, seeing this movement of Blucher, resolves to follow him, and throw him upon the Marne, resorting to a stratagem to deceive the Austrians as to his being in front of them. Moving by Sezanne, he reached Ferté on the Marne, March 2. Blucher, now finding Napoleon on his rear, and Marmont and Victor in front, moved off rapidly, March 3, hoping to connect with the Russians at Soissons on the Aisne. Napoleon immediately passed the Marne

in pursuit, passing by Oulchy to Fismes, to cut off Blucher's retreat in that direction, and force him to accept battle with the Aisne behind him.

625. There hemmed in, there was no door of escape for Blucher but through Soissons, which was secure from a *coup-de-main*, and could have withstood any attempt to take it, at least twenty-four hours. Unfortunately for the fortunes of Napoleon, this key of the Aisne was given up, through the imbecility of its commandant. The Russians, to the number of 40,000, not only escaped, but were joined by 60,000 Russians on the other side of the Aisne.

626. Having lost this opportunity, and being under the necessity of beating Blucher before again moving on Schwartzenberg, Napoleon surprised a passage of the Aisne, at three points above Soissons, on March 6th, and, on the 7th, attacked the strong position of the Russians and Prussians on the heights of Craonne, which he carried after a fierce struggle and considerable losses. Giving his army some rest, on March 8, he moved in pursuit of the Allies towards Laon on the 9th; Marmont, at the same time, closing in on the left of the Allies, took up, at night, a position too open and advanced, from which he was stampeded and forced back with loss. On the 10th, a desperate assault was made on Laon, a small place of great natural strength, in which having failed, Napoleon was forced to fall back on Soissons, having only about 40,000 men and leaving the Allies with 90,000.

627. With this disaster closed all hope of retrieving the fortunes of the day. To use his own words, "Providence had in this case shown himself on the side of the heavy battalions."

Though still struggling with the same firmness, activity, and fertility of resources; checking and causing his opponents to retrograde at his every movement; displaying still his unparalleled skill in handling troops; the odds against him were too great, both in the numbers of the Allies and the hopelessness of his own best officers. Fairly surrounded by the enemy's forces, he contemplated for a moment the plan of retiring towards the frontier fortresses, and there, collecting their garrisons, to force the Allies to forego their prey of Paris, which they were about to clutch, to follow his movements in their rear and on their line of retreat. This last brilliant scintillation was quenched by the stern realities of his position; and quitting St. Dizier March 28, 1814, where he had opened this marvellous campaign by storming it Dec. 26, 1813, he reached Paris only in time to take measures for his first abdication.

628. It is hardly necessary to point out the strategical features of this campaign. Selecting an interior line to operate on, we see Napoleon, with forces greatly inferior in numbers and many of them mere conscripts, throw himself first upon one column and then on the other of the Allies, operating on two exterior lines. To this advantage of position, we must add the *prest'ge* of Napoleon's presence; his wonderful activity and physical endurance; and then the characters of the two leading generals, Schwartzenberg and Blucher, with which he was well acquainted, who were opposed to him. The former slow and pushing prudence to timidity, thus losing opportunities by too tardy an advance, or retiring upon the least appearance of danger; the

latter reckless, and, in his hatred of France, following rather the dictates of his passion than
those of purely military reasons, thus constantly
putting himself and his army in jeopardy. And
last, though not least, the condition of Napoleon's own lieutenants, who, worn down by
such incessant warfare, were sighing for repose,
and who had now begun to look upon the fortunes of their leader as irretrievable. The private soldiers alone stood firm, and were ready
for every sacrifice; but in this, as in all similar
cases, discouragement commenced at the top
and descended to the ranks, only when the latter found there were none to head them.

629. *Influence of Fortifications.*—In this as well
as in several of the preceding campaigns, particularly the one of 1806 against Prussia, the invading armies passed by the fortified places,
leaving them in their rear, and taking no other
precautions than, in some cases, to detach a
small force to watch their garrisons. These examples have caused some military writers to call
in question the utility of fortified places in any
defensive system; a view fortunately unsupported by any eminent military authority. With
the immense invading armies with which Napoleon operated in Germany and Russia, from the
campaign of 1805 up to that of 1814, he was enabled to pursue this system of depending on
beating and dispersing the enemy's armies in the
field, looking, as a natural consequence, to the
fall of the fortified places, the garrisons of which,
being feeble and unsupported, could not be expected to offer any resistance to the overwhelming forces that could be brought against them.
The same was true of the invasion of France by

the Allies in 1814. But we have seen that, in the campaign of 1796, Bonaparte, although he had driven the Austrians, in a demoralized condition, into the German Tyrol, and wished to push forward by the same route to Vienna, did not think it prudent to leave the strong place of Mantua, with a competent garrison, in his rear. In the campaigns in the Spanish Peninsula, where the armies were smaller and more evenly matched, sieges were frequent and indispensable operations, and the success or failure of a campaign depended upon the termination of these means of gaining time and consuming the enemy's active forces. Had Napoleon in 1813 been able to have held in check the Allied armies, he would have found the fortified places in Germany, in which, to the weakening of his active force, he·had thrown garrisons sufficiently strong to hold them against a *coup-de-main*, of the most essential importance, in any favorable turn in his affairs. Had Soissons been stronger, or even been resolutely held for a few hours, or had the inconsiderable place of Laon not afforded the support it did to the Allies, Blucher and his army would, in all likelihood, have been destroyed, and the Russians on the other side of the Aisne have been driven far beyond the zone of operations of the Allies on the Seine. But still more important to the success of Napoleon's plans would have been even one or two places of some moment on his central position, between the Aube and Paris, and especially had Paris itself been encircled with fortifications secure from an open assault. With these aids, his comparatively small active forces would have been doubled in value. The audacity of Blucher would have

been checked, or severely punished, and the
timid Schwartzenberg would have put still less
than he did, to the hazards of Napoleon's skill
and daring.

630. *Marches.*—In the descriptions of the preceding campaigns, the influence of marches skilfully combined and executed has been fully demonstrated. No general perhaps of any age has
shown such striking abilities as Napoleon in this
respect. This was the result not only of administrative and executive talents of the highest
order, but of the intimate knowledge he had acquired of the most minute details of every branch
of the service, by the most indefatigable industry.

631. As strategical operations, marches may
be divided into two principal classes; those of
concentration beyond the sphere of action of the
enemy; and those of *manœuvre* executed within
this sphere. In the former the forces are only
brought to that point where the latter commences. In the campaign of 1805, we have
seen how the two corps in Hanover and Holland, under Bernadotte and Marmont, were directed upon Wurtzburg, whilst those on the
English channel were directed on the Rhine, between Mannheim and Strasburg. Having reached these points without any apprehension of an
enemy's presence, the grand manœuvre for
throwing them on the enemy's right flank and
rear commenced; those columns on the right,
being nearer the enemy, moving more slowly,
and having their flank nearest the enemy carefully guarded by a corps assigned to this service;
those on the left, moving more rapidly and pivoting on the right, whilst the whole was so com-

bined that in a few hours a large force could be concentrated on any fraction, if unexpectedly attacked whilst carrying out this grand movement.

632. In the second splendid campaign of Napoleon in Germany against the Austrians, that of 1809, the same admirable series of provisions is to be seen. Seeing the evidently hostile attitude of Austria, the first step of Napoleon was to mass his forces at those points from which they could be rapidly thrown upon the Austrian dominions. For this purpose, he chose Wurtzburg, Augsburg, and Strasburg, Pl. XI., as the points for concentration. On and towards the first point, he directed the major part of his forces from Saxony and from the north of Germany. On the second, the forces in the neighborhood of Hanau. On the third; those from the interior of France. Whilst in Italy he directed Prince Eugene, with 50,000 men, to approach the Frioul. These, with other minor movements, drew around Austria another of those Napoleonic meshworks which had already proved so disastrous to her. The Austrian army of 200,000 men were to concentrate in the neighborhood of Ratisbonne, on the Danube; part on one side, and a part on the other side of this stream, but so as to render mutual assistance. Not knowing where he with certainty should find the main body of the Austrians, Napoleon decided upon trusting nothing to mere hazard, but to be governed in his movements by recognised military principles. To this end he withdrew Davoust from Ratisbonne, on the Danube, and threw forward Massena, so as to concentrate his entire force at Abensberg, a small place on the

river Abens, and about midway between Ingoldstadt and Ratisbonne. Here he decided to
break through the Austrian centre, thus separating the two Archdukes, Charles and Louis.
In these plans, he was aided by the tardiness of
movement of the Austrians upon which he
counted, and also by the state of the weather, by
which the roads were much injured. The result
of these skilfully combined marches was that the
Archduke Charles was forced upon Ratisbonne,
and obliged to retreat across the Danube into
Bohemia; the other main fraction of the Austrian army retiring successively behind the Inn
and the Traunn, leaving the road to Vienna
open to Napoleon.

633. In this conjuncture of operations, Napoleon, after considering the military aspect of
affairs, decided to march direct upon Vienna. In
taking this step he had not only to follow up the
Archduke Louis, but to provide against the
junction of the Archduke Charles with him, by
recrossing the Danube. The principal points
where this passage might have been effected are
Straubing, Passau, Lintz, and Krems. These it
was of the first importance to secure by anticipating the Austrian movements on them. To
carry out these measures, Massena received
orders to descend along the Danube, to be followed by Davoust, and by General Dupas; and
each, in succession, to occupy the places just
mentioned, thus securing the army from an attack either in flank or in rear, by the Austrians
on the left bank of the Danube. At the same
time, Bessières was ordered to push forward beyond Landshut, on the Iser, and keep closely on
the heels of the enemy's retreating column;

whilst Lannes, under the immediate command
of Napoleon, moved between the columns of
Massena and Bessières, so as to throw this force
upon either of these two, as circumstances might
demand. Further to secure his right on their
flank, the Bavarians, his allies, were directed to
occupy Munich, and, pushing from there through
Salsburg into the Tyrol, observe the Archduke
John, and give timely warning of his movements.
These profound combinations met with all the
success they merited. Anticipated by the rapid
movements and daring of the French at every
point, the Archduke Charles was unable to join
the forces on the right bank of the Danube,
which last, despairing of being able to cover
Vienna, effected a crossing to the left bank at
Krems.

634. The disposal of the troops for a march
and the manner of executing it belong to the
practical details of the profession, for which specific rules are laid down in every service; and
with which it is presumed that every man who
accepts the responsibility of a general's position
has made himself acquainted. All of this may
be summed up in a few words. First, the trains
of every description must be covered by the
troops, for which purpose they must, in an
advance movement, be either in the rear, or on
that flank where they will be least exposed to
the enemy. In a retreat they must be in advance. When an army moves in several nearly
parallel columns, the combination must be such
that an imposing force can soon be concentrated
on any point threatened. The divisions of each
column must, in like manner, be in supporting
distance of each other, but, for convenience, not

23

crowded on the march. As to advanced guards, flankers and rear guards, both their strength and composition must depend on the general's judgment, founded on the force, character, and position of the enemy, and of the nature of the country through which the march is made. Just in proportion as he has read, has reflected, has had opportunities for action, will his judgment lead him to take right measures; whilst still more certainly, if he has wanted these aids to forming an enlightened judgment, will he take wrong ones. Let no man be so rash as to suppose that, in donning a general's uniform, he is forthwith competent to perform a general's functions; as reasonably might he assume that in putting on the robes of a judge he was ready to decide any point of law.

CHAPTER IX.

BATTLES.

635. BATTLES, though planned and fought almost solely on tactical principles, have in many cases important strategical bearings which it is the province of an able general to see and to take advantage of. Skilfully combined strategical marches, when ably executed, may alone decide the fate of a campaign, without the necessity of coming into collision with the enemy; but this is a rare case, and a battle is usually the necessary sequence to an important strategical movement, and, if well planned and successfully fought, may prove decisive of the war.

636. *Orders of Battle.*—Military writers designate by this expression the general combinations made to attack one or more points of an enemy's position; whilst they apply the term *line of battle* to the disposition of the troops, in their relations to each other for mutual co-operation, acting either offensively or defensively.

637. Whatever may be the disposition of the troops, the line of battle of any considerable force will present a well defined centre and two wings; thus offering to an assailant one or more of these as his point of attack. This has led to dividing orders of battle into several classes, arising from the necessary disposition of the assailing force, as it moves to attack one or more of these points.

638. If an equal effort is made to assail every

point of the enemy's line, the assailing force
must necessarily advance on a line parallel to the
one assailed, and this therefore has received the
name of the *parallel order of battle*. If the line
of the assailing force is sensibly perpendicular to
that of the assailed, the disposition is said to be
the *perpendicular order*. If the main attack is
made by one wing, the centre and other wing
being held back, or *refused* as it is termed, the
positions of the lines of the two parties become
naturally oblique to each other, and this is termed the *oblique order*. In like manner, the *concave
order* results from an attack by both wings, the
centre being refused, and the *convex order* from
refusing the wings and attacking by the centre,
&c.

639. The order of battle should result from
the position in which the enemy's forces are presented for attack; and as these, if skilfully disposed, will be posted so as to take advantage of
the points of vantage which the position they
occupy offers, the order of battle for assailing
may vary in an infinity of ways. Still it is not
to be inferred that one order is not superior to
another, or that the choice between them is one
at pleasure. In the parallel order, for example,
the opposing forces being supposed equal in all
points, there is no reason why one point of the
enemy's line should be forced rather than
another, and, therefore, success depends either
upon destroying his whole line, or simply pushing it back; as chance alone will determine a
break in any part of his line. In the oblique order, on the contrary, one wing being refused, or
merely acting as a menace, the other may be
strongly reinforced, so as to overwhelm the

wing opposed to it, and, if this succeeds, the assailing army, by its simple onward movement, is gradually brought to gain ground on the enemy's rear, and to threaten his line of retreat. Again, in crossing a river on a bridge, or passing through any other defile to assail an enemy opposing this movement, the order of battle becomes necessarily convex; the extremity of the defile itself becoming the centre from which the assailing forces radiate, to enlarge their front, whilst they are obliged to secure the defile on each flank. To lay down rules therefore as to what order of battle should, in every case, be employed would be pure pedantry. Talent, skill, and experience can alone enable a general to decide this point in any given case.

640. *Line of Battle.*—Whether acting offensively or defensively, troops of the same arm, as well as those of different arms, must be so disposed as not only to lend mutual support, but not to obstruct or impede each other's operations. On this point there are rules so self-evident that it would seem almost unnecessary to repeat them; yet they have been violated, with the loss of battles consequent on them, by some generals of fair abilities and experience; whilst others of great military skill have done the same, through necessity, with successful results. But let not this tempt any man to throw aside well established precedent to depend on the inspiration of the moment. There is no surer way to bring down defeat and disaster.

641. Defensive battles are usually fought upon positions selected beforehand, with the defensive properties of which the general is supposed to have made himself master. With this know-

270

ledge, he should be able to dispose the different arms to the best advantage for injuring and repulsing the enemy. In this case, he naturally seeks so to post his troops that he may obtain the greatest amount of fire, upon every point of approach on his position, whilst, at the same time, the troops may find shelter from that of the enemy. The occupation of heights, woods, undulations of ground, stone or brick houses, stone fences, and of slight field works thrown up at the moment, as each of these present themselves along the front and flanks of his position, by his infantry and artillery, are obvious measures. The judgment of course will find play here so to select among several points as to obtain the best results sought. The disposition of the troops will depend on the relation between their number and the extent of the position. Where the troops are in excess, they must necessarily be disposed in several successive lines; placing, as far as practicable, all who cannot take a part in the earlier phases of the action far enough beyond the range of fire to secure them from damage. Where there is a deficiency in numbers, a single line may have to be resorted to, and the intervals of battalions, &c., increased; but it is obvious that, except in ground of a very difficult nature to an enemy's approach, this would be a very weak distribution of the troops. But these are extreme cases. The normal distribution of infantry being that of two lines for mutual support; and a reserve ready to prevent or repair disaster, and to make, when the opportunity offers, a decisive stroke. As to the distances between the lines, and the intervals left in each line, these again

must depend on the judgment of the commanding general and his subordinates. Whilst they
endeavor to expose no troops to fire which are
not themselves engaged, they must see that their
second line is near enough to support the first,
at every new position taken up by the assailant.
Battalions will, to this end, be placed either immediately behind those they are to support, opposite their intervals, or more or less to the
right or left, as the ground may favor, and as, by
so doing, the necessary manœuvres of one or
both lines shall not be impeded. Like considerations apply to the battalion, brigade, and division
intervals of each line. All of this supposes at
least plain good sense, and some experience on
the part of the commanding officers.

642. The positions chosen for the artillery will
be wherever they can get the widest and longest
range. This may require the batteries, in some
cases, to be distributed throughout the front of
the position; in others to be massed. In the latter case, the effects upon any one point will be
the more staggering to the enemy, but risk of
greater loss is run, should the enemy throw himself upon and capture the artillery so massed.
A gap in a line has been filled by artillery, but the
general, who would imitate this, should be very
certain of the other arms by which his artillery
is supported. Raking fires along roads, &c.,
cross fires over wide open spaces, and concentrated fires upon openings that cannot be raked,
such are the services that the general should endeavor to secure from his artillery.

643. As for cavalry it has no passive defensive
properties; in the defensive therefore it must be
kept out of fire, until called upon to act offen-

sively to support either the infantry, or the artillery when hard pushed. This of course it can only do where horses can be led to the charge. Here the general has to show his knowledge of what this arm can reasonably be called upon to perform. That it has sometimes charged up or down steep broken ground, where infantry might have found an advance not easy, that it has swum rivers, and dashed up against fortifications, are all very creditable to the audacity of this arm; but no general, in making his distribution of it, would count upon seeing it of course perform such feats.

614. *Phases of Defensive Battle.*—The artillery, of course, opens the ball and keeps on thundering, and holding on to its position as long as its fire can be made telling from it; losing no time in shifting about. Next come into play the light troops, who, as sharpshooters, have taken up every advanced cover to meet the enemy by their fire far off; these too hold on for dear life, as every man picked off destroys not only one, but demoralizes his neighbors. When they are forced back, they judiciously, both for their own skins and to let the enemy have the benefit of it, slip into the rear, by any opening not likely to be swept by the fire of the first line. Now comes into play the deadly volley firing, which soon runs into that of every man for himself. It is now that the second line becomes all alive. Now that the reserve is kept firmly in hand and bid to keep cool. If forced to yield, the first line, without scampering, should soon leave an open field between the second and the enemy; and the second must have well made up its mind that the bayonet must be finally their re-

liance for a decisive stroke; knowing that the reserve is still behind them, untouched and ready for any work. As to throwing forward the reserve, if the commanding general's eye and instinctive appreciation of the moment do not lead him to seize it, no written rules, however elaborate, will.

645. *Offensive Batt'es.*—To know what we are going to encounter is half the battle in almost all affairs of life; for we are, thus far, secure from the surprise of finding something in our way that we had not counted upon. In no transaction is this beforehand knowledge more important than in preparing for a battle. There is hardly any labor, any personal risk to which a general should not subject himself to gain precise and accurate information on this head. Here he must see for himself, at the risk of finding his orders misconstrued, and his plans defeated by the carelessness or stupidity of his subordinates.

646. A personal reconnoissance therefore of the enemy's position is indispensable, and if this is made on the eve of the attack the general should take another last look in the morning, before moving, to see that the enemy has not anticipated him, and taken steps that call for changes on his part. Of course, whatever is advantageous to the defensive will particularly engage his attention; but, as his great object is, not only to drive back the enemy, but to bring on him a great disaster, the chief point to which he will bend his thoughts, will be to see by what mode and by what point of attack he can secure the greatest strategical results.

647. Considerations therefore both of a tactical and strategical character must receive the

careful examination of the commanding general, in deciding upon his plan of attack. The first, as carrying with it the most important advantage, is the strategical result; the two principal of which are, first, either to direct the main effort upon that wing of the enemy which, if overthrown, will naturally bring us on the line of retreat of his forces, or, second, upon some point between his two wings which, if pierced, may force his disconnected forces on divergent lines of retreat, and thus expose them to the disaster of being beaten in detail, or to the capture or destruction of one of the fractions. In the battle of Austerlitz, for example, in which the Allies at first acted offensively, their plan was made subservient wholly to the strategical result. The right of the French position was nearest to their line of retreat on Vienna; by forcing this point, the Allies would have been brought between the French and Vienna, thus throwing them further from their base. If repulsed in this attempt, the Allies still covered their own line of retreat, so long as their centre and right held firm. The strategical object of Napoleon, on the contrary, was to pierce the Allied centre, and thus secure the advantages of a successful operation of this kind.

648. Next in importance come what may be termed the *grand tactical* considerations; that is, the means of doing most damage to the enemy on the field of battle itself. For example, if the enemy's position is such that he has an impassable obstacle on one of his wings, as a river, lake, or a narrow defile, tactical considerations alone would suggest to direct our main attack on the opposite wing, as, by defeating this, the centre

and remaining wing may be thrown upon the obstruction which it either cannot pass, or must pass with difficulty, and thus be captured or greatly cut up. In like manner, tactical considerations would engage us to attack a height on the enemy's position which, if gained, would give our forces a decided advantage, or, if his line of battle presents a very salient point, upon which our efforts can be concentrated to attack this point; or if his line at any point presents a wide break, into which we can force our way, to do so; any one of these points if gained would give decided tactical advantage.

649. Though not necessarily leading to the same decisive results as the two preceding, a third consideration, in choosing the point of attack, is the facility which the natural features of the ground, over which we must move upon it, afford for the combined operation of the troops of the different arms that are to make the attack. Too much weight, however, is not to be given to this, in selecting the point of attack; as ground, however difficult, may almost always be got over by troops of all arms, and very often it more than compensates for the labor of doing so, by the cover and other advantages it may afford in advancing.

650. In the battle of Austerlitz the tactical advantages were greatly against the Allied point of attack, as they, in the first place, had to advance against the villages occupied by the French and through narrow, hollow roads, in which their columns became confused and disordered; and they had moreover, on the flank and rear, several ponds, with only narrow causeways between them, on which, if thrown, there was no outlet of escape except over these narrow defiles,

all of which were exposed to the artillery of the
French. The result, as we know, was a frightful
disaster. Prudence counsels, in all such cases,
to forego the tempting object of a grand result
if to gain it we expose ourselves, if unsuccessful,
to a great disaster. The general who looks forward alone, not providing for his own rear or
flanks, or who, intent only upon some striking
success, rushes recklessly, in the pursuit of it,
within the jaws of destruction, has learned but
half his trade, and that the most easily acquired
and the most dangerous in its application in
such hands.

651. It is in nicely weighing these considerations and selecting the best, that the great general shows his powers. Recognising settled principles as his guides, he does not apply them
blindly. Finding, for example, his opponent in
a position as Pl. VII., Fig. 19, having his line of
battle, A,B, oblique to his line of retreat, A,C; his
right resting on high ground, and his left on an
impassable marsh, or river, there could be no
hesitation as to selecting A as the point of attack ;
since, by carrying it, he naturally cuts the enemy's line of retreat, throws him back on the impassable obstacle, and obtains command of the
field of battle. This is a case where the general,
accepting battle in such a position, and his line
of battle as supposed, has committed the blunder
of following too implicitly the military *dictum*
that the wings should be secured by resting
them on strong features of the position chosen.
The wing B fulfils this condition, whilst A, occupying the heights, has a commanding view of
the field of battle ; still the position is a dangerous one, and the risk to the assailant, if repulsed,

'··it trifling. The better plan here would have
been, for the party on the defensive to have
taken the position c,D, the left resting on the
heights, and the right E,C, thrown back, e · po-
tence as it is termed, with a strong support F.
In this case, if attacked on the left, the assailant
would be obliged to place himself in the perilous
position of an impassable obstacle behind him;
if attacked on the right, the defensive has the
advantages of the heights; and, in either case,
if forced back, the line of retreat is covered.

652. As a further illustration, suppose an
army on the defensive to have taken the position A,B, Pl. VII., Fig. 20, its right wing A, uncovered, its left resting on an impassable obstacle, and its line of retreat being A,C, running
parallel to this obstacle. Here the strategical
consideration would designate B, as the point of
attack, as, this wing being driven back, the army
is cut off from its line of retreat; but, in attempting this the assailant necessarily places
himself between the assailed and the impassable
obstacle, and thus exposes himself to a great disaster if repulsed. Here prudence and sound
principle dictate rather to attack at A, and by
vigorous pursuit, if successful, endeavor to reap
every advantage.

653. Although but one point, known as the
key-point, is usually selected for the main effort
of the assailant, still the whole line of the assailed is more or less menaced, to prevent the
key-point from receiving reinforcements. A
different course, one by which we endeavor, so
to speak, to envelope the assailed, can only be
attempted with a prospect of success, when we
are greatly superior in force. Had the Allies at

24

Austerlitz, instead of pressing with such vigor
the French left whilst they weakened their centre in moving on the French right, thus leaving
the plateau of Pratzen a comparatively easy
prey to the French, simply menaced the left and
held the plateau with a strong force, not succeeded in their main attack, they would at least
have avoided the subsequent disaster.

654. Connected with enveloping attacks is
that of sending a strong detachment, by a circuitous route, to fall on the enemy's rear, whilst
an attack is made on him in front. Such manœuvres are wrong in principle, and military
history presents striking instances of their failure
in practice. The topographical features of the
immediate theatre of operations can alone determine whether to risk turning operations.
When this is in a very broken or obstructed
country so that such a movement may be concealed for the time necessary to perform it, the
risk will be less, but the chances are still against
it. As an example of such a case, let us suppose,
Pl. VII., Fig. 21, an army holding the position
N, covering Q, and that the line of operations P,Q,
of the assailant is covered on one flank by an
impassable river, whilst on the other the region
is mountainous, but having roads which lead to
the rear of N. Taking advantage of a tributary
covering his line of communication, the assailant,
by posting a detachment, M, behind it, sending
another, N, to occupy the height on the right,
behind which the road leads, so as to cover the
flank march of the main force, might move by
this road with safety, and, taking the position
M, turn the army N, and thus force it to retire, or
to accept battle under dangerous circumstances.

If repulsed, the main body, M, could retire with safety, as the two detachments, M and N, would secure it from either an attack in flank, or in rear. The principle then is, that, in all turning movements, or attacks in flank, the assailant exposes himself to a like attack, and he should, therefore, only attempt them when the ground is peculiarly favorable to the movement.

655. An attack on the centre is the obvious operation when the enemy's line is too extended for the number of his forces. It may also be the best course when the enemy's line of retreat is through a defile in the rear of his centre, as, in case of success, each wing is cut off from the line of retreat, and the troops of the centre, if forced upon the defile, cannot escape from a serious disaster. Where both flanks of the enemy's position are secure, and it becomes a case of necessity to attack, some point of the front must be selected for the main effort, which, if gained, will give a decided advantage. For example, if there is a commanding eminence on his front, every effort should be made to carry it, as, from there, the field of battle being overlooked the enemy would be obliged to fall back. In this case the order of battle would necessarily become *convex;* the divisions of the centre, to make the assault, being in advance, whilst their flanks and rear would be secured by the divisions of the wings advancing in echelon, those nearest the centre being most advanced.

656. Eliminating all exceptional local features, the general case which presents itself is that, where the entire line of the enemy is equally exposed, and where success therefore depends upon the ability of the assailant to keep the

whole line so threatened that its reserve alone can be moved with safety from one point to another, whilst a powerful effort with concentrated forces is made on some one point, usually one of the wings. In this case the assailing wing will be strongly reinforced, particularly with artillery; the centre also strengthened, whilst the opposite wing will be refused, the divisions receding from towards the centre, in echelon, so as to parry any attempt at turning them, or at making a flank attack on this part.

657. The only general rules that can be well laid down for the distribution of the different arms on the field of battle have already been given. Details on this point must be necessarily left to the subordinates, who, if well acquainted with the true functions and resources of their respective arms, will seldom fail to post them so as to do as much injury to the enemy and be exposed to as little danger to themselves as the natural features of the field of battle will admit of. The plan of the battle having been decided on, the manœuvres to carry it out should be as simple as possible, so as to guard against the failures that almost invariably attend any attempt at complex movements, within striking distance of the enemy. All distributions for what are termed passages of lines should be avoided, even in the case of thoroughly drilled troops. The distribution of infantry in echelons, wherever it can be adopted, is one of the best, as each division has its support at hand on its flank, whilst the interval left between the flank of the one in advance and that of the one next it in rear, should offer sufficient space for cavalry or artillery to move forward to the front if wanted.

658. As to the distribution of troops belonging to the separate fractions of the entire force, as an army corps, a division, &c., the rule is to so distribute them that they shall fight under the immediate eye of their respective commanders, and support each other. Having, for example, a division, composed of four brigades, to distribute in line of battle, the question may arise as to whether all four of the brigades shall be in one line, the first, for instance, or two be in the first and two in the second line. By the first distribution, the four brigades will be under the immediate eye of the division commander, but their supports of the second line may be a stranger division, and be led by a general, a rival, or enemy of their own commander. In the second case, the commanding general, being separated from the two divisions in the first line, will not be able to give them that direct supervision as in the first case; but a more hearty cooperation of the brigades and more unity of concert may be looked for than in the contrary case.

659. This branch of the subject may be closed by some examples of supposed cases which may aid in fixing the essential principles. That all may not be left to hazard, some regulations on this subject have to be laid down; variations in these, according to circumstances, must depend on the general's ability to adapt his troops to the position they are to fight on.

660. The first case, Pl. XII., one supposed by Dufour, is the distribution of an army of about 37,000 troops of all arms, to attack an enemy's position. the main effort being directed on the enemy's left wing, our left being refused. This force he supposes to be organized as follows:

24*

40 battalions of 750 men each,	30,000
12 squadrons " 120 "	1,440
18 batteries, 72 pieces, 130 men each	2,340
30 companies of sharpshooters,	3,000
2 companies engineer troops,	200

| Total, | 36,980 |

661. In this organization, it will be noticed that the proportion of cavalry to the infantry is very small, and that but two guns are allowed to every thousand men; proportions which would be only suitable for a theatre of war in which cavalry would but rarely find any but a very confined field of action, and in the case also of excellent infantry, which admits of a reduction in the amount of artillery.

662. Having divided the battalions of infantry into four divisions, one of these is taken to form part of the reserve, to which is assigned the whole of the cavalry, and all the disposable artillery, and the sharpshooters.

663. The other three divisions are designed to move on the right, the centre, and the left of the enemy's position. As the main attack is on the right, ten companies of sharpshooters are attached to it, and five to each of the other two; ten being with the reserve.

664. In the attack on the right and centre, each division, when formed in line of battle, is to occupy only a front of four battalions, the remaining six of each to be so placed, in second or third line, as the respective generals of division may deem best.

665. Five battalions of the left division will deploy, in echelon, on the left of the second di-

vision; the remaining five being in column to the rear, so as to move to the support of either the second, or third division, as circumstances may demand.

666. Having decided upon this preliminary plan of attack, the three first divisions are put in motion on their respective points, the heads of column on the same level; the reserve following the centre column.

667. The advance of each leading column will be covered by an advanced guard, composed of the sharpshooters, and the flank companies of the leading brigade of each, and by one battery of artillery.

668. The deployment will be that which naturally results from the positions of the brigades in column of march; each brigade forming one line, its artillery on the right, the sharpshooters in the intervals of the battalions, and the flank companies on the wings.

669. So soon as the three advanced guards, which are from 1,000 to 1,500 paces in advance of their respective columns, have come within good range, the sharpshooters are thrown out as skirmishers, the flank companies supporting them, each of these companies keeping nearly opposite to the battalion to which it belongs. The artillery, in the mean time, having opened at a convenient range for its round shot.

670. The skirmishers stick to their work until they are either repulsed, or called in, when they will retire behind the flank companies; one half of these last forming the new chain of skirmishers, the other half the supports; and, in this order, they fall back, but keeping up their fire, to the intervals between the battalions. The sharp-

shooters then take position to the rear of the
first line in the battalion intervals; the flank
companies doubling on the wings; and the batteries, which have thus been unmasked, proceeding, on a trot, to the front, to pour in a heavy
continued fire on the enemy. The two first divisions in this way enter into the engagement;
the third merely covering its position by its batteries.

671. This stage of the action is here shown on
the plate as the intentions of the commanding
general may have been interpreted by his subordinates. The commander of the first division
has taken a battalion from each of his lines to
form a small reserve, which he has placed in a
third line, to be ready for any emergency. The
commander of the second division has formed his
first line into two echelons, and has placed a second battalion to support the right one of the
advanced echelon, and has thrown forward all
his sharpshooters into the first line. In disposing of his second brigade, he has placed three
battalions nearer to the centre to strengthen the
troops engaged. The commander of the third
division has deployed the battalions of the first
line in echelons, at 150 paces from each other,
and has thrown out one of his batteries on his
left, giving it the companies of sharpshooters as
a support, with the view of checking any movement on this wing.

672. In the meantime, the general commanding, seeing the affair well under way, has massed
his reserve, in rear of the centre of the first division, seeing the moment come to complete his
stroke, has detached a brigade of the reserve,
four companies of sharpshooters, six batteries,

and the half of his cavalry to the front; giving the artillery orders to take position on the right and left of the batteries of the first division, so as to get a slant fire on the enemy's line; the infantry to mass itself on the right of the artillery, to cover it, and also by proper precautions to guard itself from a flank movement; the cavalry to post itself, in echelon, on the right of the infantry, to prevent a flank movement of the enemy's cavalry. At the same time, two batteries are also sent forward to reinforce those of the second division. To give room for these movements of the batteries, the flank battalions of the first line of the first division are thrown into column in mass, whilst those of the second incline towards the centre so as to avoid being behind the batteries.

673. As the reserve is weakened by these movements, the commanding general orders the second brigade of the third division to take post in rear of the centre of the second division, to be on hand for any emergency.

674. The order of battle which, in the early phase of the engagement, was parallel, has now become oblique. The first division, having kept its centre battalions of the first line deployed until ready to charge, will, for this last stage, throw these two battalions also into column, whilst the battalions of the second line will spring forward and fill the intervals of the first, so as to present an unbroken wall to the enemy. In this way the division will move forward rapidly, bringing down the bayonet, only when within ten or twenty paces of the enemy's line. If the line should be forced to deploy, to again open fire, the battalions of the first line will fall

to the rear, forming as the second, leaving this task to those of the second and the sharpshooters.

This onward movement of the right will be followed by the centre and left, care being taken that the whole movement is performed connectedly.

675. This example gives the spirit of the phases of an action for the case supposed. The problem to be resolved, with the arms now in the hands of troops, being to extend our front as much as possible, without, however, weakening too much our line of battle, so as to bring all the fire we can upon the enemy's line.

676. *Pursuit.*—The more vigorous the pursuit of a broken enemy, the less are his chances of retrieving himself. It is seldom prudent, however, unless in case of evident panic on the part of the enemy, to make a headlong pursuit. It is no unusual thing for an army to be successful on one point and to be beaten on another, thus bringing round a complication equally dangerous to both sides; and which the general, who has best kept his troops in hand, will have the greatest chance to profit from. If the enemy therefore breaks at any one point, it is always the part of good generalship to rally and speedily reorganize the main portion of the successful army, until the state of the whole field is ascertained with some certainty, detaching only a small force of the freshest troops to improve the partial advantage, and prevent the retiring enemy from rallying.

677. This reorganization for pursuit must not however be pushed too far; all that is needed, if the troops can endure more fighting at once,

is to collect the scattered fragments and put them again into marching or battle array, and then lose no further time to follow up success. This is a part of generalship that no theory can teach to one to whom nature has not given the faculties of a general.

678. *Defensive Battles.*—The fact that a party acts on the defensive supposes something wanting either in the numbers or efficiency of his troops; either of which defects can only be remedied by resorting to aids, offered either by nature or art, for restoring the equilibrium between the opposing forces. The requisites of defensive positions have been so much insisted upon, in other places, that it will hardly be necessary to repeat them here. There is but one point that needs to be strongly inculcated, which is that a position should not only be strong tactically, but good strategically. It should not only lend itself to the manœuvres of our troops and to the efficacy of their fire; but, if forced, should favor a safe retreat.

679. The advantages offered by heights for the defensive may induce into serious disaster, a general who takes a position of this kind from purely tactical considerations, without regard to their strategical bearing; or, when this latter consideration does not come up, who looks simply at the defensive properties without examining also the advantages that a skilful enemy, operating offensively, might derive from them.

680. Suppose an army, Pl. VII., Fig. 22, A,B, to occupy a ridge of heights, crossing obliquely its line of retreat x,y; its right resting on an inaccessible obstacle, as a precipice, &c. Now an army, C,I,D, advancing to the assault of this posi-

tion, might look upon it in two aspects. *First,* strategically, seeing that by making the attack on the right, although the ground there is the most difficult, it will force the assailed back, so as to expose his line of retreat, and may therefore be well worth the effort and cost. *Second,* tactically, to assail vigorously the more exposed left wing A, and, throwing it back on the right, necessarily produce a disaster; as the character of the ground, a narrow plateau, is supposed to be such that it will not admit of a change of position of the assailed to meet this attack in front. However otherwise advantageous, it would evidently be imprudent then for a general to take up a position of this kind, unless so superior to the enemy that he will be able to foil an attack on either wing.

681. *Field Works.*—There still remains, however, one more resource to the general, in a similar case, when he has ample time to employ it, and that is fortification. This is one that every great general has, at one time or another, availed himself of; and, in every case, with advantage. Military history is full of examples where the scale of great and decisive battles has turned on the taking or holding a mere field work that had occupied but a few hours time to throw it up. This, however, belongs to the domain of fortification, one of the most difficult as most important branches of the military art, and which demands for its proper exercise, military qualifications of a high order. There probably has existed no great engineer who, when called upon, has not shown himself a superior general; nor a great general who did not fully acknowledge and appreciate the art of

fortification. When persons therefore express themselves of a skilful engineer and say that he is only an engineer, they show their own ignorance, and proclaim themselves as little to be trusted with the command of large bodies of troops.

674. *Distribution of Troops.*—Where an army is forced to accept a defensive battle in an open position, which affords no points on which its flanks can rest with security, there is but one disposition of combat open to it, and that is to secure the wings by such an accumulation and distribution of troops upon them that the assailant will run a greater risk in an attack on one of them than on the front. The centre in this case will be deployed in the first line, so as to bring all its fire to bear, both direct and cross, over the approaches to it. The troops to support the wings will be massed, so as to be ready to act promptly, as the phases of the action may demand; and the reserve will occupy a central position in the rear, from which it can promptly be thrown upon any point pressed by the assailant.

675. It is in such positions that the formation of the order of battle by squares is resorted to when the assailant is very superior in cavalry. This is done either by a formation of small squares by single battalions, or by resorting to larger ones, as to those formed of four or more battalions. The first have the advantage of being very promptly formed, but they afford hardly more interior space than is wanted for their own staff, leaving whatever cavalry and artillery we have to find shelter between the squares. The large squares demand more complication of ma-

25

nœuvre, and more time in their formation, but afford a large interior space, where the caissons of the artillery, and even the cavalry, if in small numbers, may find shelter. In this last disposition some of the artillery would be in battery in front of those angles of the squares where its fires can best sweep the approaches on the two adjacent sides of the square; other portions will be in the intervals of the squares, so as to throw a flank and cross fire over the approaches to them. The sharpshooters may be advanced a little on those angles which are not occupied by the artillery so as to strengthen these weak points. The cavalry, if in sufficient force to charge opportunely, will take post between the squares, where it will be least exposed to the enemy's artillery, and be ready to seize the proper moment for entering into action.

CHAPTER X.

THE word *Army* is used, in either a general or a particular sense, to designate either the whole, or a part of the armed force of the state, whose duties are confined to the land; and, in this respect, it wants that quality which is essential to a word employed as a definition. To embrace therefore all that is comprehended under the term army, in its general sense, we have to resort to the expressions, the *land force*, or the *military force* as distinguished from the *naval force*.

The military force of the United States as at present organized may be represented under the following tabular form.

Regular Army, composed of

Officers who hold commissions for an indefinite period.

Non-Commissioned Officers and Privates who enlist or engage to serve for a definite period.

Volunteers, composed of

Commissioned Officers, Non-Commissioned Officers and Privates, all of whom are enrolled voluntarily only for a definite period.

Militia, composed of

Commissioned Officers, Non-Commissioned Officers and Privates, all persons in the U. S. between the ages of 18 and 45, who, subject to military duty, are enrolled according to law, and required to serve for a definite period.

REGULAR ARMY.

The regular army comprises the *general staff,* the *st ff corps,* and the *line.*

General Staff.—Under this head are comprised the *general officers,* and the officers attached to the departments known as the *adjutant general's department,* the *inspect.rs general,* the *quartermaster's department,* the *subsistence department,* the *medical department,* the *pay department,* the *judge advocate's department,* and the *signal department.*

Staff Corps.—These comprise the *engineer corps,* the *topographical engineer corps,* and the *ordnance corps.*

Line.—The *infantry,* the *cavalry,* and the *artillery,* are comprised under this head.

General Officers.

Major Generals.
Brigadier Generals.

By the Act of July 29, 1861, each Major General is allowed three aides-de-camp to be taken from the Captains or Lieutenants of the army, and each Brigadier General two ldes-de-camp to be taken from the Lieutenants of the army.

By an Act Aug. 5, 1861, the President is authorized " on the recommendation of any Major General of the regular army of the United States, commanding forces of the

United States in the field," to appoint, temporarily, at
discretion, aides-de-camp with the rank of Captain, Major, Lieutenant Colonel, and Colonel. This Act was re-
pealed by the Act July 17, 1862, leaving, however, those
aides-de-camp appointed under the Act Aug. 5, 1862, in
the enjoyment of their rank and offices.

Adjutant General's Department.

1 Adjutant-General with the rank of Brigadier General.
2 Assistant Adjutants General with the rank
of Colonel.
4 Assistant Adjutants General with the rank
of Lieut. Colonel.
13 Assistant Adjutants General with the rank
of Major.

Inspectors General.

3 Inspectors General with the rank of Colonel.
5 Assistant Inspectors General with the rank
of Major.

Judge Advocate's Department.

1 Judge Advocate General.
1 Judge Advocate with the rank of Major.

By the Act July 17, 1862, a Judge Advocate with the rank
of Major is allowed to each army in the field.

Signal Officers' Department.

1 Signal Officer with the rank of Major.

Quartermaster's Department.

1 Quartermaster General with the rank of
Brigadier General.

25*

2 Assistant Quartermasters General with the rank of Colonel.

4 Deputy Quartermasters General with the rank of Lieut. Colonel.

12 Quartermasters with the rank of Major.

42 Assistant Quartermasters with the rank of Captain.

> By the Act Aug. 3, 1861, each Assistant Quartermaster having served 14 years in the grade of Captain is entitled to be promoted to the grade of Major.
> Ten military storekeepers are attached to the Quartermaster's department, and as many master wagoners as sergeants, and as many wagoners as corporals, as the President shall direct.

Subsistence Department.

1 Commissary General with the rank of Colonel.

1 Assistant Commissary General with the rank of Lieut. Colonel.

6 Commissaries with the rank of Major.

16 Commissaries with the rank of Captain.

Medical Department.

1 Surgeon General with the rank of Brigadier General.

1 Assistant Surgeon General with the rank of Colonel.

1 Medical Inspector General with the rank of Colonel.

8 Medical Inspectors with the rank of Lieut. Colonel.

49 Surgeons with the rank of Major.

14 Assistant Surgeons with the rank of Captain.

100 Assistant Surgeons with the rank of a Lieutenant.

By the Act Aug. 8, 1861, fifty medical cadets are authorized, by the Act May 20, 1862, six medical storekeepers are authorized and one chaplain to each permanent hospital.
One hospital steward, as sergeant, allowed to each permanent hospital.

Pay Department.

1 Paymaster General with the rank of Colonel.
2 Deputy Paymasters General with the rank of Lieut. Colonel.
25 Paymasters with the rank of Major.

Engineer Corps.

1 Colonel.
4 Lieutenant Colonels.
8 Majors.
12 Captains.
15 First Lieutenants.
15 Second Lieutenants.

Topographical Engineer Corps.

1 Colonel.
3 Lieutenant Colonels.
8 Majors.
10 Captains.
13 First Lieutenants.
13 Second Lieutenants.

By the Act March 3, 1853, any lieutenant of the engineer, topographical engineer, or ordnance corps, who shall have served continuously for 14 years in this grade, is entitled to promotion to that of captain.

By an Act April 29, 1812, "the military academy shall consist of the corps of engineers" and certain named professors, and the cadets then appointed into the army, or appointed into it in future, "may be attached, at the discretion of the President of the United States, as students, to the military academy."

Ordnance Corps.

1 Brigadier General.
2 Colonels.
2 Lieutenant Colonels.
4 Majors.
12 Captains.
12 First Lieutenants.
12 Second Lieutenants.

Engineer Soldiers, Four Companies.

Company.
{
1 Captain.
1 First Lieutenant.
1 Second Lieutenant.
10 Sergeants.
10 Corporals.
2 Musicians.
64 Privates 1st Class, or Artificers.
64 Privates 2nd Class, or Laborers.
}

Topographical Engineer Soldiers, One Company.

Company.
{
1 Captain.
1 First Lieutenant.
1 Second Lieutenant.
10 Sergeants.
10 Corporals.
2 Musicians.
64 Privates 1st Class.
64 Privates 2nd Class.
}

Ordnance Soldiers.

One ordnance sergeant is allowed to each permanent military post, and beside these not more than one hundred and fifty enlisted men, as the President may direct.

Infantry.

This corps consists of nineteen regiments, ten of which, termed the *Old Regiments*, are each composed of *ten companies;* the remaining nine, termed the *New Regiments*, are each composed of *twenty-four companies*, divided into *three battalions* of eight companies each.

Old Regiment Staff.
1 Colonel.
1 Lieutenant Colonel.
2 Majors.
1 Adjutant.
1 Reg't'l Quar. Master.
1 Sergeant Major.
1 Quar. Master Sergeant.
2 Principal Musicians.

Company.
1 Captain.
1 First Lieutenant.
1 Second Lieutenant.
4 Sergeants.
4 Corporals.
2 Musicians.
42 to 74 Privates.

New Regiment Staff.
1 Colonel.
1 Lieutenant Colonel.
8 Majors.
1 Regt'l Adjutant
1 Regt'l Quar. Master.
1 Drum Major.
2 Principal Musicians.

Battalion.
1 Major.
8 Captains.
8 First Lieutenants.
8 Second Lieutenants.
1 Battalion Adjutant.
1 Battalion Quar. Master
1 Sergeant Major.
1 Hospital Steward.

Company.
1 Captain.
1 First Lieutenant.
1 Second Lieutenant.
1 First Sergeant.
4 Sergeants.
8 Corporals.
2 Musicians.
82 Privates.

Cavalry.

Six Regiments of twelve companies each.

Regimental Staff.
- 1 Colonel.
- 1 Lieutenant Colonel.
- 3 Majors.
- 1 Surgeon.
- 1 Assistant Surgeon.
- 1 Regimental Adjutant.
- 1 Regt'l Quar. Master.
- 1 Regt'l Commissary.
- 1 Sergeant Major.
- 1 Quar. Master Sergeant.
- 1 Commissary Sergeant.
- 9 Hospital Stewards.
- 1 Saddler Sergeant.
- 1 Chief Trumpeter
- 1 Chief Farrier.

Company.
- 1 Captain.
- 1 First Lieutenant.
- 1 Second Lieutenant.
- 1 Sup. Second Lieutenant.
- 1 First Sergeant.
- 1 Quar. Master Sergeant.
- 1 Commissary Sergeant.
- 5 Sergeants.
- 8 Corporals.
- 2 Teamsters.
- 2 Farriers.
- 1 Saddler.
- 1 Wagoner.
- 78 Privates.

Artillery.

Five Regiments. Four *Old Organization.* One *New Organization.*

Regiment, Old Organization.
- 1 Colonel.
- 1 Lieutenant Colonel.
- 2 Majors.
- 1 Adjutant.
- 1 Regt'l Quar. Master.
- 1 Sergeant Major.
- 1 Quar. Master Sergeant.
- 12 Captains.
- 24 First Lieutenants.
- 12 Second Lieutenants.
- 12 Companies.

Company, Old Organization.
- 1 Captain.
- 2 First Lieutenants.
- 1 Second Lieutenant.
- 4 Sergeants.
- 4 Corporals.
- 2 Musicians.
- 2 Artificers.
- 42 to 54 Privates.

Regiment, New Organization.		Company, New Organization.	
1 Colonel.		1 Captain.	
1 Lieutenant Colonel.		1 First Lieutenant.	
3 Majors.		1 Second Lieutenant.	
1 Adjutant.		1 First Sergeant.	
1 Regimental Quar. Mas. and Commissary.		1 Quar. Master Sergeant.	
1 Sergeant Major.		4 Sergeants.	
1 Commissary Sergeant.		8 Corporals.	
2 Principal Musicians.		2 Musicians.	
1 Hospital Steward.		2 Artificers.	
12 Captains.		1 Wagoner.	
12 First Lieutenants.		122 Privates.	
12 Second Lieutenants.			
12 Companies.			

The Adjutants, Quarter Masters and Commissaries of the regiments of the line to be taken from Lieutenants of the Regiment.

VOLUNTEERS.

By an Act approved by the President, July 22, 1861, the President was authorized to call for volunteers not to exceed 500,000 men, to be organized in such proportions that for each regiment of infantry not more than one company of artillery and one company of cavalry be allowed, these companies to be organized as in the regular army.

This force, by the same Act, may be divided into divisions of three or more brigades, each division to be commanded by a major general, each brigade to consist of four or more regiments to be commanded by a brigadier general.

A major general commanding a division to be allowed three aides-de camp and one assistant adjutant-general, each with the rank of major; a brigadier general to be allowed two aides-de-camp and one assistant adjutant-general, each with the rank of captain; and one surgeon, one assistant quartermaster and one commissary of subsistence to be also attached to each brigade.

By the Act July 25, 1861, the President is authorized to appoint as many major generals

300

and brigadier generals to command the volunteer forces as in his judgment may be requisite.

By the same Act the Governors of States are to appoint the Field, Staff and Company officers, and on their failing to do so, these offices to be filled by the President.

By an Act Aug. 6, 1861, Governors of States are authorized to fill vacancies occurring in officers of volunteers.

By an Act approved July 17, 1862, the President may accept 100,000 additional volunteers for nine months, and an additional number for twelve months for filling up the regiments of infantry then in service.

By the Act July 17, 1862, the President is authorized to organize army corps.

By the same Act the staff of the commander of an army corps is to consist of three aides-de-camp with the rank of major, and two with the rank of captain; one assistant adjutant-general, one quartermaster, one commissary of subsistence, and one assistant inspector general, each with the rank of lieutenant colonel; the senior officer of artillery to act as chief of artillery and ordnance.

Infantry.

Regiment.
{
- 1 Colonel.
- 1 Lieutenant Colonel.
- 1 Major.
- 1 Adjutant.
- 1 Quarter Master.
- 1 Surgeon.
- 1 Assistant Surgeon.
- 1 Chaplain.
- 1 Sergeant Major.
- 1 Quar. Master Sergeant.
- 1 Commissary Sergeant.
- 1 Hospital Steward.
- 2 Principal Musicians.
- 10 Captains.
- 10 First Lieutenants.
- 10 Second Lieutenants.
}

Company.
{
- 1 Captain.
- 1 First Lieutenant.
- 1 Second Lieutenant.
- 1 First Sergeant.
- 4 Sergeants.
- 8 Corporals.
- 2 Musicians.
- 1 Wagoner.
- 82 Privates.
}

Engineer Soldiers.

By an Act July 17, 1862, volunteer regiments and independent companies mustered into the service under the orders of the President or Secretary of War or commanding general of a military department, or reorganized and employed as engineers, pioneers, or sappers, are placed on same footing as engineer soldiers of the regular army.

MILITIA.

By the Act July 17, 1862, the President is authorized to call forth the militia of the States for a term of service not to exceed nine months.

By the same act, the enrolment of the militia is made to include all ablebodied male citizens between the ages of eighteen and forty-five; and it authorizes the President to make all necessary rules and regulations for enrolling if not provided for by the laws of the States.

The militia so called forth to be organized as the volunteers.

MILITARY HIERARCHY.

Commander-in-Chief.—The President, by the Constitution, is " commander-in-chief of the army and navy of the United States, and of the militia of the several states, when called into the actual service of the United States."

Under the same authority he nominates, and by and with the advice and consent of the Senate appoints, and commissions all commissioned officers of the regular army.

By an Act July 17, 1862, the President is authorized " to dismiss and discharge from the military service either in the army, navy, marine corps or volunteer force in the United States service, any officer, for any cause which, in his judgment, either renders such officer unsuitable for, or whose dismission would promote, the public service."

By a Joint Resolution, April 4, 1862, the President is authorized "whenever military operations may require the presence of two or more officers of the same grade, in the same field or department, to assign the command of the forces in such field or department, without regard to seniority of rank."

General Officers.—But two classes of this title exist permanently by law, *major general* and *brigadier general;* the first being the highest army grade, the second the next highest. Unless otherwise assigned by the President, they take rank and command according to the date of their commissions in their respective grades.

The functions of general officers are to command armies or fractions of an army greater than a regiment in the field, or to command the military forces distributed over any district and usually known as a *military department.* All the orders and military correspondence affecting their commands emanate from or pass through them if coming from or addressed to higher military authority.

Colonels.—The grade of colonel is next to that of brigadier general. Colonels rank and take command according to the dates of their commissions in this grade. Their functions are to command regiments, being also charged with their administration, good order, and discipline. All orders and military correspondence affecting their commands emanate from them, or pass through them if from a higher military source.

Lieutenant Colonel.—This grade is next to that

of colonel. The functions of the lieutenant colonel in the economy of the regiment in our service are very vague during the presence of the
colonel, although a tactical position is assigned
to the grade. It seems to form an anomaly in
almost every service. In that of the English the
lieutenant colonel is the actual commander of
the regiment, the colonelcy being usually held by
some general officer. In France the grade was
created first, and then duties for it had to be
looked up.

Major.—This grade is next to that of lieutenant colonel. No administrative functions are
specifically attached to it except to take charge
of the effects of deceased officers. In our new
regiments of the line a specific command is assigned to each major.

Captain.—The captain ranks next to major.
He is the head of the company, which may be
termed the administrative unit, as the battalion
is the tactical unit. He is held responsible for
the administration, good order and discipline of
his company, and upon the strict performance of
these duties depends the character of the army.

Lieutenant.—In our service we have the grades
of first and second lieutenants and that of brevet
second lieutenant, the last being conferred alone
on cadets, graduates of the military academy, and
non-commissioned officers, who, under certain
prescribed conditions, pass an examination for
this grade before a board of officers. The functions of the lieutenant are to assist the captain
in his company duties.

Cadet.—This grade ranks next to that of brevet second lieutenant, the cadet however not
holding a commission like those of the grades

above, but a simple warrant or letter of appointment from the President, and he is therefore termed a warrant officer. All cadets at present are attached as students to the military academy.

Non-Commissioned Officers.—Sergeant is the highest grade of this class and that of *corporal* next in rank. The functions of these grades are to assist the captain and lieutenants in their company duties.

Brevet Rank.—Besides the rank to which an officer is entitled from his position in his arm of service, the President has the authority to confer upon him, by and with the advice and consent of the Senate, a superior grade known as a brevet. This grade is conferred for distinguished services of which the President and Senate are the judges. It confers of itself no right to command in accordance with the rank, but the President is authorized to assign an officer to a command in accordance with it. It confers a right to precedence in court-martials and of command in detachments composed of troops of several arms.

Command of Staff Officers.—Officers of the general staff and of the staff corps cannot assume any command out of their own corps unless assigned by the President.

Promotion.—In the line promotions up to the grade of captain are made by seniority of grade and by regiments, from captain to colonel by corps in the arm to which the officer belongs.

General officers are appointed by selection without regard to corps or previous rank.

Promotion in the general staff and staff corps is confined to the corps and is made by seniority of rank.

MILITARY ADMINISTRATION.

The military administration of the land forces is confided to the general staff of the army; that of any fraction of an army to a particular staff termed an *army corps staff*, a *regimental staff*, &c.

Under this head may be comprised the correspondence, the quartering, the subsistence, the sanitary arrangements, legal proceedings, and the payment of troops.

Correspondence.—This is conducted through the various grades of adjutant-generals, assistant adjutant-generals and adjutants, through whom all orders and other information pass to and from the head of the force to which they are severally attached.

Quartering.—Everything connected with lodging troops in garrison or in the field, providing transportation, clothing, fuel and forage for them, is conducted by the various grades of officers and non-commissioned officers belonging to the quartermaster's department.

Subsistence.—The food of the troops is provided by and distributed under the direction of the various grades of officers and non-commissioned officers of the commissariat.

Sanitary Arrangements.—The duties under this head are performed by the officers and enlisted men of the medical staff.

Legal Proceedings.—Everything connected with the proceedings of military legal tribunals is committed to the various grades of judge advocate.

Payment.—This duty is confided to the various grades of paymasters.

26*

PLATES

TO

ILLUSTRATE

MAHAN'S OUTPOSTS.

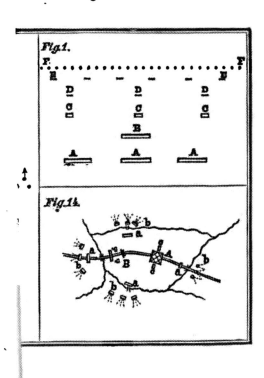

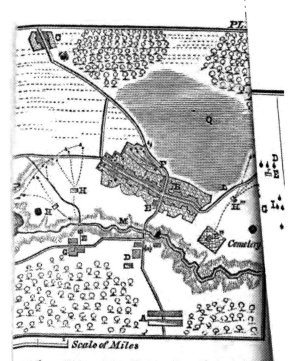

Scale of Miles

ong the outskirts of the village. These are supported
road at the outlet of the village.
an out-post of cavalry is placed at H''', and throws
supported by a grand guard of infantry E''' which

ded by two guns with infantry supports on their flanks.
cavalry and infantry of sufficient strength to support
n a suitable position to the rear of the bridge.

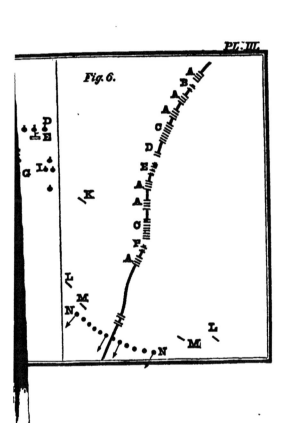

Fig. 6.

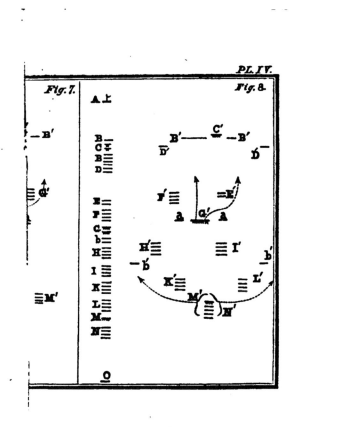

Fig. 7.

Fig. 8.

dispositions of deployment on the right.

(*Art.* 356, *p.* 132.) shows the disposi-
) to defend a bridge. At the outlet,
ie enemy, there is a saw mill with a
ilosure in advance of which stretches a
ve. Behind the bridge is a ridge along
. detachment for the defence consists of
nent of infantry; two companies of
o squadrons; and two six-pounder guns.
)mpany of cavalry will patrole beyond
i towards the enemy. One company of
rill be posted under cover in the centre
;ove, and a half company on each flank at

companies of infantry take post at *d* in
tre, and one on each flank at *e* and *f* as
s to the rifles: the enclosure will be held
st. The two guns are placed at 300 paces
of the bridge to enfilade it. Two compa-
re posted at *h* and *i* on each side of the
as skirmishers, they are supported by the
iing companies in column at *m;* and the
ider of the cavalry is posted to the rear at
i favorable position to cover a retreat.
t. 12 (*Art.* 345, *p.* 128.) shows the defensive
jitions made by a detachment consisting of
i regiments of infantry, six squadrons, and a
ry of six-pounders, to hold an enemy in
i for several hours arriving from Y towards
illage X.
; Y there is a small village through which the
i road to X passes; the road traverses the
ik S R, which discharges into the pond P on
left; this brook receives a smaller one near
the ground between the brooks and Y is gen-
undulating and interspersed with small groves.

Between the brook and the village, the ground rises so as to overlook the portion towards Y. Between the pond and village lies a wet meadow.

The main body takes position on the heights along A, B. A half battery takes position at *a*, with its support of infantry, from 4 to 600 paces in rear of the bridge to enfilade it; the other half battery in the rear at *k*. The main portion of cavalry at *m* on the right flank; a small detachment of it at *c* on the left flank. The wood skirting the brook S R is occupied by skirmishers, their supports being beyond it on the right and left of the road. A detachment of cavalry at *g* patroles on the right. The bridges at *n* and *o* are guarded and patroles pushed out on the left.

In front, skirmishers are placed at T along the brook from *i* to *f*; a small post of cavalry at Y to patrole in advance; a post of cavalry and infantry at *h* to watch the woods and roads on the left; and one of cavalry in the wood on the right at *d* to patrole towards the right.

At night the exterior posts are drawn in and join the post at T behind the brook.

If attacked and forced to retreat, the infantry and artillery will retire by alternate half batteries and regiments to the position *p*, *r*, *s*, *t* behind the small brook running to the meadow at M; the cavalry on the right flank. In the retreat through the village and around it, the ditches across the meadow can be disputed by skirmishers, as well as the outskirts of the village, these will be supported by a regiment in column occupying the open square in the centre. If the ground is favorable for cavalry on the right of the village, it will be taken advantage of for a flank attack on the enemy.